Moving to Canada

A complete guide to immigrating to Canada without an attorney

D1522412

Cori Carl

Contents

Introduction

People talk about moving to Canada all the time, but there's little helpful information explaining how to actually do it. That's what I discovered when I decided to make the move from Brooklyn to Toronto. Now that I'm a permanent resident of Canada, I've written the guide I wish I'd had when I began. I immigrated through the skilled worker program, express entry, and became a Canadian citizen in 2022.

Most of the ways you can move to Canada are the same regardless of your citizenship or where you're currently living. Many Americans and people from the Commonwealth are surprised to discover there's no fast track program for us.

Immigration, Refugees and Citizenship Canada (IRCC) has a very thorough website that's designed to enable people to apply for Canadian residency without the help of an immigration consultant or attorney. However, the website is still the product of bureaucracy. Their instructions are meant to be applicable for anyone, coming from anywhere, under any circumstances. Most of the forums and other resources available are for people coming from non-Western cultures, who have very different concerns than I did. This book is written for people coming from countries that are culturally similar to Canada, like Britain and its former colonies.

Many existing third-party guides are outdated, since the IRCC has overhauled their programs to bring them all online and continues to adjust them regularly. Other immigration guides are merely

1

advertisements to scare you into hiring someone from the author's firm to serve as your attorney.

I'm not an attorney. This book is the product of obsessive research and real life experience. You should always consult the IRCC website or a professional before forging ahead. Making a mistake on a visa application is not something you want to deal with.

Hiring someone to do your application for you will not improve your odds of having it approved, nor will it speed up the process. They can simply make sure your application is complete and doesn't contain mistakes. If you want professional legal advice, you should consult an immigration attorney or accredited immigration consultant.

Many of us move to Canada each year without getting professional help with the application or moving process. I was able to navigate the process on my own and I'm sharing everything I've learned with you in this guide.

Things to know about Canada

There are a lot of factors to consider before moving to Canada and a lot of different ways to make the move. Some people decide to move to Canada with an abundance of first-hand knowledge about what their life in Canada will be like. Others move to a city they've picked off a map or because of rumors of job prospects in a country they've never been to. I'll walk you through the basics you need to know about Canada so you can get an idea of what life in Canada is really like.

You want to move to Canada, eh?

Moving to another country is never as simple as packing your stuff and jumping on a plane. In order to legally live and work in another country, you'll have to go through the necessary government channels.

Luckily, Canada is eager for new residents from around the world. They've designed their visa and immigration programs to be simple. They may not seem simple, but that's only because you probably have nothing to compare them to. How many people immigrate to multiple countries? Not many.

To work legally in Canada, you'll need to be a Canadian citizen, permanent resident, or have a valid work permit. Depending on which country you're a citizen of, there's a good chance you can visit Canada for up to six months without needing to apply in advance for a tourist visa. This won't allow you to accept a job, but it's a good opportunity to get to know the country and start building your professional network.

If you work in a field that requires licensing or certification, you'll want to find out whether or not your credentials will be recognized and, if not, what it will take to be re-licensed or re-certified in Canada.

There's no fast track to immigrate to Canada based on your nationality. This includes you, citizens of the United States and the United Kingdom. However, the working holiday program and CUSMA (formerly NAFTA) do make it easier for people from some countries to live in Canada temporarily, which gives you an advantage if you decide to move to Canada permanently.

During the pandemic the IRCC has focused on providing permanent resident status to people who were already living and working in Canada as temporary residents. While they "welcomed" a record number of permanent residents, few of those 401,000 people arrived from outside of Canada.

Trudeau announced that in 2022 the government will continue to expand opportunities for temporary residents to become permanent residents and create a way for eligible family members to become temporary residents while they wait for their applications to be processed. They will focus on streamlining the work permit process and reducing application processing times overall. There's also talk of creating a municipal nomination program, an idea that was introduced in 2019 and delayed by the pandemic.

Things you should know about Canada

You're not alone in considering moving to Canada from abroad:

4

- Canada welcomes around a quarter of a million immigrants each year.

- Unlike most western nations, Canadians generally support their high per capita immigration rate.

- Support for immigration is increasing and all major Canadian political parties support it.

- 22% of Canadians are first-generation immigrants.

- Nearly half of people living in Toronto are foreign-born.

- Nearly half of all immigrants to Canada settle in the Greater Toronto Area.

- Because Canadian immigration is based primarily on a points system, immigrants to Canada are overall better educated and better paid than immigrants to the United States.

- Many of Canada's most highly educated (and highest paid) workers were born outside of Canada.

Let's cover the basics:

- Canada is a bilingual country. English and French are both official languages of Canada and receive equal status in the government.

- The national capital is Ottawa, Ontario.

- Canada has ten provinces and three territories, making thirteen co-sovereign jurisdictions.

- Queen Elizabeth II is the Queen of Canada and thus Canada is a member of the Commonwealth of Nations.

- Canada is a constitutional monarchy, a parliamentary democracy, and a federal state.

- Toronto is the 4th largest city in North America.

- Nearly ⅓ of Canadians live in the country's three biggest cities: Toronto, Montreal, and Vancouver.

- Québec is basically a different country.

- The Québécois aren't the only French speaking Canadians; there are also the Acadians and other scattered Francophone communities.

- Canada has a very complicated relationship with the Aboriginal peoples (First Nations, Inuit, and Métis) who originally settled the country and remain sovereign nations.

- Newfoundland was a self-governing country until 1949.

- Canada is the second largest country by area, covering 10 million square kilometers (or nearly 3.9 million square miles).

The basics of moving to another country

If you aren't currently a citizen of Canada, you can't simply apply to become one.

Typically, first you apply to become a resident of Canada. Most people do this by going to university in Canada or getting a job that qualifies them for a work permit.

Sometimes being a Canadian resident can make you eligible to become a permanent resident (PR) of Canada. Permanent residents have almost all of the same rights as Canadian citizens. The main difference is that people with PR status can't vote and they must live in the country for a certain amount of time to maintain their residency.

In some cases, people can live as residents of Canada for a long time and never qualify to become a permanent resident.

Some immigration programs, like express entry, will allow people to become a permanent resident without requiring that they be a resident first.

After having lived in Canada as a permanent resident for several years, most people become eligible to apply for citizenship.

Some people choose to remain permanent residents because their country of origin doesn't allow dual citizenship and they don't want to renounce their original nationality. Other people may simply be happy as permanent residents and don't feel the need to go through the hassle and expense of applying for citizenship.

Immigration consultants & attorneys

If you're comfortable in English and good with managing paperwork, you'll likely have no problem completing the application to move to Canada on your own, without assistance from a lawyer or immigration consultant. If you've filled out one of those online job applications where you have to upload a PDF of your resume, then link your LinkedIn profile, and then retype it all into tiny boxes that give you mysterious error messages, you're ready to manage this process on your own. If you're planning on moving to Quebec, replace "English" with "French" in that last sentence and it holds true.

You may want to get assistance with the process if you don't feel comfortable with your language skills, are worried about extenuating circumstances, or are intimidated by filling out government forms. Be sure they're authorized.

If you happen to ask an immigration consultant if their services are required, they're likely to imply that the process is so overwhelming that you'd be lost without their help, or maybe even lead you to believe that they can somehow speed up the process. Neither of those things is true.

Admissibility to Canada

If you're deemed inadmissible, you can't enter Canada, even as a tourist, until you've dealt with it. There are several things that can make you inadmissible to Canada.

Your criminal record

You may be deemed to be temporarily or permanently inadmissible to Canada based on prior arrests or convictions.

Temporary inadmissibility is for minor offenses and is up to the discretion of the border agent. Usually they don't ask about your criminal record or check you in the system, but sometimes they do. A friend of mine was turned away at the border because of an arrest and told he couldn't enter Canada until five years had passed from the date of the arrest. This may also be an issue when applying for an (electronic travel authorization) eTA.

Some things that may make you permanently inadmissible to Canada are: DUI/DWI, theft, assault, drug trafficking, or being convicted of a crime that carries a sentence of 10 years or more.

If you're criminally inadmissible, you can apply for a temporary resident permit (TRP). This requires you demonstrate that you have a valid reason for entering Canada that outweighs any risk you pose to society. It can be valid for any amount of time from a single day to three years. It can be a single entry visa or a multiple entry visa. The fee is typically $200, which can be waived.

If it's been at least five years since you completed your sentence, you can apply for individual rehabilitation to your local visa office. This requires you demonstrate that you have a stable lifestyle, a permanent home, employment, and proof of good character.

If it's been at least ten years since you completed your sentence, you can apply for deemed rehabilitation. When you're rehabilitated your criminal record is permanently resolved. In order to be eligible for PR status in Canada with a criminal record that makes you inadmissible, you need to be criminally rehabilitated.

If you have pending charges and want to enter Canada, you should contact an immigration attorney.

Your health

Your residency application could be denied if you have a high potential to place an excessive demand on health or social services. This is the case if your needs are high enough that they could impact wait times in the region you plan to relocate to or if they exceed the excessive demand cost threshold. The 2022 threshold is $120,285 over 5 years (or $24,057 per year). This amount is updated each year.

The excessive demand cost threshold doesn't apply to refugees, protected persons, and family sponsorship of dependent children, spouses, or common-law partners. This policy was updated and clarified in 2018 due to public outcry.

You can also be deemed inadmissible if you're determined to be a risk to public health or safety. This would be the case if you have an infectious disease (like active TB or syphilis), are at risk of being incapacitated by a health condition (like dementia), or demonstrate unpredictable or violent behavior.

If you are deemed medically inadmissible, the IRCC will send you a procedural fairness letter which outlines their decision and reasoning. You can reply to this letter with evidence to dispute their decision. You can also provide a mitigation plan to show how you will manage the impact of your health on Canada's public services.

Your previous visas

Having been denied entry or ordered to leave any country can cause issues when trying to enter Canada.

The US and Canada share information at the border. If you have overstayed a visa in the US or been denied entry to the US, Canadian border agents will be able to see this.

Having lived in another country without a visa

If you were deported from another country, you are considered criminally inadmissible to Canada. You can follow the procedures to resolve criminal inadmissibility.

If you are currently living in another country without a corresponding visa or have previously done so, this makes it unlikely that Canada will issue you a temporary visa for tourism, study, or as a temporary worker. It does not prevent you from qualifying to become a permanent resident.

Having been ordered to leave Canada

If you've been ordered to leave Canada previously, you may not need to do anything special in order to return.

- If you were given a direction to leave Canada, you can return to Canada normally.

- If you were given a departure order and left before the deadline, you're free to return. If you didn't comply, the departure order automatically became a deportation order.

- If you were given an exclusion order and complied with the terms, you were given a certificate of departure. If you don't have a certificate of departure or less than twelve months have passed, you need an authorization to return to Canada (ARC).

- If you were ordered deported from Canada, you need an authorization to return to Canada (ARC).

You have to apply for an ARC from outside of Canada. It cannot be done at the border.

Your country of origin

Your nationality does and doesn't change your application process and the odds of your application being approved. Officially, being a citizen of the US, the Commonwealth, or a Francophone country doesn't give you any special privileges. In reality, it does make the process easier.

The US or the Commonwealth

Canada wants new residents to be able to quickly adapt to their new home and succeed. Being from a culturally similar country increases the likelihood that you'll do well in Canada. If you're from one of these countries, you probably:

- Are fluent in English and/or French
- Have an education Canadian employers will recognize
- Have a similar office culture
- Have family in Canada, or at least know a few people
- Are used to a similar cost of living
- Have documents in English and/or French and thus don't need to be translated

While you don't get any points for being from the US, or even from the British Empire, you're more likely to meet the basic requirements, are saved from the expense of translation, and face less uncertainty in regards to education credential assessments and language exams.

Francophone and English speaking countries

People coming from countries where English or French are widely spoken have unofficial advantages. If you're from one of these countries, you probably:

- Are fluent in English and/or French
- Have some familiarity with Canadian office culture
- Have an idea of how your education will translate
- Have friends and family in Canada
- Have all or some documents in English and/or French, minimizing how many things need to be translated

Adjusting to life in Canada if you grew up in Ghana, Senegal, Pakistan, Mauritius, or Hong Kong isn't going to be as easy as if you're coming from the UK. Still, there are similarities that will help you get settled. And, in the case of people from Hong Kong, there are programs specifically designed to help you move to Canada.

Moving to Canada from other countries

There's no reason to worry if you're coming from a country that doesn't keep official documents in English or French. You're still going to follow the same process and meet the same requirements.

If you're concerned about your education being recognized, there's a free tool to see what your foreign degree will be equivalent to. This is provided by a company called World Education Services (WES), one of the IRCC approved education assessment companies.

Getting your documents translated will add time and expense to your application process. You can't just use a friend who speaks French or do it yourself, you'll need an approved translator recognized by the IRCC.

Where to move

Canada is a huge country with an incredible diversity in terms of city size, weather, and geography. There's surely somewhere that will be the right fit for you.

Best job prospects

The best place to find a job is the city you have the most professional connections in. Some cities are hubs for specific industries. Kitchener-Waterloo and Guelph are home to many tech companies and startups. Ottawa is the place to be for government jobs. Calgary is home to much of the oil and gas industry. Toronto is the leader for banking and insurance.

Generally speaking, these cities have the most available jobs:

- Toronto, ON
- Kitchener-Waterloo, ON
- Vancouver, BC
- Calgary, AB
- Abbotsford, BC
- Saskatoon, SK
- Edmonton, AB

Best cities for bilingual immigrants

New Brunswick is Canada's only bilingual province. In Quebec, much of the signage is only in French and people in small towns may not speak any English at all.

- Ottawa, ON & Gatineau, QC
- Montreal, QC
- Quebec City, QC
- Fredericton, NB
- Saint John, NB
- Moncton, NB

Easiest to get provincial nomination

Bilingual English & French: Ontario

Canadian Graduate: Ontario

Farmers: Saskatchewan & Manitoba

Investors: Yukon & Northwest Territories

If you're currently living in Canada as a student or worker, your province probably has a program to enable you to become a permanent resident.

Best weather

All of these areas are wine regions, aside from Canmore. They have opportunities for fantastic hiking. Not surprisingly, they're popular destinations for vacations and retirement.

Kelowna, BC has hot summers and rarely drops below freezing in winter. It's also rarely windy.

Osoyoos, BC stays warm year round and is rarely humid.

Victoria, BC is known for its beauty, tourist-friendly amenities, and warm weather. It gets more sun than Seattle (which isn't saying much) and very little snow (if any). The area has a Mediterranean climate and there's rainforest nearby. You can easily reach Vancouver, Seattle, and Portland by ferry and sea plane.

Niagara-on-the-Lake, ON has weather similar to upstate New York. It provides easy access to jobs and attractions in Toronto, Hamilton, Buffalo, and even Detroit.

Canmore, AB might seem like a surprising choice, but the summers are mild and the winters have spectacular skiing. You have access to the amenities of Banff and Calgary, both within an hour.

Canada is not a frigid polar land, contrary to popular misconceptions. Canada is a huge country with several climate zones. Most of the population is within 100 miles of the US border, so the climate is very similar on both sides.

I've spent a significant amount of my time in Canada hopping around from one city to another, so I can share my impression of the weather in the cities I've spent the most time in.

Toronto

While the winters in Toronto might technically be colder than what I was used to in New York, my everyday experience of getting around the city is far more pleasant. The summers aren't quite as brutal and the winters are a little rougher. It snows pretty often in Toronto, but it's usually that lovely light snow you know from the first kiss in romantic comedies. The downtown has underground walkways and the city is largely responsible for clearing the sidewalks.

I appreciate that dressing appropriately for the weather is socially acceptable in Toronto. New York is just as cold, it's simply not office appropriate to dress for it. You don't need any sort of special winter gear in Toronto besides a run of the mill coat, hat, gloves, and boots like you would have in any area that gets all four seasons.

Sadly, Toronto summers aren't any better than New York summers. It's hot and humid. Those glass box condos really heat up, so be prepared to run your AC a ridiculous percentage of the year. Toronto does lack the pervasive hot trash smell of summers in New York. It's also a lot easier to access the water for boating and swimming.

The ravines and copious waterfront make spring and fall absolutely lovely times to be in Toronto. People flock to patios, so it's easy to maximize the amount of time you spend outdoors.

Montreal & Ottawa

Montreal and Ottawa are both significantly colder than Toronto and get more snow. However, this doesn't keep people indoors. Montreal is full of street festivals featuring fires and mulled wine that run late into the evening. I found walking around all winter just fine. I was not hearty enough to stand around and enjoy outdoor concerts.

It might snow every day all winter. You probably want to shovel throughout the day so things don't get out of control. Snow accumulates rather than melts.

In Ottawa the canal system turns into a giant ice skating rink and people go skiing (cross-country or downhill across the border in Quebec) every free afternoon. Even if you don't go to an ice skating rink, a good portion of both cities effectively becomes an ice skating rink for most of the winter. Get boots with good traction.

You'll want a good winter coat and accessories in either city, but how far you go depends on what you're doing. Will you be walking from the front door to your car? Will you be going for runs with your dog every morning? Will you be waiting for an unreliable bus? Will you be drinking mulled wine at street festivals every weekend? It pays to wait and see what you actually need.

Calgary

This came as a surprise, but I enjoyed Calgary's weather. The summers are generally mild, while still getting hot enough to feel like a proper summer. Even on hot days it's cool in the shade and at night. If it gets too hot for you, go to the mountains and stick your feet in a glacial stream.

The winter weather reports sound terrifying. I found that -30C wasn't bad at all, so long as it wasn't windy. Often the wind is fine, so long as it's the chinook winds, which brings random reprieves of spring weather. The dry air meant I could easily stay comfortable with layers, unlike in Toronto where the damp chill makes it impossible for me to warm up once I get cold.

I was not in Calgary for the entire year, so perhaps I don't know how bad it can really get. I did spend part of the winter living in a tiny house with questionable electrical wiring for my little radiator and came away from the experience eager to stay longer.

I don't know if your university had that guy who wore shorts and flip flops year round, but the University of Calgary has that guy, too.

Calgary gets the most sun of any city in Canada. I really appreciated this during the winter. My biggest weather complaint was that spring and fall are so short.

The Canadian economy

Canada is one of the world's wealthiest nations. It frequently ranks among the top places to live in terms of quality of life and living standards. It has a high level of economic freedom, ranking 9th in the 2021 index. It's the most free economy in the Americas and the tenth largest economy in the world. The Toronto Stock Exchange (TSX) is the third largest stock exchange in North America, after the NYSE and Nasdaq.

Three quarters of the population works in the service industry. These include trades, healthcare, finance, education, food, retail, and government. Manufacturing is largely centered in Ontario and Quebec. Central Canada still has a farming economy, growing wheat, corn, oilseed, cattle, and pigs. The country is currently moving forward with significant infrastructure upgrades.

In addition to the second largest oil reserves in the world, Canada's natural resources include natural gas, gold, nickel, aluminum, fish, and timber. Canada has more freshwater than any other country.

Canada has trade agreements with the US and Mexico (CUSMA), the EU (CETA), the UK (CUKTCA), the Caribbean (CARICOM), non-EU countries, India, Japan, and much of South America. They're a member of the WTO and have signed the TPP.

Canada's economy is closely linked to that of the US, as the US is Canada's top export and import partner. Some economists treat both countries as a single economic entity. Half of all foreign investments in Canada come from the US. Canada is America's largest source of fuel imports.

Climate change could boost the Canadian economy. The declining ice shelves could open the northern sea route and northwest passage to commercial traffic. It could also increase the amount of land usable for agriculture and lengthen the growing season. There is strong support for green environmental policies.

Taxes in Canada are lower than that of countries with a similar standard of living, like Germany, France, and Denmark. People are taxed progressively based on their income. Canada has one of the lowest rates of corporate taxes in the world.

The Canadian Government

As capital, Ottawa is the seat of Canada's government. Canada has a Westminster style federal parliamentary democracy with a constitutional monarchy. It has one of the most stable democracies in the world and one of the most democratic nations.

The provinces of Canada are co-sovereign, meaning they hold power alongside the federal government, not beneath it. As a result, each province has a significant amount of autonomy. They are responsible for providing their social services, including health care. The federal government influences this by tying funding to federally mandated standards.

Elections in Canada

In order to vote in a Federal election, you must be a Canadian citizen aged 18 or older who lives in Canada or has been abroad for less than 5 years. Permanent residents of Canada are not eligible to vote in any elections. Government employees serving abroad are exempt from residency requirements. Provincial, territorial, and municipal elections may have other requirements.

Electoral campaigns are kept as brief as possible and parties are strictly limited in their spending. Election campaigns are legally required to last at least 36 days. The prime minister is not elected directly.

Political parties elect party leaders before an election. Candidates, including the party leader, then run for the house of commons. Candidates do not need a majority of votes (50+%), only a plurality (more votes than any other candidate). Members of the house of commons are elected for up to 5 year terms.

Canadians elect their local member of parliament (MP) to sit on the house of commons. Local districts are known as ridings. The prime minister is typically the leader of the party with the most seats in the house of commons. If a single party has the majority of the seats in the house of commons, they have a majority government. If the party with the most seats holds fewer seats than the other parties combined, the party leader to be prime minister must have support from the majority of the house.

The largest party that is not in control of the house of commons is known as the opposition party. The role of the opposition is to keep the government in check. They maintain their own cabinet and party leader.

MPs can run without being affiliated with a political party and may switch parties after they've been elected. Any time a seat of the house of commons is vacant, a by-election is held.

In the case of a no confidence motion, the governor general whom represents the monarchy will call an election on advice of the prime minister. If the budget does not pass, it results in a failure state and triggers new elections. Theoretically, the governor general can dissolve parliament at any time. Governments typically don't last more than 5 years, although there are specific exemptions to this rule. The opposition party is always ready with a new government, complete with a potential prime minister, cabinet, and senators.

The Parliamentary System

Theoretically, Canada is run by her Queen. The governor general, or viceroy, acts on her behalf, typically on the advice of the prime minister. The queen also has a privy council that advises her on important issues, members of which are appointed for life by the governor general. The prime minister is selected by elected members of parliament. The Queen then appoints a governor general, typically on advice of the prime minister. The senate is appointed by the governor general.

The governor general:

- Appoints members to open spots on the Queen's Privy Council for Canada, typically from former cabinet members.
- Appoints cabinet ministers.

- Appoints members to open spot on the senate.
- Stands in for the Queen and is a member of the monarchy.

The prime minister:

- Is typically the leader of the majority party.
- Serves as the head of the government.
- Selects cabinet ministers, who are appointed by the governor general.
- Recommends a governor general to the Queen.

The house of commons is elected by each local district. Seats are roughly tied to the population of each province or territory. While the house of commons may last for 5 years, or longer under certain circumstances, it nearly always ends within 4 years. They are responsible for taxes and uses of public funds. The house of commons is the lower house, referring to its rank, not its power.

The senate is not elected, but rather appointed by the governor general on the advice of the prime minister. Senators may serve until they've reached the age of 75 or they step down. They are responsible for providing a check on Parliament's excesses. Generally, the Senate exercises little influence on legislation. The senate is the upper house, referring to the rank of its members.

All legislation must be approved by both the house of commons and the senate. The governor general, with approval from the Queen, can appoint up to 8 extra senators to resolve a deadlock. Technically, legislation can be proposed by either the house of commons or the senate, but the vast majority of legislation arises from the house of commons.

The supreme court (SCC) makes final rulings, but only since 1949. Of the 9 judges that sit on the court, 3 must be from Quebec. This is because Quebec uses civil law, while the rest of Canada uses common law. Common law relies on judicial opinions whereas civil law tends to reference codified statutes for decision making. Generally, 3 judges will be from Ontario, 2 from the west, and 1 from the east. The Queen appoints the Chief Justice. They can hear cases from any court, as well as reference cases (which pose hypothetical questions).

Canada's political parties

There are three main political parties in Canada: the Conservative Party (Tories), the Liberal Party, and the New Democratic Party. There's also the Bloc Quebecois and the Green Party. And a bunch more.

You can read the manifestos of each party to get a more in-depth explanation of their policies.

Political parties in each province vary significantly from the parties at the federal level.

The Liberal Party

The Liberals support a free market and free trade, but support using tax money to build social services and infrastructure. The Liberal Party supports a strong social safety net and human rights causes. They aim to balance what's best for business and the public and strongly support immigration and multiculturalism.

The Liberal party was in power for 69 years of the 20th Century. They're the centrist party and represent much of the business elite. They have been the majority party in Canada since 2015.

The Conservative Party

The Conservative Party as we know it is relatively new, the result of a merger between the Progressive Conservatives and Reform Party in 2003. The Conservative Party supports small government, low taxes, gun rights, and a climate good for business and development. They also support more serious repercussions for crime. The Conservative Party is Canada's official opposition party since 2015, when Stephen Harper's government was voted out in favor or Justin Trudeau's Liberal Party.

A Canadian conservative would seem pretty liberal to an American conservative.

New Democratic Party

The NDP supports democratic socialism. The NDP is out to protect the disadvantaged and the environment. They support increasing corporate taxes and nationalization of services and infrastructure. The NDP prioritizes rehabilitation of criminals over jail time.

Traditionally the party of farmers, today it is the party of unions. While the NDP isn't a key player on its own, it works with the parties in power to pass legislation. They were the first to support bringing socialized medicine to Canada.

Bloc Quebecois

The BQ represents the Quebec separatist movement. They advocate specifically for Quebec's interests.

Quebec holds a large amount of power. Prime ministers from Quebec served nearly continuously from 1968 to 2006, in both liberal and conservative governments. Politicians are expected to speak both English and French. At least 3 of the 9 supreme court judges must be from Quebec, since Quebec has its own system of law.

Quality of life compared to the US

Canadian cities frequently place at or near the top of quality of life rankings.

- Canadians have a higher level of life satisfaction compared to Americans.

- Canadians get more paid time off than Americans.

- Parents get 50 weeks of paid leave to welcome new children, compared to 0 in the US.

- Canadians work fewer hours than Americans.

- The median net worth is higher in Canada than the US.

- Canada has a lower divorce rate.

- The infant mortality rate is lower and the life expectancy is longer in Canada.

Safety

Canada is much safer than the US. Non-violent crime rates are roughly similar, but violent crimes are much lower in Canada. There are 5.5 murders each year for every 100k people living in the US, compared to 1.3 in Canada.

Canada is lauded for its anti-discrimination policies. Canadian law embraces diversity, inclusion, and multiculturalism. Of course, there is a vast chasm between Canadian ideals and reality. Canada hasn't actually overcome discrimination, but Canada is an easier place to live than many other countries. If you're a visible minority, your odds are better in Canada. It's certainly preferable to the US. There are fewer incidences of bias and they're less extreme. The OECD named Canada the best country in the world for acceptance and tolerance of visible minorities.

Cost of living

Income disparity is a problem in Canada, but a much smaller problem compared to the US. In Canada, the top 20% earns about six times as much as the bottom 20%. In the US they earn nine times as much.

Unions are much more prevalent in Canada than in the US. In Canada, 26% of workers are in a union, compared to 10% in the US. Canada has a higher percentage of working-age adults who are currently employed. In the US, 11% of workers put in very long hours, compared to only 4% in Canada.

Canadians who live in Vancouver, Toronto, or Montreal will complain endlessly about how expensive it is. Coming from New York City, I find this ridiculous. Life in Canadian cities is significantly less expensive than their American counterparts.

The best example is real estate, which seems very expensive in Canadian cities, unless you've ever looked at renting or buying in New York or San Francisco…or Tokyo. They'll say that it's irrelevant because of higher incomes in other major cities. However, New York has plenty of jobs paying poverty level wages, a far lower minimum wage, and spotty access to healthcare. Housing costs in parts of Canada have risen rapidly in the past few years, so it's understandable that people who have spent all or most of their lives in one place are upset about the increased cost of living.

Some things in Canada are more expensive than in the US. The price of goods in Canada reflects the actual cost of the items, whereas, in the US, the government covers the cost of corporate pollution and allows higher levels of worker exploitation. There are also different tariffs. You can always use your personal exemption and shop when you're abroad. This is a popular solution and the reason Apple stores in New York are full of foreigners.

Overall, you'll likely find the cost of living in Canada to be lower and, importantly, more predictable.

Finance

The Canadian dollar and the US dollar are not the same, although they often have a similar value.

Most of the goods flowing in and out of Canada are through trade with the United States. China is Canada's second biggest trading partner.

The Canadian banking system is one of the most stable in the world. Canada's economy fared better than the US during the most recent recession, in part because Canada didn't have the subprime mortgage implosion.

Government

Canada is regularly ranked as the most democratic nation in the Americas. It is a constitutional monarchy with a federal parliamentary democracy, in contrast to the federal constitutional republic of the US.

The Canadian Crown heads the executive, legislative, and judicial branches of government. The head of state has been Queen Elizabeth II since 1952. Canadian laws are based on English Common Law, except in Québec.

Taxes for US citizens and greencard holders

It's hard to compare tax rates between the US and Canada because there are so many variables. Overall, the actual amount of money you pay in taxes is comparable between the US and Canada. However, taxes in Canada include nearly all healthcare costs whereas in the US you pay your taxes, pay for health insurance, and then pay much higher out of pocket costs.

The US taxes your worldwide income, it's true. Being a successful American expat comes at a cost. While living abroad, you aren't taxed in the US on the first $104k USD of foreign earned income. If you're married and both living abroad, you can exclude your first $208k USD of income. Any income above that amount can be sheltered from taxes by depositing it into a retirement account, up to the limit.

The US gives you credit for any taxes you pay in Canada. You also get tax breaks for things like housing costs. If someone is complaining about double taxation, they either make *a lot* of money or they need a new accountant.

The US has agreements with Canada so you're covered under Social Security in whatever country you end up in, with credit for your employment in both countries.

For detailed information on taxes for US citizens and greencard holders living in Canada, see *Cross Border Taxes: A complete guide to filing taxes as an American in Canada.*

Healthcare

In OECD surveys, the same percentage of people in the US and Canada identified themselves as being in good health. What's different is how that result is achieved.

Canada has a publicly funded single payer healthcare system, with private organizations providing services and the government health insurance covering most costs. The government doesn't provide any care directly and all patient information remains confidential. If you're from a country with universal healthcare, this all seems normal. If you're from the US, it's magic.

Imagine never having to fill out—or dispute—insurance claims again. Changing jobs or being unemployed has no impact on your health insurance coverage. You don't have to switch doctors when your plan changes or call around trying to find doctors who accept your plan. There are no lifetime limits or clauses about pre-existing conditions. You won't get hit by unexpected bills for pre-approved surgeries because someone who treated you while you were unconscious was out of network. There are no surprise facility fees that vary for no rhyme or reason.

There are no deductibles on basic healthcare and co-pays are very low compared to what most people pay in the US. Each province and territory manages its own system and they may have residency requirements for enrollment.

Patients choose their general practitioner (GP) and the GP makes referrals to specialists as needed. Preventive care is encouraged.

As you may have heard, there can be waiting lists for treatments that aren't urgent. There is often a difference between what a doctor considers urgent and what seems urgent to a patient and their family. Wait times seem comparable to similar services in the US, depending on your insurance coverage and ability to pay. I say "seems" because in the US there is no system for tracking wait times.

To put this into perspective, remember that Canadians have a longer life expectancy than Americans.

If you encounter a rare disease and a proven treatment is only available in another country, the government will pay for you to fly there and get the care you need.

People unhappy with provincial coverage can opt to receive care from anywhere in the world so long as they're willing and able to pay out-of-pocket for those services. You'll occasionally see news coverage of people whose care was denied because Canadian doctors deemed treatment to be not medically necessary or because the patient would like a treatment that is unproven.

The Canadian health insurance system doesn't cover everything. Mental health care is covered in only some circumstances. Alternative medicine is not covered. You're likely to be on your own for prescription drugs, home care, long-term care, vision, and dental. Most employers cover these with supplemental insurance plans. Only about 15% of healthcare costs are paid out-of-pocket in Canada.

Prescription drug prices are negotiated by the provincial governments to keep costs down. This is why many Americans buy their medications from Canadian pharmacies.

People in Canada simply don't die of curable diseases. The *survivorship* rate for serious diseases like cancer are much higher in the US than in countries with public healthcare systems, but the *mortality* rates are the same. That suggests people in the US are being diagnosed and treated for conditions that could have been safely left untreated. Diagnostics, surgeries, and medications can have major, potentially irreversible side effects, so over-treatment has serious negative impacts on quality of life. And, in the US, over-treatment can lead to bankruptcy. Healthcare costs are the leading cause of bankruptcy in the US.

Canada has no restrictions on abortion. Medical and recreational marijuana is legal.

The clearest, shortest explanation of the Canadian health care system I've come across is chapter two of Ezekiel J. Emanuel's *Which Country Has the World's Best Health Care?*

Education

Education is provided at no cost through high school. School systems are managed by the provinces. Schooling is offered in both English and French. Canadian 15-year-olds score above Americans on standardized tests.

The thing that stands out to me as an American is that there are publicly funded religious schools in Ontario, Saskatchewan, and Alberta. This is because separate schooling was guaranteed in 1867 and it's never gone away.

More than half of Canadians have a college degree, a rate far higher than any other country.

Canadian colleges and universities may not be as internationally known as big name US schools, but all Canadian universities provide a high-quality academic experience, while the US struggles with diploma mills and predatory for-profit colleges. Canadian schools generally have much lower tuition rates, sometimes half as much as you're likely to find in America, even when students are paying international tuition rates.

The Options

When decided I wanted to move to Toronto, my chances didn't seem particularly promising:

- I wasn't secretly a dual citizen.
- I was already married to an American.
- I didn't have any relatives in Canada.
- I didn't have a job offer from a Canadian company.
- I don't have any particularly noteworthy or in-demand skills.
- I wanted to follow international laws.

Luckily, Canada is eager for new residents and they make it easy for people to move here. In fact, one of the most confusing things about moving to Canada is the number of options. It's not uncommon for people to qualify for multiple programs.

Most people move to Canada as either a temporary resident or a permanent resident. Most temporary residents qualify to apply for permanent resident status after a year. Once you've been living in Canada as a permanent resident for three years you can apply for citizenship.

Before you read any further, there are a couple reasons why you wouldn't be able to apply for any of these programs. These include any situation where:

- You are considered a security risk,

- You have committed human or international rights violations,

- You have been convicted of a crime,

- You have ties to organized crime,

- You have a serious health problem requiring expensive ongoing treatments,

- You have a serious financial problem,

- You've previously been deported from any country, or

- One of your immediate family members is not allowed into Canada.

If you have a criminal conviction, not all hope is lost. If the conviction is from before you turned 18, you're likely still eligible for immigration. If you can get a record suspension or discharge, or convince them you've been rehabilitated, you might be fine.

If any of the above is relevant to you, you will want to hire an immigration attorney to decide if moving to Canada is really an option and to help you with your application.

One more important detail: Québec is different. In all things. They have their own work and immigration requirements that are different from the rest of Canada. I'll get into Québec-specific immigration later.

All the ways to live in Canada, legally

There are a lot of different ways to move to Canada. I'm going to explain all of the options briefly so you can decide which ones might be right for you. Once you've narrowed it down, you can learn more about each one later in the book.

Many of the ways you can move to Canada are designed to be temporary and provide a way to extend your stay permanently. Generally, if you can become a resident of Canada there will be a way for you to become a citizen eventually.

While few of these programs take your nationality into consideration, there are certain perks to being from a culturally similar country.

Live in Canada as an expat

There are a number of ways you can live in Canada as a temporary resident. These programs allow you to live in Canada for a few months to a few years. Some of these programs can be renewed indefinitely.

Take an extended vacation

If you don't plan on working while in Canada, you can stay in Canada as a tourist. Most tourist visas are issued for six months. At the end of your time, you can either apply to extend your tourist visa or simply leave the country and come right back. Doing this too often might raise some red flags at the border.

Visiting Canada can help you decide if you really want to move and where in Canada you'd like to live. It also gives you the opportunity to look for a job, check out schools, and look for love. Just remember, marrying someone for residency is a bad idea.

Visit your kids or grandkids

If you're the parent or grandparent of a Canadian citizen or permanent resident, you can get a super visa that allows you to stay for up to two years at a time.

Take a working holiday

Canada has agreements with a number of countries that allow young professionals under the age of 35 to work for up to two years in Canada through the International Experience Canada (IEC) program. After a year, you might be eligible to apply for permanent resident status.

Go (back) to school

Getting a university degree in Canada isn't the only way to get a student visa. You can also qualify by enrolling in a career training center, vocational school, or language school. As a student, you can work part-time during your studies. After you complete your program you can get a work permit for up to three years. You'll likely be eligible to apply to become a permanent resident before your work permit expires.

If you have a spouse or common law partner, they can work full-time during your studies. Depending on their job, you could both become permanent residents based on their work experience before you graduate.

Engage in free trade

Free trade agreements provide people from certain countries access to work permits with streamlined application processes. If you're from a country not mentioned here, it's worth checking, as Canada has similar free trade agreements with many countries.

US & Mexico

Thanks to the Canada-United States-Mexico Agreement (CUSMA), Canadian employers can easily hire American and Mexican citizens. You can work in Canada for up to six months without a work permit as a business visitor, trader, or investor. You can also get a work permit quickly.

Professionals can file for a TN work permit online and be issued a visa for up to three years within days. This is a streamlined process specifically for CUSMA. You can apply for a new visa every three years with no limit on the number of times you get a TN visa. If your company has an office in Canada they can transfer you up with little hassle.

The UK

Citizens of the UK have access to work permits through the Canada-UK Trade Continuity Agreement (CUKTCA). If you're a UK citizen who was working in Canada under CETA, you need to apply for a CUKTCA work permit.

Short-term business investors can stay up to 90 days in six months. Business visitors can spend up to a year in Canada.

Companies can transfer employees to their Canadian offices through CUKTCA.

The EU

If you're a citizen of an EU member country, you can qualify for a work permit through the Canada-European Union Comprehensive Economic and Trade Agreement (CETA). You can work for up to 90 days in six months as a business visitor. You can work on site to support your Canadian client(s) as a contractual service provider or independent professional for up to a year. Your company can transfer you to their Canadian branch. You can start a business in Canada or invest a substantial amount in one.

MERCOSUR

Canada is in negotiations to establish a free trade agreement with the MERCOSUR countries. Currently, no agreement exists.

Speak French

If you speak French you can get a temporary work permit through the Francophone Mobility program.

Find a job

Depending on your career and your professional network, you may find it easy to get a job in Canada or you may find it impossible. In order to hire you, a company will have to get you a work permit, which might require that they show there's no Canadian worker available to take the job.

Become a migrant laborer

The Seasonal Agricultural Worker Program (SAWP) is one of the few programs that's different depending on your citizenship. If you're interested in this program, you'll need to go through your government directly.

Moving to Canada permanently

One potential hurdle to moving to Canada is the amount of savings required. Most of the programs that allow people to become permanent residents of Canada require you to demonstrate that you have enough money to support yourself and your family while you get settled. This requirement is waived if you have a qualifying Canadian job offer or if you're already living in Canada as a temporary resident. This amount starts at C$13,200 and increases with the size of your family.

It doesn't matter if your family is moving to Canada with you or not, since you're still expected to support them. If you're in a relationship, your partner's savings can count toward the requirement. Aside from the legal requirement, it's wise to have savings when you immigrate. If you don't have a job lined up when you arrive or some sort of income, you'll burn through your savings pretty quickly. Moving is expensive.

One of the (few) perks of applying for the Quebec Skilled Worker Program is that the proof of settlement funds starts at the considerably smaller C$3,200.

If you don't have enough money in the bank, you'll need to be sponsored by a family member who can support you, apply with a valid job offer, apply from within Canada, or apply as a refugee. Or you can wait until you have more money saved up.

You don't need to be legally married to your partner in order for them to bring you to Canada. Canada recognizes common law and conjugal partnerships.

If you immigrate to Canada, they won't make you leave your kids behind. Anyone under the age of 22 who's not married is considered a dependent that is eligible to come with you, as is anyone who relies on you because of a physical or mental condition.

Already be a Canadian citizen

If you have a Canadian parent, it's likely that you're already a Canadian citizen.

Get serious with your Canadian sweetie

Are you married to or in a serious relationship with a Canadian citizen or permanent resident? They can sponsor you to become a permanent resident. If you apply from inside of Canada, you can get a work permit while you wait for your application to be approved.

Use your family connections

If you have a parent who's a Canadian citizen or permanent resident and you're under the age of 22, they can probably sponsor you for PR status. If your parent immigrated to Canada after you were born or adopted by them, they must have declared you on their application in order to be eligible to sponsor you.

If you're the parent or grandparent of a Canadian citizen or resident, they can sponsor you for PR status. However, this program has a limited number of spots each year and a huge number of applicants.

If you have another relative in Canada who's willing to sponsor you, you might be able to become a permanent resident. There are a lot of restrictions, so it's only the best option if it's the only option.

Be a business person

Running a startup? Canada is looking to hold its own against Silicon Valley, so they're building an excellent network to nurture startups and attract top talent. Up to five people can move to Canada under each startup visa. You'll need support from a designated VC fund, angel investor, or business incubator.

If you're an established entrepreneur or aspire to be one, most provinces have a Provincial Nominee Program (PNP) to help you move your business to Canada, start a new business in Canada, or buy an existing business.

Be uniquely talented and/or self-employed

The self-employment immigration program is an example of how bureaucracy lumps weird things together sometimes. There are three categories of self-employed people who qualify for this program:

- World-class authors, writers, actors, musicians, etc.,
- World-class athletes, and
- Farmers.

If you're a celebrity and you want to move to Canada, this is for you. You don't have to be a household name to qualify, since Canada is well aware that experts in certain fields are under-appreciated. However, if you qualify for Express Entry, it's faster for you to immigrate using that program.

The federal agri-food pilot program is accepting applications and there are various provincial programs.

Fun fact: Russia's Grand Duchess Olga immigrated to Canada as a farmer after fleeing the Russian Revolution.

Have skills they want

Express entry is Canada's skilled worker program. You don't need a job offer to be accepted. You also don't need to have advanced degrees or highly specialized skills. This program uses a points system, based on your age, language skills, education, work experience, connections to Canada, and adaptability.

The IRCC has a quiz to tell you if you qualify for express entry. It's a great tool to decide if it's worth it to start the process.

Live in Canada

If you're living and working in Canada, there's probably a way for you to become a permanent resident. If you don't qualify for express entry's Canadian experience class, there's likely a provincial program you'll qualify for.

Speak French

If you speak French, you're more likely to be selected for the various skilled worker programs and you may qualify for provincial programs.

Use your community ties

There are programs in some provinces for people with strong personal connections to someone in the province, such as a family member or close friend. You can also get a community group to sponsor you, such as if you are part of a faith or subculture with a tight-knit community in Canada.

These programs change regularly to meet the needs of the provinces and the application requires the complicated step of finding someone who is willing and eligible to sponsor you. Each province and each program has their own requirements and procedures.

These programs include:

- Manitoba Community Support
- Manitoba Family Support
- Nova Scotia Family Business Worker
- Prince Edward Islands Immigrant Connections
- Saskatchewan Family Members Category

Work as a caregiver

The live-in caregiver program (LCP) is closed to new applicants, as are several other caregiver programs.

The caregiver programs that are open now are pilot programs, meaning they may not be renewed when they end in five years.

These pilot programs only accept people who will meet the requirements for permanent resident status once they have two years of work experience through the pilot program. Once you've completed your two years, there will be a pathway to PR status and then citizenship.

Spouses or common-law partners of participants in these pilots will receive open work permits and dependent children will be able to accompany their parents.

If you don't qualify for any of these pilot programs, you can get a regular work permit if you have a job offer as a caregiver. However, your employer will need to get a LMIA and your work permit will only be valid for that employer.

It's also likely that new pilot programs will open in the future, as caregivers address a major and ongoing need.

Home Child Care Provider Pilot & Home Support Worker Pilot

In order to apply for either of these pilots, you need a job offer. However, your employer does not need to obtain a LMIA and you will be granted an occupation-specific open work permit. This means you are not forced to stay with the employer who originally hires you, but you can't switch careers.

The application process is different depending on the experience you have as a professional caregiver and if you have worked as a caregiver in Canada before.

Each of these programs is limited to 2,750 principal applicants per year.

Closed caregiver pilot programs

The Live-in Caregiver Program (LCP) was a pilot program and is not open to new applicants. The Interim Pathway for Caregivers is closed to new applicants. The Caring for Children and Caring for People with High Medical Needs programs are also closed to new applicants.

Other provincial nomination programs

If you don't qualify for express entry, you may still be able to become a permanent resident through the provincial nomination programs (PNP). These allow provinces and territories to select candidates based on their needs.

These programs change often. Most provinces have programs designed to retain people with connections to the province, especially people who are currently living, studying, or working there. Some communities with severe worker shortages have their own programs within the PNP system. PNPs are the best option for someone without a degree or work experience that's considered a skilled trade.

There are over 100 PNP programs. If the federal government doesn't want to try to keep a current list, I'm certainly not going to try. The best resource for information on PNPs is the CanadaVisa website.

Claim asylum

Twitter was full of eye-roll-inducing jokes about Americans moving to Canada as refugees during the Trump years, but there are legitimate reasons people qualify to move to Canada as a refugee.

Conventional refugees are living outside of their home country and can't return because of their: race, religion, political beliefs, nationality, sexual orientation, gender, or group membership. For example, a queer person from Nigeria might qualify for this status. If you're LBGTQ+ and interested in claiming refugee status in Canada, contact the Rainbow Refugee Society.

A person in need of protection is in Canada and can't return to their home country because they face the danger of torture, risk to their life, or risk of cruel or unusual treatment. Temporary workers from Afghanistan found themselves in this position in 2021.

Country of asylum class refugees have to live outside of their home country because of civil war, armed conflict, or because they are denied basic human rights on an ongoing basis. Refugees from the civil war in Syria qualify under this category.

If your claim is deemed eligible by the CBSA, you can live and work in Canada while your claim is considered. If your claim is accepted you become a protected person and can then apply for PR status.

Programs that are no longer open

In 2021 there was a lot of media attention around the pathway to PR status for essential workers who worked in Canada during the pandemic. This program closed on November 5, 2021.

Pathways to Canadian citizenship

These are the most common paths to citizenship for economic migrants.

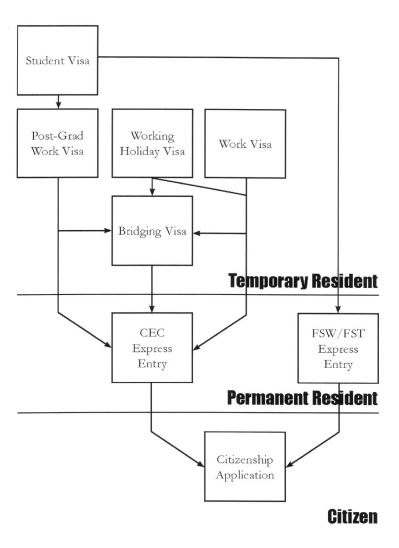

Retiring to Canada

There are no programs designed specifically to allow people to move to Canada for their retirement. The aging population is one of the reasons Canada is so friendly to immigrants—they want young people to balance out the 'silver tsunami' of aging baby boomers. Most immigration programs are designed to bring young professionals to Canada.

However, you may still be able to qualify to move to Canada, especially if you're excited about embarking on a second career while in Canada.

Long stays in Canada

If you're looking to spend your summers in beautiful Cape Breton, you're in luck. Visitors can spend up to six months a year in Canada without doing anything special. There's nothing stopping you from buying a vacation home on Prince Edward Island or in Prince Edward County. Theoretically you can stay for six months, leave the country for a day, and come right back for another six months. I imagine you'd face some extra questions at the border, though.

If you'd like to stay for more than six months, the easiest option is to extend your tourist visa. You need to do this at least 30 days before your current visitor visa expires. You have maintained status while your application is processed, meaning your visa is considered to remain valid while the new application goes through. If you dream of spending a year exploring Canada before moving back home (or on to your next adventure) this is your best option. As a visitor, you'll need to have your own health insurance coverage and, depending on how long you stay, you may need to file taxes in Canada.

The parent and grandparent super visa will allow you to live in Canada for up to two years at a time, assuming you have kids or grandkids living in Canada.

Going back to school is another great temporary option. Have you always dreamed of studying your passion, getting your PhD, or becoming fluent in French? Doing so will provide you (and your romantic partner) with residency for the duration of your program. You can even apply for a post-graduation work permit after your studies are complete, adding up to three years to your time in Canada.

Moving to Canada permanently

If you have children or grandchildren in Canada, they can sponsor you for permanent resident status through the family class program. If you don't have family to sponsor you, all other options require you to work in Canada.

Many people dream of starting a business once they've become financially independent. Canada has various entrepreneur and investor programs that you may qualify for.

If none of these options is right for you, there are plenty of other places that are eager to welcome retirees.

Retire in Quebec

The Québec Experience Program (Programme de l'expérience Québécoise or PEQ) doesn't take age into account. If you can legally work full-time in Quebec for two years or get a degree in Quebec and then land a job with your post-graduation work permit, you'll be able to apply for PR through PEQ.

Express entry for established professionals

Canada's skilled worker program, express entry, is designed to bring young professionals into the country. While it's relatively easy to qualify if you're under 35, it's still possible to qualify into your 40s if you have previous Canadian work experience, speak French, have advanced degrees, and especially if you have a qualifying job offer. There's no obligation to continue working once you get PR status through express entry.

Use your Canadian ties

You're not living in Canada now, but if you've lived in Canada at any point in your life, this can help you accumulate enough points to qualify for express entry.

If your degree is from Canada, you'll be awarded more points than if your degree is from any other country. You get additional points if you've worked in Canada previously. If you have a sibling who's a citizen or permanent resident, you'll get points.

Leverage your expertise to get a job

Getting a job offer can easily get you an invitation to apply. If you're an experienced professional who can use your network to land a job, this is a great way to get permanent resident status.

Statuses and rights in Canada

Everyone in Canada is protected by the Canadian Charter of Rights and Freedoms. Your rights as a visitor, student, temporary worker, or resident in Canada are the same, regardless of your nationality.

Visitors

Visitors to Canada can do things like open bank accounts, buy a home, buy a car, and enroll in courses lasting less than six months.

Depending on your nationality, you may have to apply for a visitor visa. Your nationality also determines how long that visa is for. Visitors from many countries, including the US, Australia, EU, and the UK don't have to apply for a visa to visit Canada, as they are automatically granted one at the border. Generally, you can spend up to six months in Canada as a visitor, but this is at the discretion of the border agent. If you're not from the US, you'll need an electronic Travel Authorization (eTA), which you can apply for online and only takes a few minutes. When you get to the border, you may also have to:

- Provide detailed information about the reason for your trip and your plans,

- Undergo a search,

- Prove that you're the guardian of any kids with you,

- Prove you have enough money for your trip,

- Prove you have plans to return home, and

- Demonstrate ties to your home country.

As a visitor, you can bring your own personal baggage and vehicles into Canada, but you may owe taxes on anything you leave in Canada. If you declare goods when you arrive and take them with you when you leave, you won't owe duty, but may be required to leave a security deposit for items with a high resale value.

You can be turned away at the border for any number of reasons. You need to be in good health, have proper travel documents, and convince the immigration officer that you will leave Canada when you are legally obligated to.

Dual intent

Dual intent is any situation where your intentions for your trip to Canada are unclear because you're doing two different things: entering Canada as a visitor while intending to stay permanently. You may be visiting Canada while waiting for your immigration paperwork to go through or intending to get married to a Canadian on your trip.

Dual intent can be a reason to turn you away at the border. However, this is rarely the case. If you qualify for multiple statuses or have a pending application for residency, be upfront about this with the border agent. Be ready to demonstrate that you understand immigration procedures, intend to follow them, and are really returning to your home country if your application is denied.

I entered Canada as a visitor several times after my express entry profile was submitted and even after my landing documents were issued. This attracted extra scrutiny at the border, but never caused anything more than a few minutes of delay. Be prepared to explain your situation and have any relevant documents on hand when traveling.

Temporary workers in Canada

There are two types of work permits that would allow you to reside in Canada as a temporary worker:

1. Open work permits allow you to work for any employer in Canada except those deemed to be ineligible to hire foreign workers by the government.

2. Employer specific work permits allow you to be employed by a specific company for a set amount of time, and sometimes in a specific location. You are permitted to look for a new job, but you will have to apply for a new work permit in order to switch jobs.

Temporary workers in Canada are protected by Canadian laws and must pay Canadian taxes.

Each province has its own worker protection laws, so they vary depending on where you're living in Canada. Regardless of where you are, temporary workers have the right to a safe and equitable workplace. Your employer:

- Cannot hold your passport or work permit,

- Must compensate you for all work, including overtime,

- Must allow for breaks and days off,

- Cannot threaten your legal status in Canada, and

- Cannot force you to perform tasks that you were not hired for.

If you're granted a work permit, you can bring your spouse and children with you to Canada. However, they cannot work without getting their own work permit. A working holiday visa does not allow you to bring your partner or children.

As a temporary worker, you will need private health insurance until you become eligible for provincial health insurance. They may ask to see proof of your insurance coverage at the port of entry. If you have family members coming with you, they'll also need health insurance.

Canadian permanent residents

You may be able to move to Canada as a permanent resident, like I did, or you may become eligible to become a permanent resident after living in Canada as a temporary resident. With PR status, you:

- Can live, work, or study in Canada,

- Are able to get most of the same benefits as citizens,

- Must pay taxes and follow all laws at the federal, provincial, and municipal levels,

- Can't vote or run for public office,

- Can join the Canadian armed forces,

- Can't hold certain jobs that require high-level security clearance, and

- May be deported if convicted of a serious criminal offense.

Healthcare in Canada is managed at the provincial level, so while you're eligible for government health insurance, you may need to meet other requirements, such as living in that province for a certain amount of time.

As a permanent resident, you're expected to live in Canada for two out of every five years, on a rolling basis. If you're living outside of the country for more than three years, you can lose your PR status.

You'll need to carry your passport and your PR card when traveling outside the country. Allowing the card to expire doesn't mean you've lost PR status, it just makes life a little more complicated.

If you were granted PR status in Canada and did not meet residency requirements, you don't automatically lose your PR status.

Canadian citizens

After you've been physically present in Canada for 1,095 days (three years) as a permanent resident, you're eligible to apply for citizenship. The days do not have to be consecutive, but they need to be within 1,825 days (five years). Some government employees (and their families) can be fast tracked to citizenship.

If you've stayed in Canada for three years since you obtained PR status, determining when you're eligible to apply for citizenship is simple. If you've traveled outside the country, you'll need to calculate the days using a tool provided by the IRCC.

Time spent as a temporary resident (student, temporary worker, etc) can add up to a year to your residency requirements. Time spent in prison does not count. Even if you don't plan on applying for citizenship yet, you'll need to use the physical presence calculator to demonstrate that you've met your residency requirements to renew your PR card.

Your application will need to include proof that you can speak English or French and that you've paid your taxes. You'll also have to take a citizenship test, covering aspects of Canadian history, government, and culture.

New Canadian citizens get Canoo, formerly the Cultural Access Pass, allowing you to visit cultural institutions for free during their first year of citizenship. This includes access to Canada's parks and historic sites run by Parks Canada.

If your original nationality allows dual citizenship, you do not have to renounce your citizenship in order to become a Canadian citizen. As a US, UK, or Australian citizen, you can be a dual citizen.

Canadian citizens have the right to:

- Live, work, or go to school in Canada.

- Vote in federal, provincial, territorial, or local elections, unless they've been living outside of Canada for more than five years.

- Express yourself, gather peacefully and groups, and practice your religion freely.

- Enter, remain in, or leave the country.

- Be treated with the same respect, dignity, and consideration regardless of personal characteristics.

- Have information presented, participate in government, and receive services in either English or French.

Canadian citizens can:

- Join the armed forces.

- Benefit from social welfare programs, such as healthcare, which may have residency requirements.

- Eliminate discrimination and injustice, help others in the community, and protect our heritage and environment.

Canadian citizens have the duty to:

- Respect the rights and freedoms of others.
- Obey Canada's laws and pay taxes.
- Participate in the democratic process by serving on a jury.
- Respect Canada's official languages and multicultural heritage.

Special circumstances

When you're already Canadian

If you have a Canadian parent, you're probably a Canadian citizen. You're a Canadian citizen if your parent was:

- granted Canadian citizenship on or after April 17, 2009, or
- born in Canada on or after February 15, 1977.

Things get tricky if your parent was born outside of Canada and you were also born outside of Canada.

- If you were born before April 17, 2009 and your parent was a Canadian citizen at the time, you are probably already a Canadian citizen, even if your parent was born outside of Canada. You just need to apply for proof of citizenship.

- If you were born outside of Canada on or after April 17, 2009 and your parent was also born outside of Canada, you are probably out of luck unless your parent was in the Canadian Armed Forces, in the federal public administration, or in the public service of a province or territory and stationed abroad when you were born.

If you're already a Canadian citizen, you can apply for a citizenship certificate online. Be warned that the processing time to get proof of citizenship is nearly as long as the processing time to become a citizen. There are some other less common instances where you may be a Canadian citizen outlined on the IRCC website, in which case you need to apply for a citizenship certificate using the paper application.

If you've secretly been Canadian all along, it'll be $75 to search for your record of citizenship and another $75 for proof of citizenship.

Why aren't I a citizen?

Before 1947 (or before 1949 in Newfoundland and Labrador) Canadians were British subjects. For various reasons, not everyone became a Canadian citizen when they made the switch. These people became Canadian citizens in 2015 when the laws were amended.

Between 1947 and 1977, being the child of a Canadian citizen didn't automatically make you a citizen if you were born abroad. Only children who were born in wedlock to a Canadian father or to a single Canadian mother and had their birth registered within two years were citizens. Children born to Canadian women and foreign fathers or unmarried foreign mothers had no right to citizenship. You were also out of luck if you were adopted by Canadians.

They fixed this later and people could apply for retroactive citizenship until 2004. However, the new rules still didn't include everyone. If the new rules excluded you, you had to apply to retain citizenship before your 28th birthday in order to stay a citizen. If you didn't apply, you lost your citizenship. In order to be eligible to retain your citizenship, you had to have a substantial connection with Canada after the age of 14 and before the age of 28 or have lived in Canada for a year before your application. People may have not known this and continued living their lives, not realizing they no longer had the legal status to stay in Canada. If this is the case, you can apply for permanent resident status and then resume your citizenship.

When you're from Hong Kong

In 2020 the IRCC announced they were taking special measures to attract immigrants from Hong Kong. The IRCC has promised priority processing for applicants from Hong Kong. In 2021 they even waived processing fees for people from Hong Kong that were already living in Canada and wanted to stay.

Open work permit

If you've recently graduated from a university program anywhere in the world, you may be eligible for an open work permit valid for up to three years. To qualify you need:

- A passport issued by the Hong Kong Special Administrative Region (HKSAR) or the United Kingdom for a British National Overseas (BNO), and
- A degree or diploma from a university program of at least two years issued within the past five years.

You can apply from inside or outside of Canada. You can include your immediate family members in your application.

Permanent resident program

People holding HKSAR or BNO passports who are already living in Canada can apply for PR status. Your immediate family members can be included in your application. This pathway is open from June 1, 2021, to August 31, 2026.

While the paper application is used, the IRCC encourages you to fill out the forms digitally and requires you to submit scans through Canada Post's online platform.

You can apply for this program from Quebec, but you must show that you intend to live in a province other than Quebec once you're approved. This means lining up a job and a place to live somewhere else, showing that you have family and friends in the area, or at least indicating that you're interviewing for jobs and preparing to relocate.

Recent graduates

In order to qualify as a recent graduate, you must have graduated from a designated learning institution in Canada within the previous three years. Two year diploma programs, degree programs (associate's, bachelor's, master's, or PhD), and one year certificate programs all qualify. At least half of your program must have been completed in Canada, even if the program was online.

Canadian work experience

In order to qualify based on your Canadian work experience, you must have graduated within the previous five years and have worked for at least 12 months full-time, or the part-time equivalent, in the previous three years. That's 1,560 hours of work in Canada performed with a valid work permit. You cannot count hours worked as a student or through self-employment.

When you're currently out of status

People living in the US, or any other country, without legal resident status can become legal permanent residents of Canada. If you're tired of waiting for the DREAM Act to provide you with a greencard or found yourself not qualifying, consider moving to Canada.

Your undocumented status in another country will not interfere with your ability to apply for permanent residence in Canada, but it will make things a little more complicated. You'll want to carefully check the information on the IRCC website and consider hiring an immigration attorney to help you. Don't make major life decisions without carefully checking the information you're given, as mistakes can have big consequences.

If you've significantly overstayed your visa in the US (or any country) or entered a country without passing through an official port of entry, you won't qualify for any sort of temporary visa from Canada. An illegal stay shows that you don't wish to return to your home country, so you won't be given a visitor visa, student visa, working holiday visa, or temporary foreign worker visa. You can, however, still apply for permanent resident status.

If you're able to obtain permanent resident status, you're free to work, attend school, and generally live your life as you see fit anywhere in Canada.

Most people can apply for a visa, PR status, and citizenship in Canada without the need for an immigration attorney. However, if you have any sort of criminal record or if you have been living as an undocumented immigrant for several years, you will likely benefit from working with an experienced immigration attorney.

Many immigration attorneys will consider the details of your case and let you know if moving to Canada is a realistic option in an initial consultation.

Move to Canada as a skilled worker

Assuming that you qualify for express entry, it's possible to apply without legal status in your current country. The IRCC is unlikely to request any confirmation of your current status as part of your application.

This is a great option for those of you who have a degree or skilled trade, at least one year of work experience, and are fluent in English or French. The process will take about six months.

If you're facing deportation proceedings, we've heard of people successfully getting their deportation hearing delayed by providing proof that they had applied for permanent resident status in Canada. A judge may give you time for your application to be processed.

Some applicants are required to attend an in-person interview at a visa application centre (VAC) as part of the application process. These interviews take place in whichever country you indicate that you currently reside in.

You may run into some complications when putting your application together.

Police certificates

The IRCC will require police certificates for all countries that you have lived in for six or more months since turning 18. This may be difficult in places that are particularly unfriendly to people without legal status.

If you indicate on your application that you have been living in the US, then you'll have to provide a FBI report. To get your fingerprints, you'll need to show a current, valid photo ID. When I applied for PR, I got my fingerprints done through the NYPD, but it's also possible to do this without going through local law enforcement. Some legal offices do fingerprints. I found reports of people that have gotten fingerprints in the US who were undocumented and didn't have any issues.

Job verification

Your application will have to include information about each job that you have had for the last ten years or since you turned 18. You'll also have to provide letters of employment from each employer.

This may prove difficult if you were working under the table. However, you do not need to provide pay stubs or tax returns, only a letter from your employer. At the very least, as the primary applicant, you'll need letters to verify the qualifying NOC work experience you have that counts towards the program.

Spousal sponsorship

The CIC frowns upon fake marriages, so they're not going to be thrilled if you met your beloved on Maple Match.

However, the US and UK are full of dual citizens (and people with permanent resident status). If you marry one (or live with one for a year and are in a serious relationship) they can sponsor you for permanent resident status as long as they demonstrate that they intend to move back to Canada once your application is approved.

Claim refugee status

It's unlikely that people who are undocumented in the US would qualify for asylum based on their experience in the US. However, some people fled their country of origin for reasons that would qualify them for asylum in Canada.

This is a complicated situation, since technically people are required to apply for asylum in the country they first enter due to the Safe Third Country Agreement. There are limited exceptions, but it's likely that your refugee claim will not be heard if you enter the country from the US border unless you have a family member already living in Canada.

Another complication is the amount of proof required in an asylum application. It's an incredible challenge to provide documentation of some situations and to show that you still face danger if you return to your country of origin.

Leaving the country you're currently in

If you own property or a business, you'll want to sell it or make a plan for continued management once you leave the country.

While it's unlikely that border patrol will arrest someone who is attempting to leave the country, it is technically possible. It is likely that they will ban you from re-entry. Some countries will fine people who've overstayed a visa. Enforcement tends to vary from one port of entry to another, so it's worth researching to see where you have the best odds and planning your travel accordingly.

One thing to keep in mind is that leaving the US after remaining in the country for a year without legal status will trigger a three or ten year ban on re-entry. You can apply for a waiver from this ban, but you must do so before you leave the US. You will likely qualify for a waiver if you were under 18 when you were brought to the US, have a pending adjustment of status case, or were a victim of abuse or human trafficking. After the ban expires, you'll be able to return to the US like a regular tourist or apply for resident status like anyone else.

When you're from Afghanistan

If you're a citizen of Afghanistan, you can contact the IRCC by phone at 1-613-321-4243 (reverse charges permitted) or through the web form. Mention that you're an Afghan national and you will actually get a timely response. If you have ties to the Canadian government, they will work with you to see how you can move to Canada.

Family sponsorship applications for people currently living in Afghanistan are being expedited.

You have a family member living in Canada because of their work as an interpreter

This program is open to the children (of any age), grandchildren, parents, grandparents, and siblings of people who immigrated to Canada under the 2009 or 2012 public policies.

These were special programs for local staff in Kandahar who supported Canada's mission in Kandahar Province in 2009 and certain local staff who provided direct support to the Canadian mission in Kandahar as of February 2012. If this applies to you, you can apply for PR status in Canada.

You have ties to Canada

People from Afghanistan who worked for Canada as interpreters for the Canadian Armed Forces, cooks, drivers, cleaners, construction workers, security guards and locally engaged staff employed at the Embassy of Canada to Afghanistan, and their family members are all eligible for PR status under expedited processing.

Approval is based on your ability to show a "significant or enduring relationship with the Government of Canada."

You qualify for humanitarian consideration

If you're living in Afghanistan and don't have a long-term solution to where you can safely live, you may be eligible to apply for PR in Canada. To qualify, you have to be a woman leader, human rights advocate, member of a persecuted religious or ethnic minority, LGBTI, or a journalist or someone who helped Canadian journalists.

Communicating with the IRCC

The IRCC communicates with applicants through email, physical mail, and online portals. The type of communication used is not consistent.

You can call the IRCC National Call Centre at 1-888-242-2100. They have an email address as well: question@cic.gc.ca.

The IRCC says that incomplete or incorrect applications will be returned to you. As far as I can tell, this isn't generally the case. They'll contact you via email or the postal system and request additional or corrected documents.

Mail from the IRCC

The IRCC sometimes mails letters confirming the receipt of an application. They may both email this letter (as an attached PDF) and send a letter through the postal system. They may only email the letter and not send a physical copy through the mail.

These letters may arrive months after application processing has begun or they may not arrive at all. Thankfully, you do not need this confirmation of receipt letter to check the status of your application online.

You may occasionally get other mail sent to your home address on file from the IRCC, typically with requests for additional documents.

Email from IRCC

The IRCC seems to be shifting to prioritize email communication.

Email from the main IRCC office tends to come from "CE CSC Do Not Reply / Ne Pas Repondre CSC EC (IRCC)" with the subject line "Immigration, Refugees and Citizenship Canada // Immigration, Réfugiés et Citoyenneté Canada" or something similar, making it abundantly clear who is sending it. Of course, be careful to check the actual address and content of the letter if things ever seem suspicious, as scam artists have been known to spoof IRCC communications.

Email from individual departments and offices will come from different addresses. The IRCC was known as Citizenship and Immigration Canada (CIC) until 2015. Some offices have not updated their wording. As of 2021, email from the Etobicoke IRCC office arrives with the subject heading "Etobicoke CIC - Communication to client /Communication auprès de la clientèle".

The webform

Submitting requests for information through the IRCC webform is a bit like sending a letter in a bottle out to sea. You may or may not ever get a response and you shouldn't expect to hear back right away.

Make sure your messages are clear and concise. IRCC agents are skimming this and if they don't understand your message or don't immediately decide it's important, they will either not respond or reply with a generic message.

Updating contact information

If you move or any of your contact information changes, let the IRCC know right away. You can update this information online through the webform. They will confirm receipt of your updated contact information within a few days.

Application modifications

There is one time the IRCC wants to hear from you: when something in your application needs to be updated. You should submit information through the webform if you:

- Change your contact information
- Hire (or fire) an attorney or immigration consultant
- Have a change in the number of people included in your application (such as you get divorced, you get married, you have a child, you adopt a child, or someone on your application dies)
- Change jobs, if that's relevant to your pending application

If there is a form to use to request a change, such as correcting a typo on a document, you need to use the correct form and submit that along with your request. Submitting a request through the typeform without the form or mailing a letter to the IRCC will lead to low-priority processing. This is a bureaucracy and you need to work with how they do things. Anything requiring processing outside of normal guidelines will cause a lengthy delay.

The IRCC will respond with a confirmation that they've received these documents within a few days.

General questions

If you have a question about how things work, the IRCC prefers you use their help center, figure things out on your own, or hire an expert. The webform is primarily used to update your application after it has been submitted. If the IRCC does respond, it's likely you'll get a generic message:

"Thank you for contacting Immigration, Refugees and Citizenship Canada (IRCC).

IRCC is always striving to improve our customer service. Rest assured that our priority is to answer your needs.

If your enquiry has yet to be answered via other channels such as our phone agents, paid representatives, community centres, etc., please write back to us using the IRCC Web form."

Application status updates

If they decide you aren't being patient enough and your application is still within normal processing times, they likely won't respond. During the pandemic, there is no such thing as normal processing times, so no matter how long you've been waiting it's too soon to ask for an update. The official response is going to be:

"Even if you haven't heard from us recently, your application remains in process. You don't need to do anything else at this time. We'll contact you if we need more information. You can also check the status of your application online."

If they're particularly busy, due to the pandemic or a political crisis, they won't respond. The message is:

"Thank you for contacting Immigration, Refugees and Citizenship Canada (IRCC).

In order to respond to the high volume of enquiries related to the situation in Afghanistan we have shifted resources in our Client Support Centre and are responding to priority enquiries only.

We will respond to these priority enquiries only:

- *Clients in crisis situations (like those affected by the situation in Afghanistan)*
- *Clients facing vulnerable circumstances (emergency and urgent requests)*
- *Clients who need to tell us about a change in their circumstances, which has a direct impact on their application (like marriage, birth of a child, or similar)*
- *Clients who are submitting documents requested by one of our officers*
- *Changes in contact information*
- *Requests to withdraw an application or refunds*
- *Ask questions about the 2021 invitations to apply to sponsor parents and grandparents*

If your enquiry is NOT one of the priority enquiries listed above, you will not receive a reply.

If you included attachments with your enquiry, rest assured that they will be added to your file shortly."

The official line is that the people responding to webform inquiries have no more information on your application status than you do, but I have successfully gotten status updates in response to the webfom. When the IRCC requested additional paperwork and I never got a confirmation of receipt, an agent emailed me back and confirmed they had gotten the documents and were no longer waiting on me. They have more information than is given to you in the various IRCC portals and they also know which portal messages are inaccurate.

I've also gotten generic requests for more information I included in my initial inquiry and no response to my follow-up:

"Thank you for contacting Immigration, Refugees and Citizenship Canada.

We thank you for your patience and understanding regarding the delay for answering your enquiry due to the ongoing situation related to COVID-19.

We verified the information you provided; however, we require further information in order to access the file.

In order to better assist you, we invite you to resubmit your request by filling out the IRCC Web form and include the following information:

- *Surname and complete given name (including middle name, if applicable) - exactly as they appear on the passport or identity document,*
- *Date of birth (YYYY-MM-DD),*
- *Client ID Number, UCI or Application Number,*
- *Country of birth,*
- *Type of application,*
- *Date on which the application was submitted or received,*
- *Mailing method (courier, Canada Post (registered or regular mail), etc.),*
  - ○ *company used,*
  - ○ *confirmation no.,*

- *Complete address (including the postal code and the unit number) where the application was sent,*
- *Receipt number,*
- *Current address,*
- *Telephone number(s),*
- *Email address, and*
- *All documents submitted with your previous request.*

If you are contacting us on behalf of someone else:
- *Please make sure to enter their information under the Applicant Information section and your information under the Enquirer Information section, and*
  - *if you are not an authorized representative or designated individual, please also include the following information in the Your enquiry box of the Web form:*
    - *your surname and complete given name (including middle name, if applicable),*
    - *your date of birth (YYYY-MM-DD), and*
    - *your country of birth.*
- *If applicable, provide a Use of a Representative (IMM 5476) form, a Release of Information to an Individual (IMM 5475) form or a Power of Attorney in order to be authorized to receive the requested information.*

We will gladly reply to your enquiry following reception of the above information. Usually, it takes us 5 business days to respond. Due to the impacts of COVID-19 however, it may take us longer to respond to your enquiry.

We invite you to consult regularly the How the coronavirus disease (COVID-19) is affecting immigration, refugees, citizenship and passport services page for the latest updates.

Furthermore, please note that there are two ways you can check your application status online. You can verify the status of your application:

- Submitted by mail (if it was not linked to an online account):
    - by using the e-Client Application Status (e-CAS) online tool, which is updated daily.
- Submitted online or submitted by mail and linked to an online account:
    - through your online account.

We hope the information provided is helpful in assisting you with your enquiry."

In response to missing communications

You may find yourself wondering if the IRCC sent you an email or paper correspondence that was never delivered.

There are times when the IRCC portals provide incorrect information. For example:

- The IRCC tracking tool for PR card renewals says they've mailed you instructions on how to pick up your PR card in person when no letter has been sent. This may mean your card is in production and the card will be sent to you. It can also mean you'll eventually be contacted for an in-person review of your file.
- The citizenship tracking tool provides a date for a citizenship ceremony and says an invitation has been emailed when no

email has been sent. It will be sent until within a week of the ceremony, sometimes within 24 hours of the ceremony.

In cases like this, there is no point in contacting the IRCC, because they will reply with a generic message that doesn't answer your question, if they reply at all. Instead, search online for the exact wording of the problematic messaging and you'll likely find someone else who has already solved the mystery.

IRCC online portals

The IRCC uses several online portals to accept applications online, conduct tests and meetings, and update applicants about the status of their application. Not all of these portals offer email notifications when information is updated. Even if email notifications are sent, they are often filtered out as spam. It's wise to check these portals periodically.

Messages in these portals tend to be vague, such as saying "decision made" without giving any indication as to what that decision has been.

Messages may also be out of date, such as saying a letter will be mailed within four weeks despite considerable processing delays or saying a letter has been mailed when it's standard procedure not to mail a letter at all. Online forums are an excellent resource for finding out when the information in the portal is not accurate.

If the IRCC has sent you email or physical mail requesting additional documents or assigning you an appointment time, this information will not be shown on your portal. Thus, if a letter is lost in the post or an email ends up in spam, there is no way to know.

Living in Canada as an Expat

Not every move has to be a permanent one. Many people want to live in Canada for a while before returning home or moving on to their next destination. In popular tourist spots and major cities it can seem like everyone you meet is there on a working holiday visa. Canadian universities are full of international students. Canadian offices thrive thanks to international workers spicing up their CVs to make them more marketable back home.

Perhaps you are interested in potentially staying forever, but you want to make sure it's the right choice for you before you commit. Maybe you don't qualify to become a permanent resident right away, but you'd like to become one in the future. I'll go over whether or not each of these options sets you on a pathway to citizenship.

Life as a perpetual tourist

If you can get a tourist visa to enter Canada, you can generally stay for six months. Many countries are visa-exempt and don't require you

71

to do anything to get a tourist visa other than showing up at a port of entry. The length of your visa is at the discretion of the border agent, but it's rare for them to not give you six months automatically.

This is the simplest solution if you'd like to spend some time in Canada, but don't really want to uproot your life and move. An extended visit to Canada is great if you're confident that you can use this time to decide where you want to live, get a job offer, or find a Canadian to settle down with. It's not a long-term solution on its own if you really want to move to Canada.

I went back and forth between Toronto and New York for almost two years and had no problem. Occasionally I'd get a few extra questions at the border, but it never took more than a few minutes. I had a home in both cities, a job in New York, and usually had a return flight booked. It's easy to split your life between Canada and the US, thanks in part to Canadian snowbirds.

The most common problem with life as a perpetual tourist is figuring out how to continue to support yourself without the legal right to work. You'll want to be prepared to show that you have enough money in your bank account to support yourself while in Canada. If you're staying with someone during your time in Canada your expenses will be lower, but you could be asked for a letter from them saying that they'll be providing you with room and board.

You'll need to get health insurance that covers you for your time in Canada. If you're staying in Canada for more than six months a year, you'll likely be considered a resident for tax purposes.

eTAs

If you're a citizen of a country that doesn't require a tourist visa to enter Canada but not a US citizen, you need an electronic travel authorization (eTA) to enter Canada by air. If you're a US greencard holder, you'll need an eTA, regardless of your country of citizenship.

You can apply online for a small fee, currently $7. There are fraudulent websites out there, so make sure you're applying through canada.ca. Most of the time people receive their eTA within minutes of applying. Your eTA is valid for five years. If you're traveling with your family, each person needs a separate eTA.

The eTA application will ask about your criminal record and health. They verify the information you provide with their databases. Being approved for an eTA does not guarantee you'll be allowed to enter Canada, which is at the discretion of the border guard.

If you're denied an eTA, you can apply for a temporary resident permit (TRP).

Tourist visas

If you're from a country that requires a tourist visa to enter Canada, you'll need to apply for one ahead of time. You'll need to show your itinerary, travel history, proof of funds, family information, and identity documents.

If you're denied a tourist visa, you can apply for a temporary resident permit (TRP).

Extending your stay beyond six months

When your visitor visa expires, technically you can cross the border and come back again for another six months. Border agents may be concerned about the likelihood of you overstaying your visitor visa. Any documents you can provide to show that you have ties to your home country, like a job or property, make it easier to alleviate their concerns.

You can also apply to extend your visitor visa, rather than making visa runs to the border. As long as you've applied to extend or change your visa before it expires, you can stay in Canada while you wait for them to make a decision, thanks to maintained status.

If you want to spend your gap year or sabbatical traveling around Canada, this is a simple process that can be done online.

Working remotely as a tourist

Since I work remotely, I was able to continue working while I was in Toronto. I was honest with the border agents I spoke with and let them know I would be working remotely for US companies while in Canada.

The border agents I spoke to said working remotely during my time in Canada as a tourist was okay. It all depends on whether what you're doing is legally considered work. The IRCC states that "long distance (by telephone or Internet) work done by a temporary resident whose employer is outside Canada and who is remunerated from outside Canada" is not considered work.

You can also work for a foreign company while in Canada if your work falls under CUSMA's business visitor provision, which doesn't require any paperwork, or a similar free trade agreement. This allows you to attend conferences, buy and sell goods and services, provide after-sales support, and get and lead training.

I work for a nonprofit providing free services, so things may be more complicated if you have a job where money is involved. From talking to other people who've worked remotely while on a tourist visa in Canada, it seems that working remotely is permitted as long as the actual business transactions are taking place abroad. Payments need to be processed outside of Canada. Processing and shipping of goods needs to be done outside of Canada. Other sorts of work, where the goods and money are not crossing into Canada's jurisdiction, seem to be allowed. Your company's legal department likely has an opinion on this, especially if you work in finance.

Traveling affordably

The perennial question is how anyone without a trust fund can afford to spend six months or more traveling around a high cost of living country like Canada. It's easy to spend a lot of money quickly. With creativity and planning it's also easy to travel around Canada, meet people, and learn new skills without spending much money at all.

Housing

If you want to travel around Canada without spending all of your money on hotels and hostels, CouchSurfing and house sitting are potential solutions for free places to stay. CouchSurfing connects hosts and travelers for cultural exchanges. It's a very short homestay you organize yourself. If you're 40+ you can join the Affordable Travel Club and if you're 50+ the Evergreen Club is another option for affordable home stays. As a house sitter you take care of whatever the resident would typically take care of, such as pets and a garden.

WWOOF connects small farms with volunteer workers. Volunteers work half-time in exchange for room and board. HelpX, WorkAway, and WorldPackers combine the features of CouchSurfing, WWOOF, and House Sitters Canada, while also including other types of situations providing housing, including helping in B&Bs and providing companion care to people with disabilities. The work expected and the living conditions vary significantly, so check each host's listing and reviews carefully.

These sites all have nominal annual membership fees and then provide access to opportunities for free accommodation and potentially free meals, transportation, training, and other perks. The fees may or may not be worth it for you, but these are all legitimate sites with numerous real opportunities. You can look through the listings before joining to help you decide if it's something you're seriously interested in. This sort of travel is a completely different experience from staying in a hotel and it's certainly not for everyone. If your only motivation is to save money, it's not going to be worth it.

Questions at the border

It's wise to anticipate potential questions and come up with simple, true ways to explain what you'll be doing in Canada and how you'll be supporting yourself without working. Be prepared to show an itinerary, at least for the first few weeks of your trip, including the names, addresses, and contact information for where you'll be staying. Most work exchange sites allow you to download this easily for confirmed stays.

Volunteering in exchange for room (and board) is considered tourism, so it's important to be clear that you're entering Canada for the purpose of tourism. Any home stay program, including staying on farms, is a cultural exchange and educational opportunity. You need to ensure the border agent understands that your volunteer work is incidental to the main reason for your visit to Canada and you are not in competition with Canadian workers.

Volunteering without a work permit

Volunteering in exchange for room and board is legal without a work permit with non-commercial hosts for up to four weeks per host. Still, mentioning any of these programs to a border agent can raise red flags that you might be working illegally. Things like pet sitting and farm work are commonly done as both volunteer work and paid labor and border agents are trained to be suspicious. Mentioning CouchSurfing raises red flags at the border just like visiting an internet girlfriend does. They suspect there's more to the story and switch into interrogation mode.

It's important to remember that you can only stay with non-commercial hosts without a work permit. The vast majority of farms listed on WWOOF are non-commercial and each listing indicates if it's commercial or not. The IRCC defines a non-commercial farm as: "A non-commercial farm generally means a farm where the farm family provides much of the capital and labour for the farm and where the production of agricultural products is to provide for the basic needs of the family, with little extra to sell for the profit of the family. This form of farming is commonly known as 'subsistence', 'hobby' or 'family' farming." If you aren't sure, check with the host. You can also only stay with each host for a maximum of four weeks without a work permit. In some areas it'd still be quite easy to spend a whole year in the same area by hopping from one farm to another.

As long as you follow these guidelines, you are not considered a worker. When perusing listings on HelpX, Workaway, and other sites, be careful to consider whether it would be legal to accept an assignment. Staying with a family in exchange for household help or language lessons is considered tourism. Volunteering in a hostel is considered working for a commercial enterprise, even if it's operated by a non-profit.

If you have a working holiday visa through International Experience Canada or an open work permit, you're free to volunteer for commercial enterprises or take paid employment.

Getting a work permit to volunteer

If you're volunteering meets the legal definition of work, you may be able to get a work permit. Charitable and religious work is LMIA exempt, streamlining the application process and reducing the cost. If you are not being paid or only receiving a stipend, you and the organization may have all processing fees waived. There are three Camphill communities in Canada that sponsor work permits for volunteers, as well as a similar community outside of Montreal. If you're a member of a faith community, look into opportunities to volunteer in Canada.

If you are given an employer-specific work permit for your charitable work, your spouse or common-law partner becomes eligible to apply for an open work permit.

Transportation

Canada is a very large country and getting around can be difficult. Flying within Canada is quite expensive compared to flights in Europe and even the US. Train service is limited, infrequent, and expensive. Often the bus is the most affordable option. It can be confusing because there are so many different regional services. BusBud and Rome2Rio help you find your transit options and choose the best one for your budget and timeline.

Another option, especially when there is no public transportation, is finding a ride share. Poparide and Amigo Express both connect riders with drivers. You can also find rideshares and travel buddies in numerous Facebook groups.

Buying a car as a tourist

You'll have no problem buying a car as a tourist. Registering and insuring it can be a different matter. Both are mandatory. You can't insure a car in Ontario or Alberta without a local drivers license. Regardless of where you are, you'll need to list a local address for registration and insurance.

I've been told that British Columbia is the best province to buy a car in terms of being able to register and insure a car with a foreign license. You can even get a safe driver discount by providing a driving record from your home country. If you're planning on road tripping around Canada, it might be worthwhile to start your trip in BC. If you're moving to Canada and plan on staying in one location, you'll need to register the car in that province and probably need to update your license.

If you opt to trade your foreign license for a Canadian license, know that they'll confiscate your foreign license. You'll need to get a new license abroad when you leave Canada.

Many drivers sign up with CAA to get roadside assistance.

International Experience Canada

Canada has agreements with a number of countries that allow people under the age of 35 to work for up to two years in Canada through the international experience Canada (IEC) program. It's also commonly known as the permis vacances travail (PVT), especially if you're in Quebec and people are complaining about their neighborhood filling up with PVTistes.

There are actually three IEC programs. You can:

- Travel while working with a working holiday.

- Gain international work experience as a young professional.

- Get work experience in your field with an international co-op.

You have to be at least 18 to apply, but the cutoff ranges from 30 to 35, depending on your nationality. You can't begin the application process until you're 18, but once you're approved you can enter Canada after you're too old to apply as long as you are selected before you age out of the program.

Here are the age cutoffs for common countries that are eligible for the IEC program:

Australia (30), Austria (30), Belgium (30), Chile (30), Costa Rica (35), Croatia (35), Czech Republic (35), Denmark (35), Estonia (35), France (35), Germany (35), Greece (35), Hong Kong (30), Ireland (35), Italy (35), Japan (30), Korea (30), Latvia (35), Lithuania (35), Mexico (29), Netherlands (30), New Zealand (35), Norway (35), Poland (35), Slovakia (35), Slovenia (35), South Korea (35), Spain (35), Sweden (30), Switzerland (35), Taiwan (35), Ukraine (35), UK (30)

Some countries are part of one IEC program, while others are part of two or all three. Each participating IEC country has an annual quota of places based on reciprocal agreements with Canada. Some nationalities have their spaces fill up quickly because demand far exceeds supply.

The IEC year runs from autumn to autumn, so it's worthwhile to enter the pool as soon as it opens for the year. It's not first-come, first-served anymore, so submitting your information within the first week or two is sufficient.

Now there's a points system that assesses your ability to be successful in Canada. This is because Canada really wants young people to come establish a career here, so they prioritize people who would likely qualify to become permanent residents.

The length of the work permit depends on the program and your country of nationality. If you're a dual citizen you can use each passport separately, doubling your opportunities to use the program.

If your nationality isn't on the list, like the US, that means your country doesn't have a bilateral youth mobility agreement. You can still do the IEC program as long as you apply through a recognized organization (RO). It adds to the cost. It also means there's an organization helping you with the application, moving, and finding jobs once you arrive.

You'll need to show you have access to at least C$2,500 to prove you won't go broke while you're in Canada. Yes, you'll have a work permit, but presumably you'll be doing touristy things for part of the time and won't necessarily be working from the day you arrive. You'll need a bank statement or letter from your bank issued within a week of your arrival to Canada. If you're doing an unpaid internship you'll need to show that you can support yourself for the entire length of your stay. You don't need a year's worth of money in your bank account. You can show a letter of support from a family member or proof of a scholarship.

Typically, you don't need a job offer for the working holiday visa program. In 2021 the IRCC did require job offers for all applicants in order to limit non-essential travel during the pandemic. It doesn't appear that participants were required to work for a single employer the whole time, like with a typical work permit. It appears that a job offer for several weeks of work was sufficient. The requirements are much less stringent than for standard work permits, so if someone qualifies for IEC, it's in an employer's best interest to use this program.

Unlike other types of work permits, the IEC program does not allow you to bring your family. If your partner wishes to come, they'd need to apply for their own IEC visa.

The IEC application process

1. See if you're eligible using the Come to Canada tool on the IRCC website.

2. Use your personal reference code to create a MyCIC account. Select the option to Apply for Visitor Visa, Study, and/or Work Permit and complete your IEC profile.

   o If a field doesn't apply to you, enter N/A.

   o Some countries require you to be a current resident in order to apply for IEC using their bilateral agreement.

   o You may need to combine multiple PDFs into one document or print, sign, and scan files for your application.

   o It's advisable to print your application for your records.

3. You're placed in the pool and must wait for your invitation to apply (ITA). Be sure to set up email notifications for your MyCIC account and add the email to your address book. If you do not receive an ITA, your profile expires after a year. Don't worry, you can just create a new profile until you age out of eligibility.

4. When you're sent an ITA, you must accept it within 10 days or it will expire. If it expires, you'll be put back in the pool and

may be given another invitation in the future. If you have a job offer, your employer needs to submit that to the IRCC at this point.

5. Once you've accepted the ITA, you have 20 days to apply for your work permit. This is when you pay the fees for your program.

6. After submitting your work permit application, you'll be sent a request to submit biometrics. You have 30 days to submit your biometrics.

7. It takes about eight weeks for your application to be processed. You can check current processing times. If you don't hear back in eight weeks, you can request an update. If it's approved, you'll receive a Port of Entry (POE) letter in your myCIC mailbox.

8. Depending on your nationality, you may need to send your passport to the embassy to get a visa.

9. Take your POE letter with you to the airport and present it to customs when you land. The visa officer at customs will give you your work permit. You must enter Canada within 12 months of when your medical exam was done. If you don't, it expires and you'd have to start over from the beginning.

Don't book your flight, enroll in health insurance, lease an apartment, or otherwise cut ties with your home country until you have your POE letter.

If you'd like to visit Canada as a tourist before you activate your IEC visa, you can do that. When you arrive in Canada, let the border agent know that you have an IEC permit, but you would like to enter Canada on a tourist visa and activate your IEC permit at a later date. I know several people who've done this without a problem. Just be sure to activate it before it expires.

Types of IEC permits and the selection process

There are three IEC programs: Working Holiday, Young Professionals, and International Co-op. Candidates are invited to apply in rounds based on their nationality and points scores.

Working holiday visas

Working holiday visas provide you with an open work permit, meaning you can work for anyone you'd like. You can work for one employer the whole time or you can work for several different employers. Applicants are selected from the pool at random.

If you're applying for a working holiday permit and you are asked for an offer of employment number, type "A9999999" in the field. Even if you have work arranged in Canada, the working holiday visa is an open work permit, so you should not include their information unless it's required as part of the temporary pandemic changes.

Young Professional & International Co-op

Young Professional & International Co-op applicants will be invited to apply for a work permit as long as there are spots available. These programs require that you have a job, co-op, or internship arranged when you apply for your IEC work permit. Your permit will only be valid for that specific employer. You can't get a second job with another employer.

You can change your employer if the company has closed, you are not being paid the wages you were promised, your working conditions are unsafe, or if you have been fired. You'll need to contact the IRCC to update your permit.

If your work contract ends before your work permit does, you can renew your contract with the same employer, stay in Canada as a visitor until your permit expires, or leave Canada before your permit expires.

Documents you need for IEC

Once you're invited to apply, you have 30 days to submit your application. It can easily take more than 30 days to gather all of the paperwork, so you should start the process before getting your ITA.

International Co-op applicants must provide proof of school registration and an internship agreement outlining the position title, description of tasks to be performed, the start and end dates, the address of the internship site, and the employer's contact information.

Applicants applying through an RO must include a copy of the confirmation letter from the RO.

Proof of funds

You can show you have the money to support yourself during your time in Canada by showing:

- A bank statement from the last week showing at least C$2,500.

- A letter from your bank from the previous week saying you have at least C$2,500 in your account.

- A bank cheque for C$2,500.

- Pay stubs.

- Proof of a student loan providing funds.

- A letter of support from the person or institution funding you.

Resume

This is not a resume like you would provide to a potential employer. This is a timeline of your education, work, travel, and life in general. You want to account for all of your time, with no gaps. If you were unemployed, caring for an ill relative, or backpacking you should include that. If there are any gaps in your resume the IRCC will likely ask you for more information, which could delay your application.

Police certificate

Depending on your nationality, you'll likely need to provide a police certificate. You will need to provide a police certificate for any country you've lived in since you turned 18, including any country where you spend more than six months in a row.

When including multiple certificates, you'll need to provide them all in one document, as there is only one upload field.

Getting a police certificate can take a very long time. You can upload your receipt or a screenshot of the confirmation page as proof that you've requested the police certificate and they'll provide you with a new deadline.

Medical exam

Not every applicant requires a medical exam. This depends on what type of job you're applying for and if you've lived in or traveled to certain countries.

If you need a medical exam, you have to go to a panel physician. They'll give you a form for you to upload with your application. If you can't get a medical exam before your 30 days are up, you can upload proof that you've scheduled one.

Digital photo

You must provide a passport photo that meets IRCC specifications. They are very fussy about this, so make sure you follow instructions carefully.

Passport

Your work permit will only be issued for as long as your passport is valid. You also need at least one blank page in your passport, other than the last page.

Visitor visa application

If you come from a country that requires visitor visas, you'll need to apply for a visitor visa. You will automatically get an eTA once your work permit application is approved. Your eTA is valid for five years, so you can leave and enter Canada without needing a new one.

Letter of explanation

If you were unable to provide all documentation by the deadline through no fault of your own, you can write a letter of explanation and ask for the deadline to be extended or for the requirement to be waived. It's important to provide whatever proof you can that you requested the documents (such as a police certificate) in a timely manner.

You have the option of including a letter of explanation with your application. Some people find that the system requires this, due to a bug. To get around this, you can upload a blank document and then delete it before submission.

Biometrics

You may be required to submit biometrics: a photo and fingerprints. This must be done at a visa application centre (VAC) or application support centre (ASC). There are no VACs or ASCs in Canada, so if you are applying from within Canada you may need to leave the country to do this. This was not required prior to 2018. The

IRCC has a tool to help you determine if you need to provide biometrics.

You are responsible for getting yourself to a VAC or ASC and paying C$85 to have the biometrics done.

Arriving in Canada

When you arrive in Canada, you'll need to provide the following documents to a border services officer:

- Your passport

- Your POE letter

- Proof of funds

- Proof of health insurance

- A ticket to leave Canada at the end of your stay or proof of funds to purchase a ticket.

- If you are doing an unpaid co-op, you may be asked to provide proof of enough money to support yourself for the entire time.

You can be refused entry into Canada if you're missing any of these documents.

If you are bringing C$10k or more across the border with you, you have to let them know. You may be asked to show proof of where the money came from.

If you've lost your POE letter, they'll print you a new one.

Your health insurance must be valid for your entire stay. It needs to cover medical care, hospitalization, and repatriation. If your insurance coverage ends before your expected stay, your work permit will expire when your insurance does. A provincial health card will not meet this requirement. The IEC cannot be extended, so if insufficient insurance shortens your work permit's validity, you may not be able to work long enough to qualify for PR through a skilled worker program.

When you've been given your work permit, check it over carefully before you leave the international zone. Check the bilateral agreement between Canada and your country of nationality to make sure the length of your work permit is correct. Make sure your work location is correct. If you're doing a working holiday, it should say "open."

If there's a mistake on the permit, tell a border services officer immediately. If there's a mistake it's much more difficult (or impossible) to fix it once you leave.

Planning your trip

You're responsible for everything about planning your time in Canada, from completing the application to finding a job and getting a place to stay. If you'd like to have help organizing these details, you can work with a RO.

Some other countries have restrictions on how long you can work for a single employer during a working holiday. There are no such restrictions in Canada and working for a single employer for a full year will simplify your eligibility for permanent resident status.

Costs

The fees vary depending on your nationality and the program. There is no fee to enter the applicant pool. The fees for the US:

- International Experience Canada: C$156

- Working Holiday: additional C$100

- Young Professional & International Co-op: your employer must pay a C$230 compliance fee and submit your offer of employment to IRCC before you submit your work permit application.

Additional paperwork

You'll have to pay for things besides just IRCC fees. These are the costs for New York City, so they'll vary depending on where you're living when you apply.

- Police certificate: $18

- Fingerprinting: $25

- Medical exam: $350

- Passport photos: $20

- Biometrics: C$85

Staying in Canada after your IEC permit expires

You generally cannot renew or extend your IEC work permit. You can apply to change employers, extend your employment, update your passport information, remove medical restrictions, and correct the expiration date.

Some countries allow you to participate multiple times. If you're a citizen of more than one country, you can apply for the maximum number of times using each passport. You may also be eligible to get a work permit through another program.

If you're applying for a new work permit, you must apply at least 30 days before your current work permit expires. Your SIN expires when your work permit does. It should reactivate automatically when your new permit is approved.

You may be able to extend your stay in Canada as a visitor after your work permit expires. You need to do this before your work permit expires. If you're from a country that doesn't require visas to visit Canada and the US, you can also simply cross from Canada into the US and re-enter Canada as a tourist.

After a year of working in Canada, you might be eligible to apply for permanent resident status through the express entry Canadian experience (CEC) program. You might have fallen in love with a Canadian (hopefully they love you back). If you'd like to stay but don't qualify for PR or an additional IEC visa, you can look into other work or study permit options.

Studying in Canada

Attending a university, training program, or language school in Canada doesn't just get you a great education, it also puts you on the pathway to Canadian citizenship.

Acceptance into a designated learning institution (DLI) in Canada makes you eligible for a study permit. You don't have to enroll in a university degree program in order to qualify, since many vocational schools and language schools can also get you a student visa.

Not all schools in Canada are approved by the government to qualify you for a student visa, so make sure your school is on the DLI list before you apply. If your school loses its designated learning institution status, you can complete your current study permit term, but you can't renew it unless you change schools.

You need an acceptance letter from the school first before you can apply for a study permit. Your school will walk you through the permit application process. Any programs that are six months or less will simply have you enter on a tourist visa, so be sure that both your school and your program qualify for a visa.

Student direct stream

If you are currently living in and a citizen of certain countries, the student direct stream (SDS) provides faster visa application processing times. Typically your student visa is approved within 20 days through the SDS.

Countries that participate in the SDS include:

- Antigua and Barbuda
- Brazil
- China
- Columbia
- Costa Rica
- India
- Morocco
- Pakistan
- Peru
- Philippines
- Saint Vincent and the Grenadines
- Senegal
- Trinidad and Tobago
- Vietnam

If you have a spouse, common-law partner, or dependents, they can also get faster processing for work or study permits. Indicate that you have family members coming with you and you'll be able to submit their applications along with yours. If you submit them separately they will not be processed together.

In order to participate, you will need to:

- Have been accepted to a designated learning institution and paid your first year of tuition.

- Have a score of 6 on the IELTS or a 7 in the Test d'évaluation de français (TEF).

- Have a guaranteed investment certificate (GIC) of C$10k.

- Submit your most recent school transcript.

- Get your medical exam, if required.

- Get your police certificate, if required.

- Submit your biometrics (fingerprints and photo), if required.

You need to apply online. The process is slightly different for each country and you may need to supply additional documents.

If you don't qualify for the student direct stream, you can still apply through the regular study permit process.

What your study permit includes

Once approved for a study permit, you'll be able to live in Canada for the length of your educational program, plus an additional six months after your program is completed.

Your student visa will allow you to bring your spouse (or common law partner) and your kids with you. Your spouse or partner can even apply for an open work permit for the length of your student visa.

As a student, you can apply for a work permit, too. Because you need to be enrolled in classes full-time in order to qualify for a study permit, you can work up to 20 hours a week while school is in session and full-time during breaks.

Your learning institution will report your academic status to the IRCC, so make sure you stay in good academic standing in order to keep your study permit (and any associated work permits) from being canceled. If you enter Canada on a study permit and never show up to classes or stop going, your study permit will be canceled.

Post-graduation work permit

Once you complete your studies, you can stay in Canada on a post-graduation work permit. There are specific criteria you need to meet in order to be eligible for a post-graduation work permit, so keep this in mind. You have to:

- Apply within six months of your receipt of confirmation that you met all requirements for your program (your transcript and a letter from the DLI).

- Completed studies in an academic, vocational, or training program at a DLI that was at least eight months long.

- Have maintained full-time student status for the duration of your program.

Your post-graduation work permit can be valid for as long as three years. Be sure to plan ahead and not miss the opportunity to take advantage of this.

- If your program was less than two years, your work permit is valid for as long as you studied. If you studied for eight months, you'll have an open work permit for eight months, which is not long enough to make you eligible for PR status through express entry.

- If your program was two years or more, your work permit will be valid for three years.

If there is a delay in receiving your transcript or other proof that you qualify for a PGWP, you can remain in Canada by applying for a visitor visa or leave Canada and apply from abroad.

Typically post-graduation work permits cannot be extended. The IRCC made a special exception to this rule because of the pandemic, allowing them to be extended for up to 18 months. This exception expired in July 2021. They are also considering applicants whose studies were interrupted by the pandemic.

While you can't renew or extend a PGWP, you can combine them if you completed multiple programs. You can also go back to school and get additional PGWPs after you graduate.

In 2021, the IRCC changed their policy so that students who complete their studies virtually through a Canadian university still qualify for a post-graduation work permit. This option is valid for people who were already enrolled in a Canadian DLI prior to March 2020 or who began their studies in Spring 2020 or Fall 2021. You are still required to have or apply for a study permit, even if you anticipate remaining outside of Canada.

Becoming a permanent resident

The most common route from student visa to Canadian citizenship is to use the PGWP to get the experience required for express entry's Canadian experience class. Most Canadian graduates will qualify for express entry after a year of working full-time.

If you already have professional experience from outside of Canada, you may be eligible for express entry as soon as you graduate. Your work experience doesn't have to be connected to your topic of study in Canada.

There are provincial nomination programs that encourage you to stay in Canada after you graduate from a Canadian university. These change depending on the needs of each province and the whims of politics. If you've earned your Masters or PhD at a Canadian university, but don't qualify for express entry or are short on points, check with your province to see if they'll nominate you to become a permanent resident. Your university will have information on current programs.

Work permits

Many people assume that the easiest way to move to Canada is by getting a job offer or that you need a job offer in order to move to Canada. As you know by now, this isn't the case. If you're a young professional or work in a skilled trade, you can probably move to Canada as a permanent resident, especially if you're bilingual in French.

Not everyone qualifies for PR status or wants to go through the hassle of obtaining it. If you're able to find an employer willing to sponsor you for a work permit, the process is straight-forward and generally quick.

One interesting detail is that you can't get a work permit for any employer "who, on a regular basis, offers striptease, erotic dance, escort services or erotic massages." That suggests they're banned from hiring foreign workers, even if you're doing the accounting. Blame sex trafficking. The IRCC also maintains a list of employers who are banned from sponsoring foreign workers.

Employer-specific work permit

Your odds of finding a company to sponsor you for a temporary work permit vary greatly, based on your professional experience and personal network.

If you do find a company to sponsor you, their attorney will take care of getting you a work permit. Some small businesses may try to get you to do this work, but they're the ones who have to apply, not you.

Your prospective employer will likely need to get a Labour Market Impact Assessment (LMIA) to show that they couldn't hire a Canadian for the job and that hiring you won't have a negative impact on the economy. The LMIA is generally the longest part of the process.

Some jobs don't require a LMIA. This is generally the case if it's determined that the job meets a "significant social or cultural benefit."

Unlike some countries, getting a temporary work permit issued can happen in a matter of weeks. If your job is LMIA exempt, you might want to start packing as soon as you accept the job offer.

They'll need to provide:

- the application,

- the job offer letter,

- a copy of the LMIA or offer of employment number,

- proof of experience or education, based on the job requirements, and

- an eTA or visitor visa, if you need one.

They can do this all online.

You may be required to have an interview with an IRCC official and/or get a medical exam. Typically the "interview" is speaking to a border agent when you activate your work permit at the port of entry.

If your job requires a medical exam, it can add significantly to the processing time. This is generally required based on the type of work you'll be performing.

Your work permit will be specific to your employer and will say how long it's valid for. It may even specify a location if your company has multiple locations. If any of these terms change, or your responsibilities or pay changes, you will need to modify your work permit or get a new one. If you have an employer specific work permit you can't get a second job.

LMIA exemptions

Your chances of getting a job offer qualifying for a work permit are greatly increased if your potential employer is exempt from the obligation to get a LMIA.

Mobilité Francophone

The Francophone mobility program is an exception to the requirement to get a LMIA. If you are fluent in French and have a job offer outside of Quebec, this is an easy pathway to getting a temporary work permit. The job must be at a National Occupation Code (NOC) skill level of 0, A or B under the 2016 system, but the job does not have to be performed in French. Whether or not a language exam is required is at the discretion of the visa officer.

Your work permit application will use LMIA exemption code C16. Because you do not need a LMIA, the LMIA application fee is not required under the Mobilité Francophone program.

Prior to 2017, you were only eligible for this program if you were recruited through a government job fair abroad. While Canadian government offices abroad continue to recruit French speaking foreign workers for this program, you no longer need to be recruited at an event to be eligible.

International mobility program

The International mobility program (IMP) exists to fill worker shortages and exempts companies from needing LMIAs to hire foreign workers.

Film and TV production

Essential workers for film and television, including graphic designers, are LMIA exempt.

Academics and researchers

Your role may be LMIA exempt and may qualify for expedited processing.

Camp counselors

Overnight camp counselors generally do not need an LMIA. Camps taking place outside of the summer months have to demonstrate that reciprocal agreements exist for Canadians to work in similar roles internationally in order to be considered LMIA exempt.

Day camp counselors do require a LMIA.

Charitable work

Some charities have volunteer roles and staff positions that are LMIA exempt. To be a charity worker, your role must "directly help to relieve poverty, advance education or address another community need". Generally office roles do not qualify. Participants must be working with the people the charity serves (like someone preparing meals for clients or teaching a class) or contributing skills to projects that serve them directly (like a carpenter renovating homes for people with limited mobility).

Charitable employers may have processing fees waived.

If you're interested in living and working alongside people with disabilities, the Camphill Association has communities on Vancouver Island, Vancouver, and Lake Simco. They sponsor work permits, provide training, and encourage people to build careers within the Camphill movement. They provide their volunteers with support for paying student loans. If you're interested in going to Quebec, Maison Emmanuel provides similar volunteering opportunities.

You can find job listings for Canadian charities on Charity Village. Many charities advertising opportunities to volunteer abroad do not sponsor work permits.

Religious work

Employees of religious organizations in roles specifically tied to celebrating, teaching, and promoting a faith are LMIA exempt. A teacher at a religious school would be LMIA exempt. A cafeteria worker would not.

Employers may have processing fees waived.

You can find opportunities for religious work that would qualify for a work permit by reaching out to different organizations in your faith community.

Working during the pandemic

Temporary residents in Canada who do not have a work permit are eligible to get one in order to address the worker shortage during the pandemic. If you are in Canada already, you can apply for an employer-specific work permit.

The program deadline was extended to February 28, 2022 and may be extended again.

Open work permit

In order to qualify for an open work permit, you need to be:

- The spouse or common-law partner of someone with a valid work or study permit that qualifies you for an open work permit.

- A refugee claimant or protected person.

- Are an applicant for PR or the immediate family member of someone whose PR application is pending.

- A student with a study permit who needs to work to support themselves.

- Someone with a temporary resident visa, or their spouse, that's valid for six months or more.

- Someone with an employer specific work permit that is being abused at work.

Even with an open work permit, you cannot work for employers who are on the IRCC's blacklist.

You can apply from inside of Canada, outside of Canada, or at the border.

If you're applying from inside of Canada, they strongly encourage you to apply online. Your work permit will be mailed to the address you provided once it's approved. Be sure to keep your mailing address up to date.

If you're applying from outside of Canada, they encourage you to apply online, but the paper application is still available. When it's approved you can take your approval letter to the border to get your open work permit. If you applied from outside of Canada and are inside Canada when it's approved, you can either go to the border or, during the pandemic, contact the IRCC and request they mail it to you. If you request they mail it to you, it will take at least eight weeks to process.

If you're applying at the border and you need a medical exam for your field of work, you need to have your medical exam paperwork with you. They will issue your work permit at the border.

During the pandemic people who are applying for an open work permit from outside of Canada are required to show a valid job offer letter in order to enter the country. Check to see if this is still a requirement.

Entering Canada with a work permit

Once your application is approved, you'll get a letter of introduction. When you arrive at the port of entry, you'll show this to a border services officer. Hopefully they'll go over the details on your application, check your passport, and give you a work permit.

Sometimes they'll ask for piles of documentation. I know people who've only gotten their work permit after going back for additional documents three times! Sometimes they approve work permits without looking at anything. This is at the discretion of the border agent.

It's important that you carefully look over your work permit before you leave the border to verify that all of the information is correct. It's much more difficult to correct any errors once you've left.

Free trade agreements

Thanks to CUSMA, citizens of the USA and Mexico have access to special work permits in Canada. Canada has other free trade agreements with labor mobility provisions modeled on NAFTA with Chile, Peru, Columbia, South Korea and is a participant in the General Agreement on Trade in Services (GATS). Thus, this may apply to you, even if you're not a citizen of the US or Mexico.

The North American Free Trade Agreement (NAFTA) was recently replaced with the Canada-United States-Mexico Agreement (CUSMA). This makes little difference to you, as the labor mobility provisions regarding business visitors, professionals, intra-company transferees, traders, and investors between the three countries remain unchanged.

Getting a TN visa is much simpler, and faster, than getting a temporary work permit. In fact, under CUSMA you may not even require a work permit in order to work in Canada if you're conducting certain types of business or are involved in trading and investing.

You can get a TN visa at the port of entry. Remember that even with a TN visa, you can be denied entry at the border if an agent determines that you are inadmissible.

Each TN visa can be valid for up to three years and there's no limit to how many times you can get a new visa. Working in Canada under CUSMA doesn't provide a direct pathway to stay in Canada permanently. However, your time working in Canada under a TN visa can make you eligible for permanent resident status through express entry.

Business visitors

Most business visitors are only in Canada for a few days, but you can stay for up to six months without needing a work permit, thanks to CUSMA. You can spend time in Canada looking for ways to grow your business, making investments, or building business relationships. Conferences, meetings, and standard business training or support are all fine.

Whenever I traveled to Canada as a business visitor, I made sure to have a letter from my employer briefly explaining what I was doing and for how long. No one ever asked me for the letter, but being overly prepared is my style. Taking a couple minutes to get the papers together seemed better than potentially being denied entry at the border.

While no one ever asked to see my paperwork, they would ask me basic questions about who the meetings were with and when they were taking place. They'd ask to see my business card and quiz me about what it is I do. They don't really care about your work, they're just making sure you're being truthful about your intentions. If your job is difficult to explain, keep it simple. Yes, you want to be honest, but you also don't want to accidentally end up spending your whole day at customs because you got too in-depth and set off red flags for no reason.

Border agents don't want to hear your life story or be treated like a career coach. They want to know that you aren't going to stay longer than six months and that your main source of income is outside of Canada. Finding a few new Canadian clients is fine.

Of course, they may ask for proof that you have funds to support yourself during your stay, like pay stubs, W-2s, or bank account statements. Having a return ticket booked never hurts.

Professionals

To be a professional under CUSMA, you still have to jump through some hoops. Why is it worth it? As a professional, whatever company is hiring you doesn't need to get approval from the Employment and Social Development Canada to hire you.

In order to qualify, you need to have experience working one of the jobs mentioned in CUSMA. CUSMA states what sort of degrees or licenses you need to demonstrate your qualifications. You also need to have a written job offer.

You won't be surprised to hear that anyone working in medicine or science will probably see themselves on this list. College and seminary instructors are in the clear. Quite a few general business people are there, including graphic designers, librarians, landscape architects, social workers, and hotel managers.

The final step is to get a work permit. You can apply online. You get your actual work permit at the border.

While the type of work I do showed up on the NAFTA list, which is virtually unchanged on the CUSMA list, getting a written job offer from a Canadian employer wasn't so easy. Several companies let me know during the phone interview that they were not interested in hiring someone who wasn't a resident, even if they didn't need to get an LMIA. In spite of having gone on several interviews, I was a permanent resident before I got any job offers. However, I didn't put a huge amount of effort into this, since I was pretty sure I could keep my current job, which is what I ultimately did.

The amount of effort required to find a company willing to hire someone on a TN visa varies greatly depending on your industry and personal factors.

Intra-company transferees

Does your company have an office in Canada? If you've worked there for a year and can convince them to transfer you, you're good to go.

You'll need to be working as a manager or a specialist and you'll still need a work permit. You can apply online.

Traders and investors

If your company is involved in a significant amount of trade between the US and Canada, you can stay for up to six months. Your company's attorney can advise you on the CUSMA rules you'll need to meet and the process for getting a work permit.

Parent & grandparent super visa

If you want to live in Canada temporarily and are the parent or grandparent of a Canadian citizen or permanent resident, you can apply for a super visa. This will allow you to live in Canada for up to two years at a time over the course of 10 years. You can check current processing times online.

A super visa doesn't last forever, so you'll have to convince the border agent that you plan to return to your home country at the end of your stay. This can be difficult if your home country is unstable or there are other reasons you might not want to or be able to return home after your visit to Canada.

Your child or grandchild will need to provide a letter of invitation. The letter needs to confirm that they will support you financially during your visit and list all members of their household. It also needs to contain:

- Their complete name, date of birth, address and telephone number in Canada, employment information, status in

Canada, and a list of all immediate family members (if it's different from the members of their household).

- Your complete name, date of birth, address and telephone number outside of Canada, relationship to them (if you are their parent or grandparent), the purpose of your visit, how long you plan to stay in Canada, where you will stay, how you will pay for things, and when you plan to leave Canada.

In order for your child or grandchild to sponsor your super visa, they will need to meet income criteria to prove that they will be able to support you financially. This is the case, even if you can support yourself. The minimum income depends on the number of people in their household, starting at $25,921 if your child or grandchild lives alone. That's the number required for 2020, which is still listed on the IRCC website as of January 2022. They can provide their most tax returns, bank statements, pay stubs, or other documents to prove their financial suitability.

They also need to include proof of their status as a permanent resident or citizen.

You'll need proof of payment for Canadian insurance coverage for at least a year. The policy needs to cover at least $100k. You won't be eligible for provincial health insurance.

You will need to pass a medical exam. This doesn't require you to be in excellent health, only to not be determined to pose a public health risk.

You may be asked to provide a police certificate.

You can apply online or on paper.

The super visa will not allow you to work in Canada, nor will it provide a pathway to permanent residency. You will need to leave Canada at the end of the visa unless you successfully apply for another type of visa.

Visiting with the intent to stay

Lots of people think you can just show up at the border with all of your worldly possessions and stay. If you do it right, that's actually an option.

This is called "dual intent." You're entering Canada as a visitor with a plan to change your visa type during your stay.

The thing is, border agents are responsible for figuring out who is at risk of overstaying their visa and preventing them from entering the country in the first place. Someone asking for a visitor visa who is clearly planning on staying for longer than six months is obviously at a very high risk of overstaying their visa. Thus, the border agent will only allow you to enter Canada if it is abundantly clear that you:

- qualify for permanent resident status or another visa,

- actually intend to go through the legal process to obtain PR status or another visa, and

- can support yourself (or be supported by your Canadian romantic partner) for at least a year, including having private health insurance.

Most people who enter Canada with dual intent are being sponsored for PR by their Canadian romantic partner. You can request a "visitor record" to extend your visitor visa from six months to a year, giving you more time to process your application.

Being able to answer questions about the immigration process and provide documentation to show that you qualify for PR goes far in demonstrating your honest intentions to follow the law.

Remember, being allowed to enter Canada as a visitor with dual intent is at the discretion of the border agent.

Immigration Programs

There are two common paths for permanent resident status in Canada: your career and your family. There are several different programs for each of those pathways.

Immigrating to Canada is fairly straightforward. It involves a significant amount of paperwork, all of which will need to be scanned and uploaded to the IRCC website or mailed in as a paper application. While the process is tedious, it's not difficult or complicated. Canada's requirements are clearly outlined and the process generally follows the official process, unlike countries where rules aren't explicitly written and the process can vary significantly.

Canada has been updating all of their immigration programs. They've digitized the system, encouraged pathways to citizenship, and adjusted it to better meet Canada's economic and cultural interests. There have been major overhauls as well as regular tweaks. Given all the changes, there's conflicting and confusing information out there. Verify anything you read on the IRCC website before doing anything. Information on the IRCC website is up-to-date and accurate.

Application processing times can vary significantly from year to year and from application to application. In addition to checking current processing times on the IRCC website, other applicants commonly post their timelines on Reddit, in forums, and in Facebook groups.

Express Entry

Immigrating to Canada through express entry feels sort of like being a contestant on a dating show. You want to highlight your best qualities so they'll choose you. Only every challenge is incredibly boring and involves calling your boss from six years ago to get paperwork or filling out a thousand tiny boxes online. If you win you become a permanent resident of Canada.

How express entry works

Like any good reality TV show, they need to stretch it out to fill a whole season, so the process can feel a little convoluted. I'll explain the whole process briefly here and then walk you through it in more detail. There are a lot of steps, but none of them are difficult.

First, find out if you meet the basic eligibility requirements to apply by filling out a short questionnaire on the IRCC website.

Assuming you're eligible, you'll create an express entry profile, detailing your skills, work experience, language abilities, education, along with everything you've done in your life and every country you've visited in the past ten years. If you meet the basic criteria, you'll be accepted into the candidate pool.

Your profile is your expression of interest (EOI) in immigrating to Canada.

You will be assigned a comprehensive ranking system (CRS) score based on the information you provided in your profile. Perhaps you took a quiz online or calculated your CRS points yourself to estimate your score, but this is your official score.

If you don't already have a qualifying job offer, you can register with the job bank. Theoretically this connects employees to employers. If you get a job offer through the job bank, you can get a work permit in as little as two weeks and will move right to the next step, without languishing in the candidate pool. You're encouraged to look for a job while you're in the pool and there's no reason to limit yourself to postings in the job bank.

If you're selected from the pool, you receive an invitation to apply (ITA). You have 60 days to add more information to your profile and submit it as your application for permanent residence. The IRCC has adjusted this number a couple times since express entry launched, so double check to see how much time you have.

Gathering paperwork and getting it translated can be a lengthy process, so it's best to begin getting your paperwork ready before you have your ITA. If you don't submit your application within 60 days and you don't respond to the ITA, your profile is removed from the system and you have to start over again. There isn't any penalty for letting an invitation expire, so it's likely you'll receive another ITA once you're back in the pool.

If you can't get your documents in time, you can decline the ITA and you will be placed back in the candidate pool, without having to start over.

Once your application is submitted, you wait. The IRCC may request additional information or schedule an interview. You'll get occasional email updates to let you know where your application is in the process.

The process is designed to take six months from when you submit your complete application to when you get final approval to move. Some people have their application processed in weeks, especially if you are already living and working in Canada. A few people wait significantly longer than six months for their application to be processed. If you're not in Canada, this is a great time to visit Canada and start getting ready to move. Just remember that you haven't been approved yet and your application could still hit a snag.

Once you're approved, you get documents allowing you to travel to the border and declare yourself a landed immigrant. You have a year from the date of your medical exam to immigrate. If you don't move before your medical exam expires, you will have to start the process over again from the beginning.

If you don't get an ITA, your profile expires after a year. You can make a new profile and try again.

Express Entry

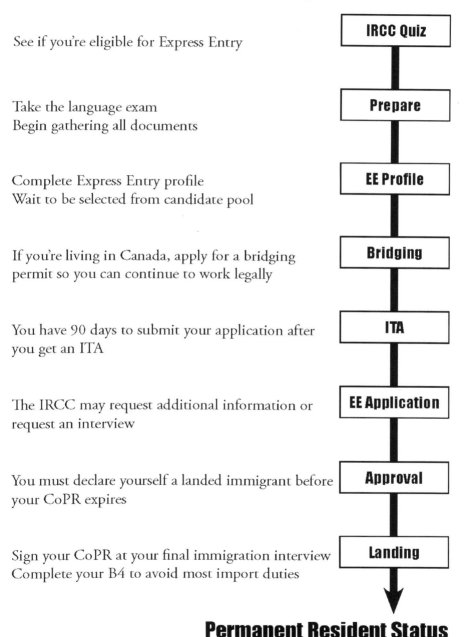

See if you're eligible for Express Entry — **IRCC Quiz**

Take the language exam
Begin gathering all documents — **Prepare**

Complete Express Entry profile
Wait to be selected from candidate pool — **EE Profile**

If you're living in Canada, apply for a bridging
permit so you can continue to work legally — **Bridging**

You have 90 days to submit your application after
you get an ITA — **ITA**

The IRCC may request additional information or
request an interview — **EE Application**

You must declare yourself a landed immigrant before
your CoPR expires — **Approval**

Sign your CoPR at your final immigration interview
Complete your B4 to avoid most import duties — **Landing**

Permanent Resident Status

Changes during the pandemic

Prior to the pandemic, people who entered the express entry pool with scores over 450 CRS points were quickly issued ITAs. Those with certain skills and abilities, such as speaking French, were quickly invited to integrated PNPs. Those who submitted applications had them approved within six months. People applying from inside Canada sometimes had their applications approved within a month. However, this has changed during the pandemic.

Canada "welcomed" a record number of immigrants in 2021. However, this is misleading, since virtually all of them were already living in Canada and simply had a change in status. When the borders closed, the IRCC shifted to issuing ITAs only to people already living in Canada, most of whom were applying through the Canadian experience class. They also welcomed people through the temporary resident to permanent resident pathway program, which was only open to applicants briefly. Almost no one moved from abroad in 2021 through express entry.

In January 2022, the IRCC had 76,000 applications pending. Processing times have slowed to nearly two years. The express entry pool ballooned to 207,000 potential applicants.

The IRCC has temporarily paused issuing new ITAs. Officials say the pause is only to allow the IRCC to reduce the backlog of pending applications. An internal memo suggested the CRS score cutoff would increase from 450 to 500.

People in politics and business are unhappy with this situation. Businesses are reporting a critical worker shortage. All major political parties in Canada support immigration, so the Conservatives are publicly criticizing the Liberal government for application processing delays and fewer applications being accepted. If more resources are allocated to application processing, this pause may be brief.

The IRCC did not make any public announcement when they decided to stop issuing new ITAs. They may or may not make an announcement when they resume issuing ITAs.

Basic requirements

- You must be admissible to Canada.

- You'll need to prove that you are fluent in English or French by taking a language test, even if you are a native speaker.

- You'll need to demonstrate that you are in relatively good health.

- You have at least a year of work experience as a manager, professional, or skilled trades person.

- You can provide all of the necessary documentation or convince the IRCC to waive the requirement.

- You intend to live in any province or territory except Québec, unless you have a CSQ.

Who can come with you?

You'll need to include personal details for all the members of your family as part of your own application, even if they are not moving with you. Assuming you are invited to immigrate, your spouse or common law partner and dependent children would automatically be invited along with you.

All dependents need to have a medical examination, even if they are not accompanying you. If any of your children are between the ages of 18 and 22, they will also need to provide a police certificate, even if they are not coming with you. If they refuse to do this, you can get permission to remove them from your application.

If you fail to disclose a spouse on your application, perhaps to avoid having their inclusion reduce your CRS score, you will not be able to sponsor them in the future and you are not eligible to use the pilot program that currently overrides the lifetime ban on family class sponsorship.

The comprehensive ranking system

The comprehensive ranking system (CRS) is EE's points system. It aims to assess your likelihood of adapting to life in Canada and doing well there, as well as your ability to improve the Canadian economy. Scores range from 0 to 1,200.

Unfortunately for those of us over the age of 29, the Canadian express entry program is specifically designed for young professionals. The younger you are, the easier it is to qualify.

After the age of 35, your chances of being accepted into the express entry program decline significantly. It's nearly impossible to get an ITA if you're over 45 unless you have a valid job offer or a provincial nomination. The IRCC even adjusted the number of points a job offer gets you in order to reduce the number of older workers who were being given ITAs.

Your CRS is based on you and your romantic partner, if you're married or in a common law relationship. If your partner is not coming with you to Canada, you can calculate your CRS as if you were single. You can also calculate your points as if you were single if your partner is already a Canadian citizen or permanent resident.

Theoretically, an invitation to apply is offered to people who:

- Are among the top ranked in the express entry pool
- Are nominated by a province or territory
- Have a qualifying job offer

You'll know your score and the scores for the most recent batch of prospective immigrants to be invited to apply, but you won't know where you rank in the current pool.

Needing to be top ranked seems a little intimidating. Living in New York City made me feel like a loser because I hadn't made our first million by the age of 30. I didn't get a perfect score on the SATs. I didn't graduate top in my class, except that one year when I was the only student in my grade. I'm not pursued by eager headhunters. When I tried to get a mortgage every bank turned me down. No one is really sure what I do for a living. Thankfully, the IRCC is less judgmental than your average New Yorker.

How many points do I need?

There is no official minimum score to get an ITA – and no number of points guarantees an invitation. Based on who's been invited to apply so far, if you have a score of 450 or higher, you'll get an ITA right away. My score was 451 and I got an ITA within a week.

You only need to get 67 points in order to enter the pool. People with scores below 450 get ITAs every year. People in the FSTC have gotten ITAs with scores as low as 199.

The IRCC publishes the scores for each EE class after every draw. Once you calculate your score – using either an online score calculator, the CRS matrix, or actually creating a profile – you can decide if it's worth getting your paperwork ready in hopes of getting an ITA.

Speaking French and your CRS score

In addition to getting points for your language ability, being bilingual in Canada's official languages boosts your chances of getting a provincial nomination.

If you are fluent in French, have an advanced degree, and can demonstrate three or more years of professional experience, then you might qualify for the Ontario immigrant nominee program (OINP).

OINP seeks specifically to bring French speakers into the predominantly English-speaking province. There's no way to apply directly to this program, instead just submit your express entry profile and enter that you intend to live in Ontario. Once your profile is reviewed, you'd receive a notification letting you know that you qualify for the OINP program along with instructions for how to continue.

This is great if you wouldn't otherwise score high enough to get an ITA. If you already have a CRS score high enough to get you an ITA, PNP is an unnecessary layer of paperwork and fees.

Ways to increase your CRS score

- Get a qualifying job offer
- Increase your English language exam score
- Learn French
- Increase your work experience
- Get more educational training, especially from a Canadian university
- Work in Canada under a work permit or working holiday
- Get provincial nomination
- If you have a spouse, have them increase their language proficiency or education level
- Talk your sibling into moving to Canada

The best way to increase your score is to find a Canadian employer willing to offer you a job or get a provincial nomination. Almost everyone with a low personal CRS score who has been invited to apply has had a provincial nomination.

Things that don't increase your score

The IRCC is not interested in your current salary or your remote job. The only thing you need to prove is that you meet the basic funds requirement; it's a yes or no question. If you have a qualifying job offer they don't even look at your finances. Having an income source, such as remote work, rental properties, or annuities, does not get you points.

If you're wealthy or an entrepreneur and have a low CRS score, consider immigrating through one of the business class programs.

You might think that owning a home in Canada would count for something. It doesn't.

Working with an immigration attorney

Your express entry points are based on your personal factors. An immigration attorney or consultant can't increase your score unless you initially filled the forms out incorrectly and you weren't allocated the correct number of points as a result. The other way they can increase your score is if they're committing fraud. Immigration attorneys occasionally make the news for fake job offers and other tricks to increase CRS points.

If your immigration consultant boosts your score illegally and is caught, you (and your family) can be deported.

Your NOC code

Canada uses the national occupation classification (NOC) system to determine what counts as skilled work for EE. You'll need to find the NOC code that matches the types of job(s) you worked at for at least 12 months in order to apply to express entry. Chances are that you'll need to do some research to find the right code. Start broad and look for the most appropriate unit group. The job title listed in the code might not match up exactly with your official title. The job description is more important than the actual title, so choose the NOC whose job description is the best match for your role and responsibilities.

If you worked multiple types of jobs that are in eligible categories, you can apply so long as they add up to at least 12 months of full time work over the last 10 years.

If you've been self-employed you'll need to provide proof of income and verification letters from clients, vendors, or buyers that document your experience. I didn't have any trouble with this and it was nice to have an excuse to get lunch with former clients.

If a company you worked for or a former client has gone out of business, don't worry. If you hoard paperwork, you can provide old documents to verify your work. If you're still in touch with former co-workers, they can write a letter for you. You can also include proof that the business has dissolved. I've worked for a lot of small businesses and startups, so I provided a lot of non-standard documents and the IRCC accepted these without issue.

Changes to the NOC system

The NOC system is being updated to include the Training, Education, Experience and Responsibilities (TEER) system. The new system is intended to update roles to reflect the modern job market and to be more specific. While 0 and A level roles in the old NOC system have largely simply been assigned a new code, some roles in the B level have been downgraded. As of January 2022, the IRCC hasn't released which TEER categories or major groups qualify for express entry.

The TEER system will be implemented in the fall of 2022. Depending on your work history, you may fare better under one system than another. The IRCC has a tool to see which NOC you fall into for both systems. If you qualify under one system and not another it makes sense to either submit your expression of interest before the switch or wait until it's implemented.

2016 NOC system

If you submit your expression of interest before fall 2022, you'll need work experience in an NOC that falls within skill level 0, A, or B.

- If you manage a team, regardless of whether that team works in an office, restaurant, or on a boat, you likely fit into class 0.

- If you sit at a desk all day and have a degree, you're probably in class A.

- If you went to vocational school, did an apprenticeship, or have a degree from a trade school, you're probably in class B.

- If you have a high school diploma and job-specific training, you're probably in class C.

- If you were trained on the job, you're probably in class D.

2021 NOC/TEER system

The NOC has been updated with Training, Education, Experience and Responsibilities (TEER) levels. If you submit your expression of interest in the fall of 2022 or after, your eligibility will be based on the new NOC system.

- If you manage a team, regardless of whether that team works in an office, restaurant, or on a boat, you likely fit into TEER 0.

- If you have a university degree or several years of experience in a TEER 2 occupation, you're probably in TEER 1.

- If you have a 2+ year degree/certification or safety responsibilities, you're likely in TEER 2.

- If you have more than 6 months and less than 2 years in post-secondary education, including apprenticeships or several years of experience in TEER 4, you're likely in TEER 3.

- If you have completed secondary school and have some additional training or several years of work experience in TEER 5, you're probably in TEER 4.

- TEER 5 is for people with little experience doing work with no formal education/training requirements.

The TEER is part of the NOC code. The first digit is the occupational category, the second is the TEER category. The first two digits together are the major group. Then the third, fourth, and fifth digits become increasingly specific until you reach your occupation.

Your NOC code and your ETA

Your CRS score does not consider your NOC code, beyond the level. However, the provinces do. Ontario, British Columbia, Alberta, and Saskatchewan all regularly issue invitations for their PNPs based on NOC codes. Provincial sponsorship virtually guarantees you'll receive an ETA.

Express entry classes

There are three types of express entry applicants: the federal skilled worker program, federal skilled trades program, and Canadian experience class. The majority of applicants apply through the federal skilled worker program.

The federal skilled worker

The federal skilled worker program (FSWP) program looks for qualified people that will contribute to the culture and economy of Canada. This program primarily assesses your age, work history, education, and language skills. If you are under 35, have professional experience, have an advanced degree, and are fluent in English or French, chances are you'll be invited into the FSWP program. You do not need a job offer to qualify for the FSWP and job offers have to meet specific qualifications to improve your chances of being accepted.

Basic requirements

- You've worked in an applicable NOC field full-time (30+ hours a week) for at least 12 months in the last 10 years. Or, you've worked the equivalent in part time hours, such as 15 hours a week for 24 months.

- You can prove that you held at least one job in an applicable NOC field for at least 12 continuous months.

- You can provide letters from all employers that you've worked for over the last 10 years verifying that you worked there along with your primary duties, length of employment, title, salary, benefits, hours, and NOC code (you'll still need letters for jobs that aren't related to the NOC field).

- You'll need to have your academic diplomas evaluated by a IRCC approved third party, such as World Education Services (WES), in order to prove that they are equivalent to Canadian degrees.

- If you don't have a qualifying job offer, you must have at least C$12,500. You may need more, depending on how many family members you have. The IRCC assumes you'll continue supporting your family, even if they don't come with you to Canada. If your partner is on your application, their funds can be included in this. Only accessible funds count towards this amount, so you can't include any retirement accounts.

Federal skilled trades

The federal skilled trades class (FSTC) program brings tradespeople to Canada. The FSTC requires that you have a valid job offer in Canada or are already certified to work in your trade within the country of Canada.

Certification exams are offered by governing bodies in each province and sometimes require related work experience within that province. You will likely have to appear in person to have your qualifications assessed by an employer in Canada in order for a valid job offer in your trade. If you don't already have a certificate of qualification, you can still apply if you can convince the IRCC that you would be eligible to obtain any necessary certifications required for your trade job.

FSTC applicants are often already working in Canada as temporary foreign workers with a work permit. Only 3,000 people can apply under this program each year. Some of the individual NOC titles have caps of 100 applicants per year.

People applying under this program are not required to have advanced degrees, though having one will help to increase your score.

Work experience

To qualify under the FSTC program you'll need to have at least two years of full time work experience in the past five years in one of these types of jobs:

- Major Group 72, industrial, electrical and construction trades,

- Major Group 73, maintenance and equipment operation trades,

- Major Group 82, supervisors and technical jobs in natural resources, agriculture and related production,

- Major Group 92, processing, manufacturing and utilities supervisors and central control operators,

- Minor Group 632, chefs and cooks, and

- Minor Group 633, butchers and bakers.

The IRCC has a NOC matrix that provides a good overview of the major job types that would qualify for this immigration program.

Canadian experience class

If you've worked in Canada legally for a year or more —on an open work permit through your partner, working holiday visa, post-graduation work permit, or CUSMA work permit – you may qualify to become a permanent resident through express entry.

It makes sense that Canada would want to make it easy for people who are currently living and working in Canada to stay. If you're already living here, or have lived here in the past, you've already demonstrated your ability to thrive in Canada.

Not every job qualifies you for express entry's Canadian experience class (CEC). Your work needs to have been in a qualifying profession under the NOC code system. Work done on a student visa doesn't count. Neither does working remotely for a Canadian company. You'll also need to provide proof that you were (or are) authorized to work in Canada and you filed your taxes.

Provincial nominee programs

Because different regions of Canada have different economies and cultures, these programs allow Canadian provinces and territories to select potential immigrants based on their needs. This is the purpose of provincial nominee programs (PNP). Some of these programs are integrated into EE, which is what I'm talking about here. There are also PNPs that operate independently of EE.

The requirements of these programs change regularly. If you're worried that your CRS score is too low to get an ITA, check into the current PNPs and see if you qualify for any of them. Some PNPs will choose candidates that qualify from the pool, others require a separate application first.

If your CRS score is low, but you have skills or experience that a particular province needs, you may get a provincial nomination. Provincial nomination will add 600 points to your CRS score. A PNP will also add to the amount of time it will take to process your application, as they each come with their own paperwork and fees.

Not everyone who gets a provincial nomination accepts it. If you believe you can get an ITA without PNP, you may decide it's not worth the hassle and expense of the PNP process.

Entering the express entry pool

The first step of express entry is using the Come to Canada tool on the IRCC website. That will give you a personal reference code that saves your information for 30 days.

The next step is to create your express entry profile, using your personal reference code so you don't have to re-enter all of your information.

You know those online job applications that have you upload your resume and then make you type it all out, one line at a time? That's what the express entry profile is like, only it wants to know a lot more about you and your family. It took some time for me to find start and end dates for:

- Every job I've ever had,
- Every place I've ever lived,
- Every school I've ever attended, and
- Every country I've ever visited.

Mercifully, you can save your profile and log back in later. You have 60 days to complete your profile, otherwise you'll have to start over again.

When you create your account, you'll get a MyCIC number. Save that information or you'll have a heck of a time trying to log back in.

Gmail was automatically sorting notifications from the IRCC to the trash folder, so I set up a filter rule to make sure emails from donotreply@cic.gc.ca would be marked as important and not vanish into my spam folder. You might want to do something like this for your own email account to make sure you don't miss any updates or requests for additional information from the IRCC.

Regardless, it's probably a good idea to login to your IRCC account occasionally to make sure you haven't missed any important notifications.

Things you'll need

You can't create a profile without:

- A passport or another national identity document
- Language test results
- The ability to scan and upload documents

Optional paperwork

- Education Credential Assessment (required for you and/or your spouse if either of you are trying to get points for academic degrees)
- Written job offer
- Provincial nomination

While this is the only paperwork you need to have in order to create your profile, I highly recommend you begin gathering all the paperwork you'll need before you even submit your profile. I got an ITA right away and the paperwork took so long to gather that I probably would have run out of time had I not had most things ready to go when I submitted my profile.

Work history

Calling this your work history is a bit of a misnomer. This is not intended to be a resume or CV like you'd submit in a job application, this is a timeline of everything you've done as an adult.

There's no clear way to account for time spent being unemployed, traveling, or providing care for a relative. The engineers who designed this must have had a very clear life path. I improvised. You cannot have any gaps in time, so write out what you were doing and fill in any blank fields with N/A.

I've done a lot of contract and freelance work, so it wasn't easy to complete the work history section. I did my best to accurately portray my work experience in their system. Given the number of graphic designers who've been invited to apply, they appear to be okay with that.

At this stage, you don't need to provide any documentation to prove your work history. However, if the documents in your application don't match what you put here, your application can be rejected.

Addresses

Perhaps you're the type of person who's lived in one place your whole life. The IRCC is ready for that.

I'm not one of those people.

Hopefully they've fixed this, but when I submitted my profile, they didn't allow letters or special characters in house or apartment numbers. I've had a few previous addresses that contained fractions or letters, which were rejected when I tried to enter them. I left out the offending characters and my application was accepted, so I wouldn't worry too much about this.

The address of my childhood home has changed several times, although it's the same house in the same location. My family ignored this and our friendly mailman continued to deliver our mail, regardless of which address it was sent to, but I wasn't sure how the IRCC would respond to this confusing situation. I simply used the original address and they never asked for clarification.

Language test results

Everyone needs to take a language test, even if English is the only language you speak. It seems silly, but rules are rules.

It sounds even more ridiculous when they tell native English speakers to study before the test. This is good advice. Like any standardized test, it feels more like a test of your test taking skills than on your language abilities. There are plenty of native English speakers who don't get a perfect score, but you'll certainly pass. You can take practice tests online if you'd like to get a better idea of what you're in for. Spending an hour getting familiar with the test format can really pay off.

I took the general training module test through IELTS (International English Language Testing System). They have testing locations throughout the world. If you don't live near a major city, be prepared to travel. The testing slots fill up fast, so schedule your test sooner rather than later. You will need a valid passport when you arrive for the test in order to be admitted into the testing room.

Taking the test feels a lot like the SATs. You leave all of your personal belongings in a separate room, including your wallet and cell phone. You're given a pencil to take a hand written test. The test is made up of four different parts: listening, reading, writing, and speaking. This will involve:

- Listening to an audio recording of a subject matter and answering questions about what you heard,
- Reading a short story then answering questions about what you read,
- Writing essays about two different topics, and
- Talking to a test facilitator for about 30 minutes on an assigned subject.

Expect to spend about six hours getting quizzed in how well you speak, write, and understand English.

The test is not necessarily difficult, but it is time consuming and somewhat stressful, especially if you aren't used to writing things out by hand for several hours straight or needing to ask permission to go to the bathroom. The whole experience felt a lot like being back in high school.

The test results will be mailed to you about two weeks after you complete the test. They'll include a code that you'll need to enter into your EE profile.

Education credential assessment

Canadian employers generally recognize degrees from abroad, but the IRCC doesn't. You'll need to get your credentials assessed by an approved company if you're applying under the skilled worker class.

Applicants under the skilled trades or Canadian experience class don't necessarily need an education credential assessment (ECA), but you won't get points for your education without it. If you need the points, it's worth the hassle.

If you aren't sure how your foreign training will be recognized in Canada, the World Education Services (WES) has an online tool that will tell you what your degree is equivalent to for free. You will, of course, still have to send them the documents and pay the fee for this to count toward your CRS. You may only need to have your highest degree assessed. Check the guidelines from your ECA provider to be sure.

I got a "Course-by-Course" evaluation from WES. It took about six weeks from when I submitted everything to when I received the official letters authenticating my degrees from US universities. Those six weeks don't include the three or more weeks of waiting beforehand for each school to mail transcripts directly to WES. Most universities have since switched to online systems that are instant or nearly so.

WES will ask for several different documents for each degree that you are seeking an ECA for:

- Photocopy of your actual diploma or graduation certificate.

- Academic transcripts sent directly to WES from your school (usually an additional $25-$50 each, unless they now use the Parchment system).

- A legal document verifying any name change if the name on your diploma or transcripts does not match your current legal name (such as a marriage certificate or divorce order).

Don't assume you can just mail a transcript request form and actually get one. Unexpected bureaucracy can add significantly to how long your paperwork will take to get ready. My undergraduate registrar insisted I had an outstanding debt, so they wouldn't send the transcript, but the bursar had no record of the debt, so they wouldn't let me pay it. Clearing up this $20 dispute took months.

If you didn't keep a copy of your diploma, you'll have to pay your school for them to send you a new one (which cost me $50 per diploma).

The ECA that WES provides is valid for five years.

Registering on the Canada Job Bank

After you submit your profile, you can register with the job bank. This used to be mandatory; now it's optional.

Theoretically, employers can check out resumes posted to the job bank and offer you an interview at their company. The job postings I saw weren't particularly enticing and the inquiries I got from employers were seemingly random.

If you are able to find a job through the job bank, you can get a work permit in as little as two weeks and you'll probably get an ITA in the next round of invitations.

129

Waiting for an ITA

Hopefully at this point you'll get an email letting you know you have a top secret message in your MyCIC account to let you know you've been placed in the express entry pool. You'll also be told your official CRS score.

Don't just sit back and relax. Continue gathering your paperwork and looking for a qualifying job offer. If anything you've put in your profile changes, you'll need to update your profile.

Once the IRCC has a chance to review your express entry profile and determines that you meet the criteria to immigrate, you'll receive an invitation to apply (ITA) for permanent resident status. I received my ITA about a week after I submitted my profile.

If one of your kids turns 22 while you're waiting for an ITA, they're no longer considered a dependent and would require their own application. Once you receive an ITA and your application is submitted, their (and your) age is considered to be "locked in," but until your application is submitted they can age out of dependent status and you can lose points for your age.

Preparing your application

Once you get your ITA, you have 60 days to submit your complete application. If your documents don't support the number of CRS points initially awarded or you're deemed inadmissible, your application will be denied.

If you can't get the paperwork together in time, you can decline the ITA and you'll be placed back in the pool. You may be invited to apply again.

If you don't decline the ITA or submit an application within 60 days, you'll be removed from the pool. You'll have to start over if you'd like to be invited to apply again. There's no penalty beyond having to retype and reupload.

Paperwork you'll need

- Police certificate (for you and any adult family members)
- Language test results (for you and an accompanying partner)
- Educational credential assessment (if you want points for education)
- Medical exam (for you and any family members)
- Proof of funds (if you don't have a valid job offer and are not already legally living in Canada)
- Verification of your work history
- Proof of relationship status, if applicable:
  - o Marriage certificate
  - o Divorce certificate
  - o Death certificate if you are a widow
  - o Evidence of a common law relationship
- Proof of parental status, if applicable:
  - o Birth certificates for any dependent children
  - o Adoption certificates for any adopted dependents

Other information to gather

- All addresses you've ever lived at
- All international travel within the past 10 years
- Personal information about all immediate family members, even if they will not be immigrating (such as full names, addresses, and date of birth)

Police certificates

You and any family members who are 18 or older will need police certificates for any country you've lived in for at least six consecutive months for the past ten years or since you (or they) turned 18. They're valid for six months for the country you're currently living in. For other countries it can date from any time after you left, even if it has an expiration date that's passed.

You may want to request police certificates early in the process, since some countries are slow to provide this. A quick search online will provide you with an idea of the length of time it will take. The FBI is notoriously slow and prone to error.

The IRCC will accept proof that you've requested a police certificate, so you can submit your profile before the deadline even if your police certificate hasn't arrived yet. Your application generally can't be approved without it, although in some cases the requirement can be waived, such as if your government has effectively collapsed.

Some countries require a consent form before issuing a police certificate. If you need a police certificate from one of these countries, you submit the consent form to the IRCC in place of the police certificate and the IRCC will then request a police certificate from that country on your behalf.

The FBI doesn't provide any status updates or even proof that they received your request. You need to be fingerprinted by your local police department before you can submit the request to the FBI. Since I was living in NYC, I spent an afternoon at the NYPD headquarters getting this part done. It took about two hours and wasn't nearly as unpleasant as I expected it to be.

Medical exam

Medical exams were not required for most applicants already living in Canada during 2020 and 2021. Check to see if they're being required before you go through the hassle.

The IRCC recommends you wait until you get your ITA before scheduling your medical exam. Your exam results are only valid for 12 months and need to have at least six months remaining when you submit your application. If the medical exam is valid for less than six months, you'll have to get another exam done. I scheduled my appointment as soon as I received my ITA.

The date that you get your medical exam is extremely important because the date your permanent resident visa expires is based on this. Your PR visa is the paperwork allowing you to become a permanent resident.

You can't just go to any doctor for your required medical exam. You need to see a panel physician and there aren't many of them located in each country. Be sure to mention you need an express entry medical exam when you make an appointment. Chances are the office will know exactly what you're talking about and exactly what they need to give you. If they don't, try a different panel physician in your area if you can. There's likely to be a significant wait for an appointment. The cost of the immigration medical exam will not be covered by your health insurance.

When you go to your appointment, bring two passport photos, your MyCIC number application number, and your passport.

You will need to give a general medical history, get blood work and a chest x-ray. My x-ray tech seemed very excited to tell me that I didn't have TB.

The doctor may give you a sealed letter that you will need to hold onto. In theory, the immigration office might ask to see this letter when you arrive at the port of entry to declare yourself a landed immigrant. I wasn't asked to show mine, but you'll want to hold onto this in case you are asked for it.

The doctor will submit your medical exam results directly to the IRCC and likely won't give you any actual information.

It seems like the blood work is to test for HIV and syphilis. You won't automatically be deemed inadmissible if your blood work comes back positive. However, once the IRCC has gotten your test results you have 60 days to withdraw your application or they will notify your partner of your status. If you'd like to continue with EE, you'll want to voluntarily disclose your status to your partner, if you haven't already.

A few weeks after the medical exam, you'll receive an update on your IRCC page letting you know if you passed the medical exam.

Proof of funds

The proof of funds required starts at C$12,669 for a single person and increases based on the number of people in your immediate family, regardless of whether or not they're immigrating with you.

If you don't need to show proof of funds if you:

- Have a qualifying job offer and a valid work permit, or
- Are applying through the Canadian experience class.

If you are currently living in Canada, but aren't applying through the Canadian experience class or don't have a valid work permit, you still need to provide proof of funds.

The IRCC wants to make sure you have some money to set up a home and cover your living expenses when you first arrive in the country. It's reasonable to assume you might be unemployed for a period of time while you find a job. Moving internationally can be quite expensive.

Perhaps you work remotely and will keep your current job, have passive income, or have a job offer that doesn't qualify for points through express entry. The IRCC will not take these into consideration.

If you plan to immigrate with your spouse, cash in either of your bank accounts will count towards the total amount of funds you'll need to document.

Since they want to make sure you haven't borrowed this money, you'll need to prove that you have had this money in your personal accounts for several months before applying.

You will need to get an official letter from your bank printed on letterhead that includes:

- Your name
- Bank address, telephone, and email address
- Account numbers
- Total funds in each account
- Date each account was open
- Current balance of accounts
- Average balance of each account for the past six months

Getting proof of funds ended up being more difficult than it should have been. Bank officers really wanted to give me the information that the United States immigration process requires, rather than what I needed for Canadian immigration.

If your bank refuses to provide a letter with the information the IRCC requires, try to get them to put in writing that they cannot comply with your request. You can provide this along with several months of bank statements.

Verification of your work history

If you're applying as a skilled worker, you will need to prove that you're actually a skilled worker. Makes sense, right? This is actually one of the hardest parts of the application to put together, since you have to account for the last ten years of your life. This means you'll need to reach out to every employer you've worked for in the past decade, even if it didn't end well. You'll also need to account for any time you weren't working.

Canadian experience class

If you're applying through the Canadian experience class, then you're in luck because you only have to account for whichever jobs you've worked in Canada. Since you only need a single year of qualifying work experience in Canada, this probably means only having to get a letter from a single employer. It won't hurt to account for however many years of qualifying experience you have in Canada.

If you're applying through this program, you'll also need to provide your most recent work permit, T4 tax information slips, and notice of assessments.

Proof of employment history

Proving your work experience is rarely as simple as it would seem. Even people who've worked for one company for the past ten years have probably held different job titles or even worked for different divisions. Who should write the letter? What should it contain?

Many of us have gaps in our employment history, have worked for our own companies, or were freelance workers. Plenty of companies go out of business each year. There are a lot of questions that come up when talking about how to verify your employment experience.

Thankfully, while the IRCC website doesn't give the clear instructions for non-traditional employees that we might like, these things won't disqualify you from moving to Canada as a skilled worker using express entry.

Your work verification letter should be written by either a member of your company human resources department or your supervisor.

The letter should be written on the company's letterhead and a business card for the person writing the letter should be attached. The author of the letter should sign it and include their full name and title. If your company has an official seal, be sure to get the letter stamped.

If you've had multiple positions within the same company, you can either have separate letters for each position or include the relevant information (title, responsibilities, and dates) for each position you've held included in the same letter.

Your employer is probably used to being asked for character references. While the IRCC will be happy to know you're a good employee and an upstanding citizen, they're more interested in your job duties.

You'll need to get an official letter from each employer on company letterhead that includes:

- Your legal name as it appears on your express entry profile and identity documents
- Company's address, telephone, and email address
- The full name, job title, and contact information for the person writing the letter
- Your official job title and the corresponding NOC code
- Your hire date and either that you are still employed there or the date you stopped working there
- The average number of hours worked per week
- Your salary, hourly rate, or other payment information
- Benefits included in your salary or in addition to your salary
- A detailed description of your responsibilities

I wrote a draft of what I needed each company to verify, then sent it out to the employer with a request that they review and return it on company letterhead. For larger companies, this will probably need to

137

go through the HR department. Since you don't have much control over how fast this part goes, get started on it soon so you're not stuck waiting around for it at the end.

For jobs that align to the NOC you're applying under, make sure the responsibilities of the job match the NOC description. Just like you may tailor your resume for a specific job posting, you can tailor your job description to ensure that it matches your NOC code. The person assessing your application may not be familiar with the jargon of your field, so make sure it's easy for them to see that there's a match between your role and the NOC code you're applying under.

Don't just copy/paste the NOC code description into the letter. You need to provide a description of your work responsibilities that is customized to your position that incorporates key phrases and terms from the NOC code. Your official job title is less important than the description of your role.

This part of your application will be thoroughly reviewed so make sure you demonstrate that you are qualified to immigrate as a skilled worker.

What work needs to be documented?

It's very important to document the last three years of work experience. Any other work experience related to the NOC code you're applying under should also be documented to the best of your ability.

Insufficient proof of your work history can get your express entry application rejected. The meaning of 'sufficient' proof is subjective. It's up to the person assessing your application to decide how much is enough to decide you should get PR.

If you're the accompanying spouse, you should still provide documentation for any relevant work history. However, a poorly documented work history of a spouse is less likely to lead to your application being delayed or rejected.

Do you need to spend weeks tracking down a supervisor from that defunct company you worked for seven years ago in a completely unrelated job? Probably not. However, it doesn't hurt to play it safe and provide some verification, like old pay stubs, contracts, or tax forms.

Self employment

The IRCC recognizes that many people today work for their own companies and do freelance work. This won't hold you back from immigrating through express entry.

Provide a letter explaining that you were self employed and providing a detailed description of the services you provide(d). If your services changed over time, include this information.

Include reference letters from clients to verify this information. These reference letters should follow the same format as the standard letters above.

You can include any additional documentation, such as:

- Client contracts
- Proof of payment from clients or vendors
- Business registration paperwork
- Tax filings
- Screenshots of your website or promotional materials

Alternative documentation

What happens if you can't get a work verification letter? Or if your company will not include all of the required information in the letter? You simply need to provide additional documents to ensure the people assessing your application will be able to feel you have demonstrated your work history.

Some companies have policies forbidding them from providing salary information or other details in a letter, meaning they can't provide you with the letter the IRCC is asking for. You can use additional documentation to fill in the gaps, like your original contract, paystubs, tax forms, or canceled cheques.

The IRCC has made it very clear that it is the applicant's responsibility to demonstrate their work history to the satisfaction of the person assessing your application. The less clear your work history is, the more likely your application is to be delayed while you provide additional documentation or denied outright.

I had one former employer provide me with a letter that lacked the required information. I provided their letter with additional documents to fill in the gaps and provide the information the IRCC is looking for. If you have gaps in your documents, see if you can dig up:

- The original job posting
- Your original offer letter
- Employment contracts
- Printouts from the company intranet showing your role
- Emails confirming your role
- Tax forms (W-2, 1099, T4)
- Paystubs
- Bank statements (showing your salary being deposited)
- Old proof of employment letters
- Old reference letters
- Company newsletters that mention you and your work
- Pictures of you at work
- Letters from coworkers or clients

If a company has gone out of business, you can contact your former supervisor or a former company executive to write a letter stating that the company is no longer active and verifying your employment. It's advisable to pair this with additional documents, if you have them.

If you are unable to provide any letter at all, write a letter of your own explaining why. Provide any evidence you can to demonstrate your work history and corroborate your explanation, such as:

- Newspaper articles showing that the company has shut down
- Obituary for your former supervisor
- Screenshots from the company website showing that they are no longer in business
- Bankruptcy filings
- Publicly available legal documents showing the company is no longer active

Proof of relationship status

This part only applies to you if you are married, divorced, widowed, or common law.

- Married: Marriage certificate, even if your spouse will not be immigrating with you
- Divorced: Divorce certificate if you or your spouse has ever been married in the past
- Widowed: Death certificate for your spouse

Canada will allow you to immigrate with your partner even if you're not married, but you will need to prove the validity of that common law relationship by providing:

- A completed Statutory Declaration of Common Law Union form

141

- Evidence of cohabitation for at least 12 continuous months including utility bills in both of your names
- Statements from joint bank accounts or credit cards
- Lease or mortgage in both of your names

If you do not include your partner, you may be permanently banned from sponsoring them in the future. If your partner is not accompanying you, you should include them on your application and indicate their status as non-accompanying.

Proof of parental status

If you're a parent of a dependent child, you will need to provide information about each of your dependent children, even if they will not be immigrating with you.

- Birth certificates for any dependent children
- Adoption certificates for any adopted dependents

If you do not include a child on your application, you may be permanently banned from sponsoring them for permanent resident status in the future.

Fees

You'll have to pay your right of permanent residence fees, express entry fee, and biometrics fee online before your application is considered complete.

If anything in your profile has changed since you originally created your expression of interest, be sure to update it before submitting your application.

Biometrics

Once you've submitted your application, you'll get a letter in your myCIC account requesting your biometrics. You have 30 days to do this. You need to bring this letter and your passport to your biometrics appointment. Anyone included in your application (ie. all living immediate family members, regardless of whether they're moving to Canada or not) must also provide biometrics.

Most applicants are required to submit biometrics (a photo and fingerprints) if you're between 14 and 79 years old, even if you gave your biometrics in the past and they're still valid. The IRCC has a tool to help you determine if you need to provide biometrics.

This must be done at a Visa Application Centre (VAC) or Application Support Centre (ASC). There are no VACs or ASCs in Canada, so if you are applying from within Canada you'll need to leave the country to do this. This was not required prior to 2018. The biometrics fee is $85, with a maximum of $170 per family.

If they're required, your application will not be processed until your biometrics are submitted.

Application processing

You'll get messages in your MyCIC mailbox with occasional updates or requests for any additional information. They may even request an interview.

The IRCC aims to process applications within six months and they hit that target for most applicants. In fact, some people have their paperwork processed in six weeks!

Applications that take longer than six months likely were missing documents (like the police check), required additional background screening, had unclear family situations (pending divorces, adoptions, or child custody issues), or required an in-person interview.

Ready for visa

About five months after I submitted my application and all of the fees, I got an email letting me know that I was "ready for visa." This let me know that my application was almost complete. Though this wasn't an official "approval" quite yet, I took it as a sign that I was nearly done with the process. I was asked to mail out:

- 2 photographs for my permanent resident (PR) card
- Copies of my passport
- One self-addressed stamped envelope

About a month after this, I received my permanent resident visa (also known as the confirmation of permanent residence or CoPR form), the official travel papers that granted me the right to immigrate to Canada. All told, it was almost exactly six months between when I submitted my application to when I received the paperwork I needed to actually immigrate.

If you're coming from a country that requires a visa to enter Canada, you may need to visit or mail your passport to a Visa Application Centre (VAC) for them to put a visa in your passport and provide you with paper copies of the documents you need to enter the country. People from countries where visitor visas are automatically granted upon entry will be able to download and print these documents themselves.

How much EE cost

In addition to having money in your bank account to provide proof of funds, you'll also end up paying for just about every piece of documentation you'll need to gather as part of your application.

While your experience might be a bit different, here's an overview of what I ended up paying to prepare my application while living in the US in 2015:

Document	Single	Couple
Police Certificate	$18	$36
– Fingerprinting	$25	$50
Language Test (IELTS)	$225	$550
Education Credential Assessment	$205	$410
– Transcripts (2)	$50	$100
– Diplomas (1)	$50	$50
Medical Exam	$350	$700
– Passport Photos	$20	$40
express entry Fee	$395	$790
Right of Permanent Resident Fee	$350	$700
Photographs for PR card	$20	$40
Biometrics	C$85	C$170
Total	**$1,708**	**$3,466**

In 2015 biometrics were not yet required, so they are not factored into the total, but I've included it here for your reference.

There are other costs you might have to pay, depending on your situation:

- Document translation (required for any document that is not in English or French)
- Immigration representative fees
- Copies of marriage, divorce, or death certificates

- Proof of common law partnership
- Copies of birth or adoption certificates
- Additional language test to establish French fluency

Timeline

Everyone's experience will be different, but here's how the timing worked out for me:

Event	Date
Submitted express entry profile	18-Mar-15
IRCC confirmed that profile was received	19-Mar-15
Registered with job bank	19-Mar-15
Accepted into express entry	19-Mar-15
Invited to apply for Permanent Residency	27-Mar-15
Appointment with panel physician	2-Apr-15
Submitted application for Permanent Residency	13-Apr-15
IRCC confirmed that application was received	13-Apr-15
IRCC requested additional information	29-May-15
Provided additional information	29-May-15
IRCC confirmed that information was received	30-May-15
Received "Ready for Visa" email	15-Sep-15
Mailed out pictures and copies of passports	29-Sep-15
Received travel documents (invitation to immigrate)	26-Oct-15
Primary applicant declared residency	10-Dec-15
Actually moved to Toronto	15-Jan-16
Expiration date for invitation to immigrate	2-Apr-16

There are groups and forums where people regularly share their timing, so I know my timeline is still fairly typical. I list resources for getting an idea of the latest timelines later in the book.

There are two different rounds of the application process. First you'll need to create your express entry profile on the IRCC website. Then, you'll be invited to apply for permanent residency status through one of the three economic immigration programs available through express entry.

I had all of the paperwork ready to go before I even created my profile, since once you get started it all goes so fast. The exceptions to this are the medical exam, which you won't even be eligible to schedule until you've already been invited to apply, and biometrics, which need to be done after you submit your complete application.

What you'll need to create your profile

These are the approximate times I waited for each document required to create my profile. Keep in mind that your own wait times and costs may be a bit different. Though some things are marked as optional, they are required if you'd like to receive points for it.

	Wait Time	Cost	FSWP	CEC	FSTP
Education Credential Assessment	1-3 months	$200	✓	Optional	Optional
– diplomas	2-4 weeks	$50	✓	If needed	If needed
– school transcripts	2-4 weeks	$50	✓	Optional	Optional
Language test results	1-3 months	$225	✓	✓	✓
Passport if you don't have one	6 weeks	$50	✓	✓	✓
Travel history			✓	✓	✓

Residential history			✓	✓	✓
Job history			✓	✓	✓

What you'll need for your application

After you've been invited to apply for express entry, you'll need all of these documents on hand in order to submit your application.

The table below shows the approximate times that I waited to receive the documents request at this stage, as well as the approximate costs. You may find that you wait more or less time depending on where you live, went to school, and worked. The different streams have slightly different requirements.

	Wait time	Cost	FSWP	CEC	FSTC
Police certificate	3-4 months	$20	✓	✓	✓
– fingerprints	1 day	$25	✓	✓	✓
Medical exam	1-2 months	$350	✓	✓	✓
Letters from all employers for the past 10 years	1-6 months		✓		✓
Letters from all Canadian employers	1 month			✓	
Proof of funds, valid job offer, or work permit	1 weeks		✓		✓
Provincial nomination	1+ months		Optional	Optional	Optional

Proof of relationship status	1 month	$20	if needed	if needed	, if needed
Proof of parental status	1 month	$20	if needed	if needed	if needed
Written job offer	1 month		Optional	Optional	Optional
Work permits, T4s, NOAs	1 day			✓	

Being sponsored as immediate family

If you're the immediate family member of a Canadian permanent resident or citizen, you probably qualify to become a permanent resident.

Being married to a Canadian doesn't automatically get you a Canadian passport. You'll have to submit numerous documents to the IRCC to apply for permanent resident status, assuming you qualify. You don't need to be legally married for a Canadian partner to sponsor you for PR status, although this requires more paperwork.

If your Canadian partner can sponsor you, they can also sponsor your children. There are eligibility requirements for everyone.

Once you have PR status, you can apply for citizenship in a few years. The only way you can become a Canadian citizen directly is to be adopted by a Canadian citizen who qualifies to pass their citizenship to you.

Remember that you don't actually become a permanent resident until you arrive at a port of entry, declare yourself a landed immigrant, and are approved. Each person on your application needs to do this before their landing paperwork expires.

Eligibility to be sponsored

Before you start getting the paperwork together and planning your move, remember that you still need to be admissible to Canada and your romantic partner or parent needs to be eligible to sponsor you.

If you've overstayed your visa in Canada, you can still be sponsored as long as a removal order hasn't been issued. However, it's unlikely you'd be able to get an open work permit while you wait for your application to process, as eligibility for an open work permit requires that you have valid status in Canada. If you're able to get an open work permit, it would be once the IRCC has deemed you to have approval in principle (AIP) status, which happens towards the end of the process.

Can your Canadian love sponsor you?

Not just anyone can sponsor you to become a permanent resident of Canada, even if you're married or they're your legal guardian. In order to sponsor you, they must:

- Be a Canadian citizen, member of a First Nation, or permanent resident over the age of 18.

- Not be in receipt of social assistance, other than disability payments.

- Be able to show that they can support you.

- Not be in jail, bankrupt, or have been convicted of a violent crime.

- Not have sponsored anyone in the last three years or failed to have supported a spouse or child they sponsored.

- Have paid their taxes and any court judgements (like child support and alimony).

150

If your potential sponsor is a Canadian permanent resident, they need to be living in Canada when they sponsor you. If they came to Canada through spousal sponsorship or family sponsorship themselves, they need to have been a permanent resident for at least five years.

If your sponsor immigrated to Canada and did not list you on their application, they will not be able to sponsor you unless you joined their family after they immigrated. If you were married when they applied, or got married while their application was processing, they cannot sponsor you. The IRCC will deny your application and respond with a form letter explaining this. If this applies to you, you may be able to get the IRCC to consider your application if you have a good reason for the discrepancy. This is a situation that typically requires the help of an immigration attorney.

If your potential sponsor is a Canadian citizen, they can be living anywhere in the world while they sponsor you, but you have to convince the IRCC that you plan on living together in Canada once your application is approved.

Your sponsor also needs to be willing to make a legally binding promise that they will provide for you for a certain amount of time, called an undertaking. The specifics of this guarantee depend on your relationship and where in Canada you will be moving to. Your sponsor only has to meet income requirements if you have a child that's young enough to be included in your application who also has a child.

Canada doesn't like sham marriages and has somewhat conservative ideas of what a relationship looks like. You'll need to be able to provide documents to prove that you're in a bona fide relationship. If you've been married for a decade and have kids, great. If you've been living together forever and are financially entangled, great. If you just met on Maple Match, you'll face additional scrutiny. There are plenty of legitimate relationships that struggle to come up with adequate documentation.

Governments tend to have outdated notions of what commitment looks like. Many couples maintain separate bank accounts, own property separately, and otherwise lack the sort of paper trail the IRCC will look for. You might want to take some steps now to make sure you will have some government approved proof you're really together.

Previously, people who were sponsored by their partners and had been in a relationship for less than two years were required to live with their partners for two years once they arrived in Canada or face having their permanent resident status revoked. This is no longer the case.

The IRCC is very suspicious of adult adoptions and even adoptions of unrelated teenagers. The decision is at the discretion of immigration agents.

You do not need to stay in an abusive situation in order to maintain your status in Canada. There are organizations to help you find a safe living situation.

There are three types of relationships that will allow someone to bring you to Canada as a romantic partner: marriage, common law partnerships, and conjugal partnerships. This is also the program to sponsor a dependent child.

Marriage

Are you and your partner legally married? Great, that makes things easier. Canada will recognize your marriage as long as:

- It's legally recognized in the country where it took place,
- It's legally recognized in Canada, and
- Both partners were physically present for the marriage ceremony.

If the country you were married in repealed marriage equality or no longer recognizes your marriage for whatever reason, you can either get re-married in a country that will recognize it or apply as common law partners.

If you are legally married, have been separated from your legal spouse for at least one year, and are legally prohibited from getting divorced, you can sponsor a different partner as a common-law or conjugal partner. If you are legally married to someone and live in a country where divorce is legal, you cannot sponsor someone else through common law or conjugal partnership. If you and your spouse have been separated for a year or either of you has entered into a common-law partnership, they can't sponsor you. If you fail to disclose your legal spouse in your application, you will not be able to sponsor them in the future.

Common law partnerships

If you've been in a committed relationship with your partner for two years and have lived together for at least 12 consecutive months, you can apply for family sponsorship as common law partners. If you have children together, you still have to live together for a year before you're eligible, but the two year requirement is waived.

This is a great option for people in same-sex relationships in a country that doesn't recognize marriage equality. It's also a great option for people who want to stay together badly enough to move to another country, but not badly enough to put a ring on it.

You'll need to provide documentation showing that your love is real and that you shared a home and finances. Partners who aren't legally married are more likely to have the IRCC ask for additional documentation or be required to attend an interview.

Conjugal partnerships

Sometimes there are extenuating circumstances preventing you and your partner from getting married or living together. You can still apply for spousal sponsorship as conjugal partners.

You'll need to provide documentation showing that you and your partner were unable to live together for 12 consecutive months due to immigration barriers, religious reasons, or sexual orientation. These reasons must be beyond your control.

While family responsibilities or a tough job market are a significant hurdle to living together, they wouldn't be enough to qualify you as conjugal partners. This is primarily for people coming from countries with laws against homosexuality, where they are married already and divorce is not allowed, or they face other insurmountable legal logistical challenges.

Conjugal partners are still required to prove that they are in an interdependent relationship "financially, socially, emotionally and physically – when they share household and related responsibilities, and when they have made a serious commitment to one another."

Fiancé visas

Canada used to have a fiance visa so partners could move to Canada while planning their wedding. This is no longer an option.

If you are planning your wedding and would like your partner to move to Canada prior to the wedding, I'll let you in on a secret: lots of people don't get legally married on their "wedding day." You can get married legally and hold a ceremony after your sponsorship has been approved.

You can also try moving to Canada under dual intent, entering as a visitor and then applying for PR once you're married, but this means you might be turned away at the border. It would be a real bummer to have to reschedule your big day because of issues at the border. Even if you enter Canada on a visitor visa, your chances of being allowed in with dual intent are better if you're already legally married.

Sponsoring a dependent child

The process for sponsoring a dependent child is the same as sponsoring a spouse. If you're sponsoring a partner with kids, you include them in the same application.

You can sponsor a dependent child, even if they have kids of their own, as long as they're under 22 years old when you apply and don't have a spouse or common law partner.

You can sponsor a dependent child over the age of 22 if they rely on your support because of a mental or physical condition that existed before they turned 22.

Confused? They have a quiz to help you figure out if your kids qualify.

Sponsoring a child you are adopting is different.

Being sponsored by an immediate family members *after* they receive PR

Until recently, immediate family members who were not declared on your application for permanent residence were banned from family class sponsorship in the future, since applicants had omitted key information and this was viewed as committing fraud. This information is still listed on the IRCC website in 2021.

If you were not included on their application for PR because they reasonably believed you were dead or feared reprisal for acknowledging a child born out of wedlock, you can be sponsored by them through family class. It's unclear if the IRCC is still upholding the ban in other cases.

The IRCC determined that family members were being omitted because of gender discrimination, power imbalances within relationships, and complex family situations. Thus, there's a pilot program that will allow previously ineligible family members to be sponsored. This was planned to run from September 9, 2019, to

September 9, 2021. It has been extended to September 9, 2023 due to the pandemic.

If you were included on their PR application and indicated you were not accompanying them to Canada or you were granted a CoPR and did not immigrate before it expired, you may be sponsored by them through the regular family reunification program without needing to rely on this pilot program.

Pledge of financial support

Your partner will have to sign a contract promising to financially support you for three years, known as an undertaking. If you're being sponsored by a parent, they are obligated to support you for ten years or until you turn 25, whichever is sooner. If you are immigrating to Canada with dependent children who are not related to your Canadian partner, your partner will need to pledge to support your children for ten years or until the child is 22 years old (whichever happens first).

This includes food, shelter, clothing, household supplies, personal items, and any healthcare costs not covered by provincial health insurance. They may need to meet minimum income requirements. Your income does not count toward the income requirement.

If you or your children (not related to your Canadian partner) apply for social assistance during those years, your spouse will need to repay that amount to the Canadian government, even if you are separated or divorced.

While you don't have to meet any financial requirements, you'll need to sign a pledge promising you will make all reasonable efforts to support yourself and your children once you are legally able to work.

Which is better: family sponsorship or being a skilled worker?

Many young adults with a Canadian romantic partner qualify for both express entry and spousal sponsorship. If you qualify for both, which is the best way to get PR status?

Because express entry is entirely online, it can be slightly faster. However, there often isn't a huge difference. Times can vary significantly for outland sponsorship, so if you don't need an open work permit it's worth considering. You can check current processing times online to see if one way is faster when you're ready to apply.

Just like spousal sponsorship doesn't require you to be married, the skilled worker program doesn't require you to have a job offer.

Why would you want to use a skilled worker program rather than family sponsorship?

- Your spouse or parent isn't eligible to sponsor you.

- You have been married a short time, don't have kids, and don't have strong documentation to support that you're in a committed relationship.

- You're worried your spouse or parent might withdraw their application, which they can do at any time before you become a permanent resident.

- You'd rather the IRCC scrutinize your work history than assess the strength of your family ties.

Why would you want to use family sponsorship rather than the skilled worker program?

- You've been working without legal status or have not been declaring your full income on your taxes.

- You don't want to gather documents from previous employers.
- You don't want to take the English exam.

How family sponsorship works in Canada

The paperwork you need to submit to support your application depends on the legal and residential relationship between you and your romantic partner. The application itself depends on where you're applying from: inside of Canada or outside of Canada. As usual, there's a bonus round if you're applying from inside Quebec or intend to move to Quebec.

Types of family sponsorship

There are two types of family sponsorship, which are based on where you're living while your application is processed.

In Canada class

If you and your sponsor are already living in Canada, you're eligible to apply as spouse in Canada or in Canada class. This is the case if you have a valid visa as a visitor, student, or worker.

This allows you to apply for an open work permit while you wait for your PR application to go through. If you don't already have a work permit, you cannot work legally until your open work permit application has been approved.

If you already have a work permit, make sure whatever visa you're on doesn't expire before your application is approved. You can apply to extend your current visa while your application is being processed.

Once you have an open work permit, you'll likely be eligible to register for provincial medical insurance if you aren't already covered.

158

If you leave Canada while your application is being processed, there is no guarantee that you will be allowed back into the country. Is it likely that border agents will turn you away? Not very. Consider your comfort level with risk before you leave Canada.

Family class

If you're living outside of Canada, you'll need to be sponsored under Family Class. Your application will be processed by the visa office in the country you're currently living in.

If you're planning on moving out of Canada temporarily while your application is being processed or the processing times for your country are faster than in Canada, you may want to apply through family class, even if you qualify for in canada processing.

While waiting, you should be able to visit Canada under a regular visitor visa with dual intent. Dual intent is when you're entering Canada on one visa (like a tourist visa) while also applying for (or planning to apply for) another type of visa (such as permanent resident status). You may face additional questions at the port of entry, but in most cases it just adds a few minutes to your travel time.

If you're feeling particularly brave, you can even see if you can move to Canada to live with your spouse while waiting for your application to process. This is totally up to the border agent on duty, so be prepared to be turned away. You may have to demonstrate that:

- Your sponsor has submitted the application.

- You totally qualify and understand how the process works.

- You'll leave Canada if your application is denied.

- You won't work illegally while you wait for your application to process.

- You can support yourself (or your sponsor will support you) while you wait.

- You have private medical insurance coverage.

The border agent will decide how long your visa will be valid for and you'll need to make sure you don't overstay this visa. You may also have issues bringing your things across the border before your application is approved without having to pay duties on them, depending on what visa you're currently on.

Sponsorship in Quebec

If your sponsor is living in Quebec or you plan on living in Quebec when your application is approved, the IRCC will direct you to apply for a CSQ from MIDI once they've completed processing your federal application. See the section on Quebec for more information on this process.

The application

The IRCC has played around with the order of things. They verify your eligibility to be sponsored and your partner or parent's eligibility to be a sponsor. You have to submit both applications at the same time. If you're coming with your kids, include them.

When submitting your application, be sure to have submitted the exact documents required by the IRCC in the checklist they provided, based on your specific situation. You can complete the forms digitally and then mail in printed copies for the paper section of the application.

When filling out the application:

- You must complete every field of the application. Do not leave a section blank, write "N/A."

- If you don't know a date of birth, use an asterisk in the field for the year, month, or day that you don't know.

- If you don't have a family name or given name on your ID, type "N/A" in the corresponding application field.

- Be sure to sign and date where it is required. If someone under 18 is required to sign, a parent or guardian should sign in their place.

- Check which documents need to be originals and which can be copies.

Your sponsor will get a confirmation of receipt once they've submitted the complete application. Once you get this, you can check your application status online.

While the application is done on paper, you can still link it to an online account. The IRCC provides instructions on how to link your application to your account after you create an account or sign in. They also have an FAQ to help if you encounter any problems creating or linking your account.

Document checklist

The exact documents required depend on your relationship to your sponsor, your country of residence, and the countries your key documents come from. The IRCC provides you with a custom document checklist for your specific situation.

Your immigration application requires extensive documentation of your relationship, as well as lots of information about you. Any documents that aren't in English or French will need to be translated.

If you can't submit a document included in the IRCC checklist, you must include an explanation of why you can't submit this document or your application will be returned to you for being incomplete. Keep your explanation clear and concise. If the IRCC decides your reason is legitimate, they will work with you to provide alternate documentation or waive the requirement.

Be sure to sign any places where signatures are required. The IRCC checklist provides a list of places where you need to sign. If you forget a signature the IRCC might return the application to you without

161

processing it or they might ask you to resubmit that part of the application. Either way, it'll delay things.

Documents verifying your romantic partnership

- Proof of cohabitation if you are currently living together.
- If you are not living together:
  - As much proof as possible to demonstrate the reasons why you have not been able to share a household and/or finances.
  - 10 pages of printed media to demonstrate ongoing communication (letters, text messages, social media posts, and/or emails).
  - Proof of visitation (plane tickets or boarding passes and passport pages).
- If you are married: marriage certificate and 20 photographs from your wedding.
  - A record of solemnization or marriage license are not accepted. Check the specific requirements the IRCC has for the country you were married in.
- If you are in a common law or conjugal relationship: as much information as possible to demonstrate that you share a home and finances such as:
  - Statements for joint bank accounts or credit cards
  - Mortgage documents signed by both parties
  - Property lease signed by both of you
  - Property ownership documents in both of your names
  - Declarations from people verifying your relationship

162

- Pictures from your lives demonstrating that your relationship is genuine such as from vacations, family events, holidays, etc.
- Birth certificates of any children that you have together
- Proof of three of the things below (not needed if you have been together for more than 2 years, currently live together, have children together, and have only been married to each other):
  - Joint ownership or lease of a home
  - Joint responsibility of utilities
  - Government issued identification documents showing the same address
  - Evidence of financial support between you and your spouse
  - Proof that your relationship is recognized by your friends and family (such as social media posts showing that your relationship is public, cards mailed to you for your wedding or anniversary, wedding photos)

Documents verifying your relationship to a parent

- A birth certificate listing them as your parent. There is a separate process for international adoptions.
- If your other parent is living and not accompanying you to Canada, you'll need to provide a copy of their ID and proof of the custody arrangement.
- If your other parent is not living, you'll need to include their death certificate.
- If you have children of your own, you'll need to include their documents demonstrating that you are their parent and that

you have (or do not need) permission from the other parent to bring them to Canada.

Documents your sponsor will need to provide

The IRCC may ask for additional documents or even require an interview. If they require an interview, you can request that it take place at the visa office closest to you. Even though they try to accommodate your requests, this will likely still require traveling because there aren't a lot of visa offices.

- Proof of citizenship (Canadian birth certificate, certificate of citizenship, or Canadian passport) or permanent resident status (permanent resident card, record of landing, or confirmation of permanent residence).

- Proof of income:

  o Tax returns and income slips for most recent tax year OR explanation for why you cannot provide these

  o Letter from your employer stating length of employment, salary, and hours per week (if applicable)

  o Welfare receipts and/or receipts from government payouts (if applicable)

- Required only if you will be immigrating with your children:

  o Sponsorship evaluation

  o Evidence of income for the previous 12 months

  o Evidence of savings that show they meet the financial requirements

  o Financial evaluation if you are the parent to a dependent child with a child of their own

- Required only if they have been married to another person: divorce, annulment, separation, or death certificate

- Application to sponsor, sponsorship agreement and undertaking
- Sponsorship evaluation and relationship questionnaire form

Documents you will need to provide

It's very important that you declare all family members that aren't already Canadian citizens or permanent residents, even if you're not including them in your application.

- Valid passport
- Your birth certificate
- 2 photographs for permanent resident card
- Police certificate(s) from any country that you have lived in for 6+ months since turning 18
  - o Some countries require a consent form before issuing a police certificate. If you need a police certificate from one of these countries, you submit the consent form to the IRCC in place of the police certificate and the IRCC will then request a police certificate from that country on your behalf
  - o If your application is complete except for the police certificate, you can show that you've requested the police certificate and provide the police certificate when you get it. The FBI is notorious for holding up applications.
- Required only if you have been married to another person: divorce, annulment, separation, or death certificate
- Required only if you are applying through the spouse or common law partner in Canada class: visa or permit

confirming that you are currently allowed to legally live in Canada

- Required only if you have children (even if they will not be immigrating with you): birth certificates, certificates of adoption, or custody papers for all children, including those who are already Canadian citizens

- You will need to be asked to do a medical exam by the IRCC, which is not included in your initial application. Your medical exam can't be done by just any doctor, it needs to be done by a panel physician approved by the IRCC, so follow instructions carefully.

- If you are not currently living in Canada, you will need to provide biometrics:

  - You cannot get your biometrics done until you get a biometric instruction letter (BIL) from the IRCC. This needs to be done in person at an approved location.

  - In 2020 and 2021 this requirement was waived for applicants already living in Canada.

  - If you have opted to have your application processed overseas, you will need to provide biometrics, even if you are currently living in Canada.

  - You may need to give your biometrics, even if you gave biometrics previously for another application.

  - Anyone included on your application will also need to provide biometrics.

Forms

You can fill out most of these PDFs electronically. Typing information, rather than hand writing it, will reduce the likelihood of things being illegible. Some of these forms allow you to verify that it's complete and provide a barcode you can print and include in your application.

- Schedule A – Background/Declaration [eIMM 5669]
- Relationship information and sponsorship evaluation form [IMM 5532 E]
- Generic application for Canada [IMM 0008]
- Application to Sponsor, Sponsorship Agreement and Undertaking [IMM 1344]: A copy of this form must be included for each person on the application.
- Additional Family Information [IMM 5406]: If a dependent child on your application has one or more children of their own.
- Declaration From Non-Accompanying Parent/Guardian For Minors Immigrating to Canada [IMM 5604]: If a child included in your application has a parent besides you and the person sponsoring you, you must submit this form, along with a copy of the other parent's photo ID. If this is not possible, you must include a letter of explanation.
- Use of Representative form [IMM 5476]: If you have an immigration attorney or consultant preparing your application or if you want your sponsor to be able to monitor your application for you.
- Financial Evaluation (IMM 1283) form: If a dependent child included in your application has children of their own.

Submitting your application

When mailing your application, don't put it in a binder, staple anything, or put it in a folder. It should just be a stack of documents ready to go through a document scanner. You can use a paper clip or rubber band to keep the photos in place.

Put the documents in the order provided in your custom document checklist. The last page of the checklist will help you make sure you've signed everything that needs to be signed.

- Your document checklist should be the first page when you mail in your application.

- If you are applying for an open work permit, the application for this and proof of payment should be included after the document checklist.

- Some of these PDF forms have the option to validate that they're complete. If a validated form provides a barcode, you should print this out and include it beneath the checklist page in your application. If you are applying for an open work permit, the barcodes go after your work permit application.

Regular mail

If you're currently living outside of Canada or living in Canada but choosing overseas sponsorship:

CPC Sydney

P.O. Box 9500

Sydney, NS

B1P 0H5

If you're currently living in Canada:

CPC Mississauga

P.O. Box 5040, Station B

Mississauga, ON

L5A 3A4

By courier

If you're currently living outside of Canada or living in Canada but choosing overseas sponsorship:

CPC Sydney

49 Dorchester Street

Sydney, NS

B1P 5Z2

If you're currently living in Canada:

CPC Mississauga

2 Robert Speck Parkway, Suite 300

Mississauga, ON

L4Z 1H8

After you submit your application

The IRCC will send you an acknowledgement of receipt letter (AOR). Depending on the backlog, your application may sit for quite some time before anyone looks at it. They will contact you again to let you know they've deemed the application complete.

As they go through your application to be sponsored, they'll request your biometrics, medical exam, and a CSQ, if applicable. Once you submit those, it's normal to not get any updates for a few weeks or up to four months.

They'll notify you when they've decided you're eligible to be sponsored. They'll also notify you when your potential sponsor has been found eligible to serve as a sponsor. Then the IRCC will review the documents you've submitted to demonstrate that your relationship is genuine. This generally takes somewhere between two and six months. It can take much longer if you're missing documents or have a complicated situation.

When you receive a letter with information on pre-arrival services, you know you're almost to the finish line. Soon they'll contact you to confirm your address and request updated photos. Now things move forward quickly and you'll probably have PR status in the next month, or at least have the option to land if you're ready.

If you're applying from within Canada, they'll then provide information for your virtual landing portal.

If you're applying from outside of Canada, you'll get your confirmation of permanent residence document (CoPR). Once you have your CoPR, you're ready to go to the border and declare yourself a landed immigrant.

You don't have PR status until you actually land and activate your CoPR or are issued your CoPR through the virtual landing portal. You need to declare yourself a landed immigrant before your CoPR expires. The expiration date is typically the expiration date for your medical exam. In some circumstances you may be granted a new CoPR if you're unable to land before it expires, but this is unusual. Don't assume you can extend the deadline. It's better to land and then return to your old home to tie up loose ends.

IRCC communication

The IRCC aims to process applications within a year. The IRCC website lists current processing times. If your application is incomplete or requires extra scrutiny, it can take much longer.

- It is important to keep your contact information up to date.

- If you create an online account and link it to your application, all updates will be sent through that.

- If you have a representative, including your sponsor acting as a representative, your representative can link their account to your application, but you cannot.
- I found that automated emails from the myCIC system were often filtered as spam. You want to set up a filter rule to make sure emails from donotreply@cic.gc.ca would be marked as important to make sure you don't miss any important messages.

- If you provide an email on your application and don't have an online account, they'll contact you via email. If you hand write your application forms and they are unable to read your email address, they will use your postal address.

- If you don't have an online account and don't provide an email address, they will contact you through the mailing address you provided on your application.

- If you apply using a representative, that person will receive all correspondence.

- If you authorize your sponsor to act as your representative, they will receive all correspondence.

Biometrics & medical exam

Once your application to be sponsored has been provisionally approved, you'll be contacted and instructed to do your medical exam and have biometrics taken. Everyone on your application over the age of 14 will have to have this done. In some cases, teenagers may refuse to cooperate or co-parents may block them from cooperating. In this case, you can remove them from your application in order to proceed. You will need to provide the IRCC with a letter of explanation and documents to show they are refusing to cooperate with the immigration process, like screenshots of conversations.

Sponsorship in Quebec

If your sponsor is living in Quebec or you plan on living in Quebec when your application is approved, the IRCC will direct you to apply for a CSQ from MIDI once they've completed processing your federal application. See the section on Quebec for more information.

Approval

Once your application is approved, they might request your passport or a copy of it, two passport photos, and proof that you've paid the right of permanent residence fee. If you need a visa put in your passport, they'll do this, even if you're already in Canada.

Next you'll get a Confirmation of Permanent Residence (CoPR). This document will have an expiration date. You have to go to a Canadian port of entry or visa office and declare yourself a landed immigrant before this expiration date. Everyone on your application must become a permanent resident before their CoPR expires.

Once you've landed, you'll typically get your permanent resident card in the mail within a few weeks. If you don't, you can fill out a form to request it be resent. You'll be eligible to apply for provincial health insurance, if you aren't already covered.

Deemed ineligible

If your partner or parent is found ineligible to be a sponsor, the IRCC will return your application and refund your fees, except for the sponsorship fee. If you are deemed ineligible, they won't return your fees. In either case, you can appeal this decision or resolve the issue and reapply.

Sponsoring an extended family member

Canada's family class program is designed to allow Canadian citizens and permanent residents to bring their adopted children, parents, and grandparents, to the country as new permanent residents.

In order to sponsor another type of extended family member, a sponsor must prove that they don't have any family members in Canada and have no living immediate family members (a spouse or dependent child) that they could sponsor.

If you're approved for permanent resident status through family sponsorship, you can bring your spouse (including a common law partner) and dependent children with you, so long as you include them on your application.

Adopting a child from outside of Canada

All too often, Canadians who've adopted a child abroad find themselves in the news when they're unable to get their child status in Canada or face long processing delays. Learn all of the requirements ahead of time and hire an attorney. You'll need to deal with the government of your child's home country, the federal government, and your provincial or territorial authorities.

In order to bring your adopted child to Canada, you'll need to apply to be a sponsor and then apply for them to be given permanent resident status. Once the adoption is final, you can apply for them to become a citizen.

You need to meet the general sponsor requirements, which are outlined in the family sponsorship section. You can sponsor a child under 18 if you're a citizen or permanent resident.

You can sponsor a child over 18 if you're a citizen. If your adopted child is over 18, you'll need to show that a genuine parent / child relationship existed between you before they turned 18.

You're agreeing to support the child for ten years or until they turn 25, whichever happens first.

You can sponsor the child on your own or have a co-sponsor. Co-sponsors are helpful when one might not be eligible individually.

You need to submit a separate application for each child you'd like to sponsor.

Getting the adoption recognized in Canada

Adoption procedures vary from country to country and not all countries allow international adoptions. The rules are often different when a child is being adopted by someone who is already a family member. In order to qualify for sponsorship, the adoption has to:

- Be legal both in the child's home country and the part of Canada where you live.
- End the relationship between the child and their biological parents.
- Be in the best interest of the child and not be done primarily to gain PR status for the child.

You'll have to show that the adoption conforms with the Hague Convention and informed consent was given to both biological parents, if they're alive.

The child will need a medical exam according to the requirements of your province or territory.

Once your local authorities have approved the adoption, you'll get a letter of no objection. Then you can begin the application process with the federal government.

Being approved as a sponsor

If you know which country you'll be adopting a child from, you can be approved as a sponsor before being matched for a child. This minimizes the amount of time between when your adoption begins and when you can bring your child home to Canada. If you're adopting a child and haven't yet been matched with a specific child, you can leave the name field blank on the forms.

You'll need to submit these forms:

- Document Checklist — Sponsor [IMM 5287]
- Application to Sponsor, Sponsorship Agreement and Undertaking [IMM 1344]
- Financial Evaluation [IMM 1283]
- Additional Dependants/Declaration [IMM 0008DEP], if applicable
- Schedule A – Background/Declaration [IMM 5669]
- Use of a Representative [IMM 5476], if applicable
- Medical Condition Statement [IMM 0133] if you already know what child you will adopt

Then you pay the fees online and mail in the application:

Sponsorship: Adoption
Case Processing Centre - Sydney
P.O. Box 9500
Sydney, Nova Scotia
B1P 0H5

If you send it by courier:

Sponsorship: Adoption
Case Processing Centre - Sydney
49 Dorchester Street
Sydney, Nova Scotia
B1P 5Z2

Applying for PR for your child

Once your application to be a sponsor has been approved, the Canada Visa office in your child's home country will send you a PR application. This is the Generic Application Form for Canada [IMM 0008].

You or the child's current guardian can fill it out and return it to that Canada Visa office. If the child is old enough to speak, they may be required to go to the office for an interview. There is country-specific information on the IRCC website. You'll also need to include the Medical Condition Statement [IMM 0133] if you haven't already submitted it. You'll also need to provide the Additional Family Information [IMM 5406].

Your child will need a passport from their home country both to apply for PR in Canada and to enter Canada.

Be prepared for there to be a significant delay while you wait for your child's PR status to be approved. It's unlikely you'll be able to bring your child home to Canada until they have PR status.

Once the Canada Visa office gives you landing documents for your child, you're ready to bring them home to Canada. That's when they'll become a permanent resident.

Applying for citizenship for your child

If you were born abroad and became a Canadian citizen through your parents, you may not be eligible to sponsor a child who was also born abroad for citizenship. You can still sponsor them for PR and later apply for a grant of citizenship once they meet the standard requirements for citizenship. In most cases, if you're a Canadian citizen you can pass that citizenship to your child without waiting until they meet the physical presence test.

Once again, this is a two-part application, where you prove your eligibility to sponsor them for citizenship and then prove their eligibility to be sponsored. You'll need to submit these forms:

- Document Checklist [Form CIT 0484]
- Confirmation of Canadian Citizenship of the Adoptive Parent(s) [Form CIT 0010]

Pay your fees online and mail your application to:

Citizenship and Immigration Canada
Case Processing Centre: Adoption
P.O. Box 10030
Sydney, Nova Scotia B1P 7C1

Once you're approved to sponsor them for citizenship, the IRCC will send you a letter asking you to send in the second part of the application, so they can confirm that your child qualifies to be sponsored.

- Document Checklist [Form CIT 0485]
- Adoptee's Application [Form CIT 0012]
- Use of a Representative [Form IMM 5476]
- Canadian Citizenship Certificate Preparation Form [Form CIT 0480]

If your child's application is approved, they'll be granted citizenship. If you're living in the US or Canada, the IRCC will mail your child's citizenship certificate to you. If you are living outside of Canada, they'll mail it to the local Canada Visa office. If you're outside of Canada, you may need to apply for a Canadian passport from the nearest consulate.

Parent and grandparent program

If you are the parent or grandparent of a Canadian citizen or permanent resident, they can apply to sponsor you through the parent and grandparent program (PGP). Only 10,000 people are invited to apply each year. Applicants are selected through a lottery system. The processing time is around two years.

First, you need to submit an interest to sponsor form through the IRCC website. All applicants that expressed interest will be notified even if they are not invited to apply. If you're selected, your sponsor will be invited to complete the full application for the parent and grandparent program within 60 days. That's not enough time to get the documents required, so you'll want to begin collecting documents ahead of time. Each year slots go unfilled because people don't submit their applications before the deadline.

Due to the number of applications received, it's estimated that this lottery system gives each applicant a 20% chance of getting selected. Those that aren't selected are allowed to re-apply the following year.

For the applications that are approved, Canada aims to process the immigration process within a year.

In spite of whatever finances you have yourself, your child or grandchild that sponsors you will need to demonstrate that they have the means to support you for a period of up to 20 years.

Document checklist

Forms

- Application to sponsor, sponsorship agreement, and undertaking
- Financial evaluation for parents and grandparents
- Income sources for the sponsorship of parents and grandparents (if applicable)
- Statutory declaration of common-law union (if applicable)
- Generic application form for Canada
- Additional dependants declaration

- Background declaration
- Additional family information
- Use of representative (if applicable)
- Copy of fee payment receipt

Supporting documents

- Sponsor's ID and proof of citizenship or PR status
- Spouse's ID and proof of citizenship or PR status (if applicable)
- Proof of applicant's relationship to sponsor
- Copy of passport for applicant and dependents
- Proof of relationship for applicant's dependents
- Two photos of applicant and all dependents (per IRCC specifications)

Sponsoring other family members

In order to sponsor you, your family member would have to demonstrate that they:

- Have no spouse or common law partner
- Have no living parents or grandparents anywhere in the world
- Have no relatives living in Canada, including: children, parents, grandparents, siblings, uncles, aunts, nieces, or nephews

If that's the case, they can sponsor you if you're a sibling, uncle, aunt, niece, or nephew.

Requirements for your sponsor

Your family member must be over the age of 18 and currently living in Canada. They must not:

- Have ever received government financial assistance (other than disability).

- Have defaulted on a court-ordered support order (such as alimony or child support).

- Have been convicted of a violent or sexual crime.

- Have defaulted on an immigration loan.

- Be in prison.

- Be in bankruptcy.

- Have sponsored another family member for immigration and failed to financially support them.

Financial requirements

While you are expected to make all attempts to support yourself once you become a resident of Canada, your family member must promise to support you financially for 10-20 years.

- Parent or grandparent: 20 years
- Any other family member: 10 years

They'll need to meet certain income requirements in order to be eligible to sponsor you. They'll have to promise to provide basic requirements including food, clothing, utilities, shelter, fuel, household supplies, as well as health care not covered by the provincial health care system, such as vision and dental care. They are still financially responsible for you during this time, even if you become estranged.

Sponsorship in Quebec

If your sponsor is living in Quebec or you plan on living in Quebec when your application is approved, the IRCC will direct you to apply for a CSQ from MIDI once they've completed processing your federal application. See the section on Quebec for more information.

Provincial nomination programs

Canada has a number of provincial nomination programs (PNPs) that allow provinces to sponsor people for permanent residence status. These programs change frequently. Some PNPs have online applications separate from the IRCC website, some are integrated into express entry, and others require a paper application.

Many are designed to allow temporary residents, like students and temporary workers, to stay permanently. If you have ties to a certain province or territory, you should see if you qualify for a PNP.

Others are designed to meet specific skill shortages. These skill lists change regularly, so if you don't qualify now you may qualify in the future.

Each PNP is different. Some are run by private organizations or community groups. They may provide clear instructions or you may apply only to find you didn't qualify. Some change the rules or shut down without notice. Some are well managed and will process your application quickly.

All PNPs require you to state your intent to settle permanently in whichever province sponsors your immigration into Canada. You must still meet all of the requirements for federal immigration, in addition to the requirements of the PNP you are applying for.

Canadian graduates

Provinces can nominate candidates outside of the express entry system, typically for people who do not meet EE requirements because of their age. Outside of the EE system, candidates must first get a provincial nomination. Once you have the nomination certificate, you can apply for immigration through the federal government using the paper application. You can find all the forms on the IRCC website. The paper immigration application has a much longer processing time.

If you have a degree from a Canadian university and have a valid job offer from an approved company, you likely qualify for PNP for your province.

If you've gotten your Master's degree or PhD in Canada, you'll likely qualify for PNP in your province and may even get an open work permit while your application to become a permanent resident is processed.

Business class immigration

Running a business in Canada can provide a pathway to PR status. If you're already an entrepreneur, you can bring your business to Canada. If you have a startup idea, you can build your business in Canada. You can even buy or invest in an established business.

These programs tend to be quite small. Ontario welcomed two investors in six years, although now they're planning on expanding the program to 100 investors.

Entrepreneur stream

If you have financial capital and business experience, there are several programs set up that would allow you to immigrate to Canada and invest in the economy. Each province and territory has their own PNP with entrepreneur streams to get you started on the pathway to residency. Some PNPs will grant you permanent residency status before you move, and others will sponsor permanent residency only after you've been successfully operating your new business in Canada for a specific amount of time.

These programs vary slightly between each province, but generally all require that you become an active partner in a new or existing business located within that province. They require that you prove your net worth, demonstrate the ability to contribute a certain amount of equity into a business, and to make a sizable deposit to that province that will be held by the government for a specific amount of time or until your business plan has been fully executed.

Most of the PNPs that are open to business investors have caps and only accept a certain number of applicants per year. Depending on which province you're interested in living in, you may need to wait in order to even apply. Since the PNPs aim to address specific economic needs, the requirements and selection criteria may change at any time.

You'll need to submit a viable business plan along with your application and would meet with a government representative to discuss your strategy. Priority is given to applicants that are most qualified and thought to have the greatest potential to establish themselves in that province and make the biggest contribution to the economy. Meeting the technical requirements does not guarantee your acceptance into the program.

The purpose of these programs is to contribute to the economy and to create jobs, so your business plan would need to address the creation of new full-time jobs for Canadians, not just for yourself or family members.

In addition to whichever requirements exist for each PNP, you and any accompanying family members would need to pass a medical exam and prove that you would not be an excessive burden on the health and social services offered by the government. You'd also have to prove proficiency in English and/or French and, of course, be considered admissible to Canada.

Move your start-up to Canada

Running a startup? Canada is looking to hold its own against Silicon Valley, so they're building an excellent network to nurture startups and attract top talent. If approved, you'd be able to move to Canada as a permanent resident through the start-up business class immigration stream.

Unlike most other immigration programs, this one does not necessarily favor younger applicants. Up to five people can move to Canada under the startup visa. You'll need to take a language test to prove your proficiency in English and/or French.

You need to prove you have funds to support yourself and your family. The requirements are quite reasonable and if you're moving to a city, you'll want to have access to more funds than that if you don't have some sort of income coming in.

You'll need support from a designated VC fund, angel investor, or business incubator.

Each person coming on a startup visa needs to have at least 10% of the votes and collectively, the startup applicants and designated organization need to have a majority stake.

Requirements

- Guaranteed minimum investment from a designated organization

- Own at least 10% of your business

- Verified voting rights that, along with any other applicant and designated organization, is equal to or greater than 50%

- Have completed at least a year of post-secondary education

- Ability to communicate in English or French

- Do not intend to live in the province of Quebec

- Have the minimal amount of savings to support yourself (about $12,600 and additional $2,000 per family member that would immigrate with you)

Investment

While you can obtain investments from just about anyone, you'll need to secure minimal support from at least one of the three types of designated organizations:

1. Venture capital fund: C$200k minimum investment

2. Angel investor group: C$75k minimum investment

3. Business incubator program: no investment required

Within each of these categories, there are a limited number of organizations that qualify within each option. Check the list of designated organizations provided by the IRCC in order to find the most up to date list.

Each organization has their own set of criteria in place to evaluate the potential of your business plan. You'd be responsible for establishing contact and pitching your idea in an effort to obtain their support.

If one of the organizations decides that they would like to invest in your business, you'd also be responsible for getting a Letter of Support to submit as part of your immigration application. The organization will also need to submit a Commitment Certificate directly to the IRCC to verify their support. This certificate would outline the agreement between you and the organization in regards to the business venture.

If the only way you can reach the minimum investment amount is through support from multiple organizations, you'll be considered to be in syndication. In that case, you'll need to provide letters of support from each organization. If any one of the organizations is a venture capital firm, then you will need to meet the minimum investment amount of C$200k, even if all of the other groups pledging support are angel investors.

All commitments are subject to a peer review process.

Ownership

You don't have to be the sole proprietor of your business in order to be eligible for the visa. You, along with up to four other owners, can apply for the visa. Once your investment is secured, each owner would submit their own application for the start-up visa.

If your business is owned by more than one person, the investor commitment can be conditional. That would mean that their promise of investment would only be guaranteed if whichever people are identified as "essential." In that situation, the investment would only be given if the essential applicants are approved for immigration. If that person was rejected for the visa, then all other owners would also be rejected.

Self-employed

If you're a successful author, musician, athlete, or the like, you can become a Canadian permanent resident through the self-employment visa program. You need to be working in cultural activities or athletics at a world-class level.

This is also the program farmers can immigrate through, this program has been paused since 2018.

They take your age, language skills, education, experience, and adaptability into account, on a points system. You and your family members must have a medical exam and get police certificates. You must also show that you have enough money to support yourself and your family after you get to Canada.

Refugees & asylum seekers

If you can legally move to Canada through any other immigration program, it's best to pursue that option before considering claiming asylum. If there is ever the choice, it's best to claim refugee status from inside Canada. Gaining refugee status from outside of Canada is a lengthy and uncertain process.

You're ineligible to claim refugee status if you're inadmissible to Canada, have an ongoing refugee claim in another country, or if you have already made a refugee claim in Canada.

Claiming asylum in Canada

Claiming asylum is a complicated process with a lot of paperwork. Settlement organizations can help you with paperwork, navigating the system, setting up a home, enrolling your kids in school, and other things you might need. There are also NGOs that assist refugee claimants. You can find assistance by contacting your local library, YMCA, Canadian Council for Refugees, or the IRCC. Your local library can also help you with computer use, internet access, and printing services.

If you try to claim refugee status at the US/CA border, you will be returned to the US unless:

- You can show that you have family already living in Canada.

- You are an unaccompanied minor without family in the US.

- You have to apply for a visa to enter the US but are visa-exempt in Canada.

- You face execution in the US and are not criminally inadmissible in Canada.

Some refugee claimants get around this requirement by crossing the border at unmarked crossings. They are then allowed to claim refugee status once they are detained by the Royal Canadian Mounted Police (RCMP). Not surprisingly, the CBSA discourages irregular border crossings.

If you have a valid Canadian work permit or study permit you can claim asylum from within Canada, even if you entered through the US.

Once your claim is determined to be eligible, you and any accompanying family members can apply for open work permits. If you're accepted by a designated learning institution you can apply for study permits. You need to renew work or study permits before they expire. If they expire, you'll need to reapply and stop working or attending school until you get a new permit.

There is no need to get a study permit to attend kindergarten, primary, or secondary school.

If you are from certain countries, your asylum application will be reviewed quickly. These designated countries are less likely to have legitimate refugees. If you are denied asylum, you'll have to leave Canada.

It's important to make sure the IRCC and IRB have your current contact information. You can update your contact information online.

Claiming at the border

You can claim refugee status for yourself and any accompanying family members at the border. When the border agent asks the purpose of your visit to Canada, tell them that you are claiming asylum.

They will bring you to a secondary screening area and ask you questions about your situation. They'll look at any documents and ID you have. They will also take your fingerprints and photograph.

If your claim is deemed ineligible, you will not be allowed into Canada.

If your claim is accepted at the border, it will be referred to the Immigration and Refugee Board of Canada (IRB). You'll be given a refugee protection claimant document (RPCD), a confirmation of referral letter, a basis of claim form, and instructions for getting an immigrant medical exam (IME).

You can request a work permit at the border. If they approve it, you'll get it once you've completed your IME. If you didn't apply for a work permit at the border, you can do so later.

You then have 15 days to submit the basis of claim form to the IRB's Refugee Protection Division office shown on your confirmation of referral letter.

You may also be told to submit your claim online. You'll then be assigned a time and location for an interview where they'll review your eligibility.

Claiming asylum if you're already in Canada

If you're already living in Canada, you can claim asylum online. You can request a work permit when you apply. You can also apply for a work permit later.

If you can't apply online, you'll need to contact the IRCC via email. They will respond to your request within two business days with instructions.

You'll be assigned an appointment time and location. Attendance is mandatory. You'll need to bring your original passport, if you have one, and any other IDs you have.

They'll review your application, fingerprint you, take your photo, and ask questions about your claim to determine your eligibility. They'll provide you with information about what to do next. If they can't decide your eligibility, they'll schedule an interview.

If your claim is not eligible, they'll issue a removal order and you'll have to leave Canada. They may issue a departure order, which gives you 30 days to leave Canada. You must confirm your departure with CBSA and get a document confirming that you complied with the order. You may also be ordered to leave Canada immediately. The CBSA may escort you out of the country.

Once your claim is deemed eligible, it will be referred to the Immigration and Refugee Board of Canada (IRB). You'll be given a refugee protection claimant document (RPCD), a confirmation of referral letter, a basis of claim form, and instructions for getting an immigrant medical exam (IME). You'll get a work permit once you complete your medical exam.

Interim federal health program

Your RPCD gives you access to health coverage through the interim federal health program (IFHP). You can apply for IFHP coverage online or by mail. When your application is approved you'll get an eligibility document. If you lose this document you can get a new one online.

The IFHP gives you access to healthcare providers registered with Medavie Blue Cross. You'll need to show your IFHP eligibility document each time you access health services. You may be asked to sign a form confirming that you received care from them. You may also receive mail confirming that you've received certain services.

IFHP covers:

- In-patient and out-patient hospital care; service from medical doctors, nurses, and other licensed healthcare professionals; laboratory, diagnostic, and ambulance services.

- Some vision and dental care; home care and long-term care; care from allied health-care practitioners (such as clinical psychologists, psychotherapists, counseling therapists, occupational therapists, speech language therapists, physiotherapists); and assistive devices, medical supplies, and equipment (like hearing aids, mobility aids, prosthetic equipment, diabetic supplies, incontinence supplies, oxygen equipment, and orthopedic equipment).

- Prescription medications.

Your coverage will be canceled automatically when your status changes. If you have any other insurance coverage, you are required to have that as your primary coverage.

Immigration medical exam

You'll need to get an immigrant medical exam (IME) performed by a panel physician. Your IME and any necessary related diagnostics are covered by the IFMP.

Your hearing

You'll be required to attend a hearing. The IRB will send you a notice with information on when and where it is. The IRB has a guide on how to prepare for your hearing.

Leaving Canada temporarily

If you want to leave Canada while your claim is pending, you will need to get a refugee travel document (RTD) to ensure you're able to return.

Healthcare workers and surviving spouses

If you're a refugee claimant working in healthcare while waiting for the IRB to decide on your case, or they've denied your case and you are still in Canada legally, you may be eligible for PR now.

You can also qualify for this program if you are the spouse or common-law partner of a refugee claimant who died of COVID and you have been in Canada since August 14, 2020.

This means you don't have to wait for the IRB to grant you protected person status and then apply using the paper application. Your IRB claim will be put on hold while your PR application is processed. It's important that you not withdraw your pending asylum claim or begin a new appeal. If you are under a removal order, that will also be put on hold while your application is processed.

You'll need to continue to maintain valid work and study permits while your application is processed.

To qualify as a healthcare worker, you need to have:

- Provided direct patient care as part of your job.
- Worked both:
    - 120 hours between March 13 and August 14, 2020
    - Worked full-time (30 hours/week) for at least six months or 750 part-time hours before August 31, 2021 in Quebec or before October 31, 2021 if you plan to live outside of Quebec.

It's fine if you changed jobs during this period, took vacations, or took a leave of absence, so long as you meet the hour requirements.

If you live in Quebec, you will need to be approved by the MIDI and granted a CSQ.

If your application is approved, you'll need to withdraw your pending refugee claims and appeals. You'll have a meeting with an immigration officer, where they'll go over the details of your application, verify your documentation, confirm that you can financially support yourself and your family. Then they'll give you your confirmation of permanent residence document (CoPR) and confirm the address to send your PR card.

If your application is denied, they'll notify you by mail. Whatever processes were put on hold (refugee claim, removal order, appeal) will resume.

The decision

Once the IRB has made a decision on your claim, they'll contact you.

Approval

When your claim is accepted, you become a protected person. You can now apply for PR status using the paper application. You do not need to pay the right of permanent residence fee. You do need to pay processing fees.

Once your application is received and deemed complete, you'll get a confirmation letter. It will then be passed to the visa processing center, unless you're in Quebec, in which case it will first go to MIFI for their approval. If MIFI rejects your application, you can move forward with the application provided you move to another province.

You may have an interview to confirm details of your application. You will have a final interview during which you will be given your PR status.

Denial

If your claim is denied, you can appeal with the IRB. If they deny your appeal, you can appeal to the Federal Court of Canada.

If your claim was denied because you have already made a refugee claim in Australia, New Zealand, the US, or the UK and can prove that you are in danger if you have to return to your home country, you can apply for a pre-removal risk-assessment. If it's approved you become a protected person and can then apply for PR.

You can also ask for PR status under humanitarian and compassionate grounds. You still have to comply with any removal orders and your case will continue to be processed while you're outside of Canada. There is no right to appeal.

Claiming from outside of Canada

If you're living outside of Canada, you need to be referred to the IRB through the United Nations Refugee Agency (UNHCR) or privately sponsored. Once you're referred, you can be government sponsored (government-assisted) or sponsored by a private organization. Sponsors must be members of the private sponsorship of refugees (PSR) program.

Sponsors will provide you with the things you need to initially settle in Canada, like a temporary place to live, furniture, and clothing. You'll get ongoing support for basic necessities. You'll also have access to social and emotional support programs through settlement services.

Landing in Canada

You've made it through the paperwork and you've officially been invited to move to the great white north. Now what?

I always want to know what to expect, but there was very little information about the process of actually arriving at the border and becoming a legal resident of Canada. I was hoping that meant it was so easy to move that no one had bothered to write about it. The IRCC provides instructions. They made sense to me after I'd gone through the process, but didn't help me understand what landing would be like.

The good news is that it is pretty simple, especially if you're just arriving with a few suitcases. It gets a little more complicated once you add a family and a house worth of stuff, but that's true of any move. The only things you really have to worry about are exotic pets, vehicles, and individual items over C$10k in value. Even then, you'll just want to do the research ahead of time to make sure you don't have any surprises at the border.

Pre-arrival settlement services

There are a number of organizations providing settlement services you can access before you arrive in Canada, to help you get ready to go. These are all funded by the government so there's no cost to you.

Next Stop Canada is run by the Toronto YMCA and provides access to forums, webinars, and professionals to answer your questions. They can match your needs to available programs and refer you to relevant organizations.

Your landing paperwork

Landing in Canada for the first time as a new resident doesn't necessarily mean that you have to "land" at an airport. You can just as easily drive yourself across the border, arrive on a boat, or change your status from inside the country.

If you're living outside of Canada when you receive your visa, you can enter Canada by going to any Canadian port of entry (POE). These are generally land crossings with the US or international airports.

If you're living in Canada already, you can update your status by making an appointment at an IRCC office or using their virtual landing portal. It may be simpler and faster to go to a port of entry, assuming you can legally enter the US or feel like taking an international vacation.

It used to be standard for people living in Canada to go to the border to change their status. The IRCC has put restrictions on flagpoling at major POEs, like at Niagara Falls, through a pilot program to reduce wait times at the border. Check CBSA restrictions at your intended POE before you go, since the CBSA tends to institute these policies without making a public announcement first.

In addition to the visa and my passport, I brought all of the documents that were submitted with my application. You probably won't need to show any of this stuff, but you could be required to. Technically, they can ask for original documents for anything you submitted with your application and turn you away if you don't present them. This is rare, but I've met people who've had this happen. If it happens to you, you can try again before your visa expires. That's a lot easier to do if you're entering by land.

There are things you absolutely need to have with you at the border, like your visa and your passport.

If you're bringing your stuff with you to Canada, you need:

- BSF186 form for goods on your person (two copies)
- BSF186 form for goods to follow (two copies)

I'll go over the BSF186 forms and how to actually move your things later on.

These papers probably won't be required, but you'll want to have with you if they were in your application:

- Sealed letter from your medical exam
- Police certificate
- Birth certificate
- Language test results
- Education credential assessment
- Diplomas
- Proof of funds
- Verification of your work history
- Proof of relationship status, if applicable
- Proof of parental status, if applicable
- Written job offer, if you have one

Landing as a permanent resident

When you get a letter in the mail saying your application for permanent residence in Canada has been approved, you'll also get a Confirmation of Permanent Residence (CoPR) paper for yourself and any other family members that you applied to immigrate with. The CoPR paper is very important, though it's not obvious by looking at it. This is your permanent resident visa.

You aren't a permanent resident yet, even with your PR visa. The final step is signing the paper in front of a border agent during your final immigration interview.

The CoPR is a single legal-sized piece of paper with your personal details and a big stamp across it that says "NOT VALID FOR TRAVEL." It actually looks a bit like a temporary driver's license. Keep this in a safe place – Canadian customs officers will not allow you to cross the border and declare that you are moving to Canada without your CoPR. They may be willing to issue a new one at the border.

Take careful note of the "valid to" date, which will be exactly one year from when your panel physician submitted the results of your medical exam. You need to declare landing in Canada before this date passes. The IRCC has stated that this cannot be extended for any reason. There are cases when they have issued a new CoPR, but I wouldn't count on it.

You can declare landing even if you plan to return to your home country right away to finalize your move. The border agents I spoke to said that's pretty common. You may want to return to sell your home, finish up the school year, or do other things to wrap up life in your old country. You can't, however, declare landing and then not actually move. Or you can, but you'll lose your PR status.

If you applied to immigrate with other members of your family, you can land before they do, but they can't land before the primary applicant. They can enter Canada as a visitor and declare landing after you've become a permanent resident.

Every family member who is coming with you to Canada needs to declare landing before their CoPR expires.

If your family situation has changed since you applied, you will have to make that declaration before you immigrate. If you've gotten married, divorced, entered into a common law relationship, had a new baby, or adopted a child since you submitted your application, let the IRCC know as soon as possible so that they can adjust your invitation accordingly. This will probably delay your ability to move.

Your official Permanent Resident card will arrive in the mail at the address you list on the CoPR form in about six to eight weeks. Until then, the CoPR form will serve as both your temporary proof of permanent resident status and a record of your landing in Canada. With the pandemic, people are reporting wait times of up to eight months. If your PR card doesn't arrive, you can request a new one by filling out a solemn declaration.

I've been asked for my CoPR several times since I arrived in Canada. You'll need it to access settlement services, enroll in health care, prove your legal status, renew your PR card, and apply for citizenship. You'll want to have a scan of it handy and keep the original in a safe place.

Changing your status

If you're already living in Canada, the process of changing your status is different than if you were arriving in Canada. You can change your status by going to the border, meeting with an IRCC agent at a local office, or changing your status online.

Flagpoling at the border

Those who are already living in Canada who need to update their status used to leave Canada, immediately turn around, and re-enter Canada. This is referred to as "flagpoling."

To flagpole, you need to leave Canada (which requires going through immigration to enter the US) before turning around and coming back. You can go on foot or by car. It's also possible to take the bus or train to the border, just let the driver or conductor know that you're only going to the border itself and they don't need to wait for you.

At the US border ask for a receipt to prove that you entered the US. A surprising number of people ask the US border agents if this means their Canadian visa is activated, which is a surefire way to annoy them. Remember, the US and Canada are different countries! Only a Canadian border agent can activate your Canadian visa.

Tell the Canadian border agent that you are there to change your status in Canada—to activate your student visa or work permit—or to declare yourself a landed immigrant. It's safest to use general terms, as the agents who do primary screening often aren't familiar with specific programs.

You'll be sent to the secondary screening area. There's often a wait. It may be 30 minutes or it may be several hours. You may not be allowed to use your phone, so be prepared with a book and snacks.

Someone will call you over and confirm the details of your paperwork. If you're required to have proof of private insurance, proof of funds, a medical exam, or any other documents they'll ask for them at this point.

Keep your answers to any questions simple, short, and honest. Remember: you're not confessing to your therapist, narrating your memoirs, or talking to a life coach. They're just trying to make sure you're going to follow the rules.

Carefully look over your permit or CoPR before leaving. It's much harder to change or correct your paperwork after you've walked away.

Some ports of entry discourage flagpoling. They may only process flagpolers at certain hours. They may admit you without changing your status or they may turn you away entirely. Niagara Falls is notorious for giving work permits lowest priority, leaving many people to wait eight hours in secondary screening. Once you're there, you're stuck, so plan your timing carefully to avoid peak hours. Check the CBSA website for hours and the latest updates on changing your status.

The border lacks the welcome centers that major airports have, so you'll need to get your SIN and information on settlement services at your local service center.

Landing by appointment

Staff at busy border crossings discourage flagpoling because it isn't actually necessary. You can change your status from within Canada by contacting your local IRCC office and scheduling an interview or going during walk-in hours, if they have them.

Go at your appointment time or during walk-in hours. Bring all of your other required documents. If you don't have an appointment, you'll need to show someone at the front desk a printed copy of the email saying your application was approved, or your CoPR, or whatever paperwork you received to show you're ready to change your status.

When you're called, the agent will go over the details of your visa to verify it. They'll ask to see any paperwork that's required for your visa type.

You'll be sent on your way with a signed CoPR or work permit or study permit. Check for typos and clerical errors before you leave, as changing it afterwards ranges from difficult to impossible.

It's all quite anticlimactic, so it's wise to create your own celebration to mark the occasion.

Virtual landing

In 2021 the IRCC added the option for people already living in Canada to become landed permanent residents virtually. If this is an option for you, the IRCC will invite you to land virtually using their PR portal. If you agree, you will be asked to provide them with an email address for each person on your application.

The IRCC will provide you with separate logins for each person, along with a link to the PR portal and instructions.

When you login you'll create a new password for your account, confirm that you're physically in Canada, confirm your address and contact information, and upload your photos.

Once your photos are approved, which usually happens within a week, they'll update your status in the portal and mail your PR card to the address you provided. That's it!

Flying into Canada

I decided to declare landing at Toronto Pearson Airport and paid a moving company to bring all of my stuff up later. Driving a moving truck from Brooklyn to Toronto with two cats was not something I wanted to deal with.

At the airport, the first customs agent asked me what my current status was in Canada and I explained that I was declaring myself a landed immigrant. I needed to show my completed customs declaration card, passport, and visa document at this initial stage.

If you've ever flown into Canada, you'll have filled out a customs declaration card on the airplane that asks you to identify yourself as a visitor or resident. There's no "moving to Canada" option. The customs agent I spoke to explained that since I wasn't yet living in Canada, I should put my most recent US address (even though I had an apartment in Toronto already) and mark myself as a Canadian resident.

Then, I was directed to a second customs clearing area.

Customs

The secondary customs area is where I spoke with a border patrol agent about my plans to move to Canada. They reviewed my visa and passport, verified me in their system, and asked me general questions about my life. This is also where they will review your biometrics to ensure they match the biometrics on your application.

I was asked why I decided to move to Canada, where I was going to be living, and what I did for work. They don't want to hear anyone's life story, they want the elevator pitch. Keep it short and sweet. Other people report being asked if they've ever been convicted of a crime, how long it took them to do the application, if they'd ever been deported, and even if they'd called their parents to let them know they'd landed safely.

The customs agent filled out my visa form, the CoPR, with my landing information.

Depending on what time you arrive at the airport, the secondary customs area might be empty or crowded. You might think it's best to avoid peak times, but if you arrive at an off time, you might miss out on some of the settlement services at the airport and have border agents who aren't as experienced.

I arrived at a peak time, so I waited in line for a while to talk to a customs agent. Because I was able to get my SIN and a bunch of settlement information (and a bag of welcome goodies!) it saved me time in the long run.

If you want to ask a human being some quick questions about enrolling your kids in school, setting up a bank account, or other settlement questions, you'll have an opportunity to do so at the airport.

If they don't have the answer, you'll be directed to the right agency to find assistance.

Social Insurance Number

The customs agent might not tell you this, but you can probably get your new social insurance number (SIN) at the airport. This is the number you will need to access government benefits and programs like health insurance. You'll also need it to fill out your taxes.

At Toronto Pearson they do this right in the customs area within a few minutes and you'll have the opportunity to ask questions of staff who are experts in immigration and settling. They sent me home with a goody bag of information on settlement services.

Declaring goods

After I finished up at the secondary customs clearing area and got my SIN, I was let out at the luggage area of the airport.

The final step of landing is declaring goods. You know how you're always asked if you have goods to declare? Today you have things to declare, even if you're not bringing them with you right now. *Especially* if you're not bringing them with you right now.

When you go to the exit and hand your customs declaration card to the agent, let that person know that you need to declare goods. If you don't have them with you right now, tell them you are a new resident and have goods to follow. They should then direct you to a final clearance area where you will declare your goods and get your BSF186 document or list of items stamped. Hold on to this. If you're importing goods at a later date, you will need to show this document when you bring your goods across the border to avoid paying duties.

If you don't get your BSF186 or goods list stamped at the airport, you will not be able to take advantage of duty exemptions for new residents. If you're thinking you might bring things over at any point in the future, it's worth creating a goods to follow list, which does not expire. It doesn't require you to actually import the items, but it allows you to bring them over duty free in the future.

Driving into Canada

If you're coming from the US, you'll probably be driving. Some land border crossings are putting restrictions on when foreign nationals can process their work permits, process study permits, and validate their permanent resident status. Check with CSBA if there are restrictions at the port of entry you plan on using so you don't find this out the hard way.

At the port of entry, tell the customs agent that you're landing in Canada as a new resident or activating a work or student permit. You'll be asked to drive your vehicle to a second checkpoint where you will be interviewed by a customs agent who will go over all of your documents.

If you're taking a bus or train across the border, you'll want to make sure you can take a later one the rest of the way, since your original bus or train will not wait for you.

You'll need your BSF186 or goods list ready for any of your things you're bringing into the country with you. If you're not bringing your things across the border right now, you'll need to have a BSF186 form for goods to follow. They'll stamp it and you'll need this when you bring your things into the country.

If you now have the right to work in Canada, you'll need to visit your local Service Canada location to get your Social Insurance Number (SIN). Be sure to take your passport and visa document with you when you go.

Importing your worldly possessions

If you're moving to Canada you'll need a list of all of the items you're importing for your personal use. You'll need this on your BSF186 form, previously known as a B4. While the name CBSA uses has changed, it's essentially the same form and has both identification numbers on it.

This requirement is enforced unevenly by customs agents. Some people are never asked to show their lists. Others who show up without lists are forced to unpack at the border and create a list right then and there. I'd much rather have a list and not need it.

Moving as a temporary resident

If you have a vacation home in Canada, you have one shot to bring in household and personal items. You can't sell any of these items for at least a year. You'll need to show that you've purchased a property recently or have a lease for three years or longer. You'll complete the BSF186 as a "seasonal resident."

Technically, you're not supposed to sell or get rid of anything you import without customs approval. However, this is really only an issue for high-value items. Declutter last season's clothes? Go ahead. Sell your incredibly rare vintage guitar? Check first. You may be required to pay duty.

Not everything is duty free. Any single item that's over C$10k in value will be taxed on the excess (ie. the value over $10k). Some items require special permission to bring into Canada, like plants. Check the CBSA website for complete details.

Immigrating

If you're immigrating, you'll need to complete the BSF186, as a "settler." You don't need to have everything you own with you the day you arrive in Canada as a new resident.

After you declare landing, you are free to return to your home country whenever you want and can cross back into Canada, bringing more stuff with you each time. If you do this, you will need to make sure that you have your stamped BSF186 form with you every single time you cross the border with additional belongings. Once you bring something into Canada, you can bring it back and forth across the border without needing to declare it again.

If you are bringing anything that was not included on the BSF186 form, you will need to declare it at the border and pay any associated taxes you may owe. You're better off packing any items not on the BSF186 in one section you can access easily if you need to show them to a customs officer. Of course, if the value of what you're bringing in is under your personal exception, you won't have to declare them. Currently, the personal exemption is C$800 if you've been out of Canada for 48 hours or more.

Remember that the BSF186 is a way to avoid paying taxes and anything that was not already declared can be taxed. The customs officials will not be happy if they realize you're trying to sneak additional items into the country without paying the appropriate taxes on them.

While in theory you can make as many trips as are needed, I don't suggest making more than one or two trips with belongings you need to declare. You will need to go through the entire customs process each time, which can take a few hours.

Check the CBSA website for complete details on what you can import duty free and what the restrictions are.

Vehicles

You can probably bring your car with you when you move. The Register of Imported Vehicles explains everything you need to know about the import process. It will need to meet Canadian safety standards if it's less than 15 years old. There is a $75 inspection fee and handling charges. This makes it sound simple. Based on what I've heard, it's not.

If you're on a temporary visa, you can bring an ineligible car into Canada as long as you take it with you when you leave the country. You cannot sell it or give it away in Canada.

If you have leased or financed your car, you will first need to get in touch with the company you've leased or financed it from to find out if you can bring it to Canada with you. If you can, you'll need the original Certificate of Title along with an original letter from the company that authorizes the import and identifies the car and VIN.

Pets

Bringing your pets into Canada is a pretty simple process. Canada does not require a quarantine period for domestic cats and dogs coming from most countries. You will need to prove that they are in good health.

If you're not coming from a rabies-free country, you will need to bring a current rabies vaccination certificate. The US is not rabies-free. While it's not specifically required by customs, you will probably want to have any recent paperwork from your veterinarian as well, just in case.

When you cross a border with a pet, either to immigrate or just to visit, your pets will be inspected by a customs agent to make sure that the paperwork is valid and they appear to be in good health. You might be asked to pay an inspection fee for each animal. I wasn't asked to pay this.

The government reserves the right to refuse to allow an animal to enter the country if it does not meet the necessary requirements. The IRCC website has a handy overview of the different requirements for each type of animal that you might want to bring with you.

One more issue is breed specific regulations. Pit bulls are banned in Ontario and Winnipeg, Manitoba.

Flying with a small pet

If you're flying, most airlines will allow you to book a spot for your pet so long as you let them know when you are booking the tickets. There's usually a fee for this and restrictions regarding the weight and carrier.

Some airlines will require you to provide veterinarian paperwork. The airline may require different or more extensive paperwork than the border agents. Make sure you ask about this when you book the flight so that you can make sure you have everything you'll need.

Getting a pet through airport security

If you fly often, you'll know that security is a little different at every airport and it's often different each time you fly.

US security requires that you take your pet out of the carrier and physically walk them through the metal detector while they scan the carrier. Because I was flying with cats, I was concerned about this part. I got a harness and leash for my cats, but since cats are a liquid, I'm pretty sure they could have escaped if they wanted to. Luckily, my cats were so terrified by the whole situation that they didn't try to move at all. Make sure your pet harness doesn't have any pieces that would set off the metal detector.

Don't surprise TSA agents. Give them a heads up as you walk up and let them know that you have an animal. Ask them how they want you to proceed. The TSA agents were friendly and helpful when I brought my cats.

Get yourself ready to walk through security (place your bags on the conveyor belt, take off your shoes and belt, take your laptop and liquids out of your bag, empty your pockets, etc.). This is an excellent day to wear slip on shoes and not have a belt. The more prepared you are for this part the better. While holding your pet, wait for TSA to give you the go ahead to walk through the metal detector.

Pets on a plane

It should go without saying that your pet needs to remain in the carrier for the duration of the trip. Remember that not everyone loves pets as much as you do and many people are allergic to animals. Some people are mortally afraid of both flying and animals, so try to be considerate.

When you get on the plane, let the flight attendants know that you have an animal so they can make things easy for you. Pet carriers must be kept under the seat. My cats were so terrified they didn't move or make a sound for the (mercifully short) flight.

My cats weren't traumatized by the experience. As soon as we got to our destination they were happy to explore their new home. They quickly resumed their usual routine of ignoring me and each other.

Getting your pet through customs

Let customs know that you have a pet. You'll be taken to a separate clearing area where a customs agent will inspect your pet to make sure everything is in order. Usually this is just a visual check to make sure the animal isn't obviously sick. You may also be asked for proof of vaccinations.

This part was very quick and easy. The agents just spent a minute talking about how cute my cats were and sent us on our way.

Wedding presents

You can bring your wedding presents into Canada duty free within three months of your wedding (either before or after you get married).

Inheritance

If you inherit goods while you're a resident of Canada, you can generally import them duty free as long as you provide a copy of the estate documents and the death certificate. The BSF186 refers to this as a "beneficiary" import.

The BSF186 form

Canada requires that you declare all of your goods on a Personal Affects Accounting Document, aka the BSF186 form. Anything not included on your BSF186 will be taxed at normal import rates.

You can create a single BSF186 for your family or each adult can have their own.

If you are moving up with all of your things, then you only need a single BSF186 for all of your accompanying goods. If you are landing with just a few pieces of luggage and plan to move all of your stuff up at a later date, then you will need two BSF186 forms:

- **Goods accompanying**: This is a list of all the things you have with you on the day that you land. This could be a single bag, multiple pieces of checked luggage, or everything you own.

- **Goods to follow**: This is a list of all the things you plan to bring into Canada in the future. If you're going to bring all of your stuff into Canada a few days or decades in the future you will need to let customs know the first time you land. If you don't declare them at this time you could be taxed on them later.

Looking at the form, you'll see that there are only eight lines to list goods. Use this section to list up to eight categories. For example:

Item	Description of goods (include serial numbers, if applicable)	Value (CDN Dollars)
1	Furniture	$3,000
2	Kitchen	$2,000
3	Clothing	$4,000
4	Electronics	$5,000
5	Linens	$1,000
6	Books	$2,000
7	Décor	$2,000
8		

You can create whatever categories make sense for you.

I made a list of items in each category with the approximate value. Some people advise you to list garage sale values, others recommend listing replacement costs. Technically, you don't need to provide values unless you're asked for them, but I would rather not have to guess while I'm at customs.

For each list, include the category, category number from the list you made on the BSF186 form, your full legal name, a description of the item, quantity, and approximate value in Canadian dollars.

You will also need to include the make, model, and serial number for each item, if it has one. This is usually for things like electronics and sports equipment. For items like high-value jewelry and art, they may require that you include a photo of the item. Generally, they don't really care about any item valued at less than a few thousand dollars.

Here's an example of how I made the category lists:

GOODS TO FOLLOW				
CATEGORY: Furniture				
MY NAME				
No.	Item Description	Serial #	Quantity	Value (CAD)
1	Kitchen chairs		4	$100
2	Kitchen table		1	$300
3	Armchair		2	$400
4	Bookcase		4	$550
5	Filing cabinet		1	$250

You don't need to itemize everything you own. You can group things together for the sake of simplicity. For example:

No.	Item Description	Serial #	Quantity	Value (CAD)
1	Boxes of books		6	$300
2	Boxes of toiletries		3	$150
3	Boxes of tools		3	$500

The only things that should be listed individually are high value items. Unless you have designer clothes that would fetch a tidy sum at resale, you can simply list the number of boxes.

When you're done, print out two copies of each category list along with two copies of each BSF186. The CBSA will keep one and give the other back to you.

There is no limit on the amount of time you have to import things on your goods to follow list. However, once the list is stamped by customs you cannot add anything to it.

This list will be useful when you get renters or homeowners insurance, since you now have a government approved list of everything you own and its value.

Hiring movers to move you from the US

You can't hire a random guy with a van to move your stuff across an international border. Only certain companies are properly licensed to do this. They'll ask for a copy of your passport and CoPR document when you book your move.

Customs for goods to follow

When you landed as a new resident and declared that you had goods to follow, the customs agent reviewed your list of goods and entered it all into their database. They're now going to cross reference the goods that you actually import with the goods that you declared when you land. You'll need the paperwork with you.

Even if you hire a moving company, you will still need to physically sign for and receive your belongings after they are brought across the border. You can either meet the movers at the Canadian border or at a CBSA sufferance office.

Whichever way you go about this, make sure that you get very specific instructions from your moving company about where, when, and how to meet them. The office to meet them isn't a place designed for visitors, so it can be tricky to find. Also ask about the cost, both for moving and fees associated with customs, so there aren't any last minute surprises.

Either way, you will be interviewed by a customs agent and be asked to show your passport, visa document, and stamped BSF186 form. The CBSA will stamp your BSF186 form and mark your goods as arrived.

They will also give you a completed and stamped A8A form, the Customs Cargo Control Document. This verifies that your goods were allowed into the country and cleared by customs.

It's possible that customs will go through everything in your truck and compare it to the list. In my case, they didn't even open the truck. It still took about two hours

Moving to Québec

Québec has different immigration requirements than the rest of the provinces and territories. Unfortunately, in practical terms, this just means that moving to Québec has extra hurdles, since your application needs to be approved by the province of Quebec and the federal government separately, while many other programs are entirely federal.

This doesn't appear to prevent people from moving to Quebec, at least not if you speak French. The province is growing more, not less French with time. They've had more immigrants from France in the past 20 years than they did during the time it was a French colony. That's only considering the motherland. Many more native French speakers come from former French colonies.

Do you need to speak French?

Over 80% of people in Québec speak French. Plenty of them speak English as well. While people who speak conversational French are favored over Anglophiles, it's not required that you speak French before you move to Québec. You don't need to speak French to qualify for their immigration programs.

You're encouraged to spend time learning French online or take classes before you leave your home country in order to help you integrate more quickly. If you take language classes in your current country of residence prior to immigrating, you may be able to have some or all of the fee reimbursed. Once you're in Québec, you'll have access to French courses free of charge and possibly even financial aid to help you take time off to attend classes.

Of course, the French spoken in Quebec is different from the French spoken in France. Quebec was already an English colony by the time France united the nation by standardizing its culture and language. When Quebecois films screen in Paris they have subtitles. Still, speaking any dialect of French will help and you'll become comfortable with the Quebecois dialect with practice.

Quebec values

If you're looking to become a permanent resident in Quebec, you'll need to demonstrate that you're proficient in French and pass a test on Quebec values, the Attestation of learning about democratic values and the Quebec values expressed by the Charter of Human Rights and Freedoms.

The test has 20 randomly generated questions.

You can take the test online or in-person. You have up to three chances to pass. If you're living in Quebec when you fail the test, you'll have to re-take it in-person.

The attestation is valid for two years.

Why is there so much conflicting information out there?

Immigration programs in Canada have undergone a tremendous number of changes since 2015. The federal government has been shifting from paper applications to online systems in several phases. They continually tweak them to make them easier to use. This is why my ex-wife and I wrote the first edition of this book, because all the information we found on the immigration process was about a system that no longer existed. This is also why each edition of the book has substantial changes, as they have since revamped the application processes for spousal sponsorship and citizenship.

Quebec is going through that process currently. Right now the federal portion of that program is still done on paper, while most of Quebec's programs have moved online.

Because things are changing rapidly, you should be extra careful to verify that the information you're reading here is still accurate, even if it's less than a year old.

Living and working in Québec temporarily

There are two primary ways you can live in Québec on a temporary basis: going to school or getting a work permit.

Going (back) to school

Once you choose a school, apply, and are accepted, the school will guide you through the process of getting a student visa. You'll need to provide proof that you can support yourself while you go to school.

As a student in Québec, you're agreeing that:

- Studying will be your principal activity for the entire time you're in Québec,
- You will supply your own health insurance coverage, and
- You will cover your own tuition, transportation costs (to and from Canada), living expenses, and any other costs.

You don't need to get a student visa for programs lasting six months or less.

Many students choose to extend their stay after graduation or immigrate permanently. You can do this by getting a post-graduation work permit and eventually applying for permanent resident status.

Find a job

Once you have a job offer in Québec, you and your employer have to take steps to make it legal. Your employer will work with Ministère de l'Immigration, de la Diversité et de l'Inclusion to complete the paperwork required, which will include demonstrating that they were unable to find a local employee to do the job. Your work permit will be specific to that employer.

Any time you extend your employment contract or change jobs, you'll need to file a new work authorization application.

Becoming a permanent resident in Québec

Québec has its own visa and immigration procedures for economic immigration programs. If you're applying through a Quebec PNP or express entry, you apply through MIDI first and then apply for federal approval through the IRCC.

If you qualify for family sponsorship and you wish to live in Québec, you apply through the IRCC like any other applicant and will be directed to complete an additional application through the Ministère de l'Immigration, de la Diversité et de l'Inclusion (MIDI).

Once you are living in Canada as a permanent resident, there are no restrictions on where you can live. However, it's frowned upon to apply to live in one province and immediately move to another. If you apply for PR through a PNP, you could face consequences if you move to another province right away.

Is moving to Québec right for you?

The Ministère de l'Immigration, de la Diversité et de l'Inclusion offers free online and in-person information sessions to explain what it's like to live, work, and go to school in Québec. These also go over the immigration process. They are offered in several languages and can be scheduled online.

Common values

Once you receive your Certificat de sélection du Québec (CSQ) you'll need to sign the Declaration on the Common Values of Québec Society. These values are:

- Speaking French is a necessity.
- Belief in a free and democratic society.
- A society enriched by its diversity.
- A society based on the rule of law.
- Political and religious powers are separate.
- Men and women have the same rights.
- The exercise of human rights and freedoms must respect the rights and freedoms of others and the general well-being.

Being sponsored by a resident of Québec

If your sponsor lives in Québec or you plan to live in Québec once you're granted residency, you'll need to complete an extra step after the IRCC approves your federal application. You'll need to obtain a Québec Selection Certificate (CSQ) from the MIDI. Right now this is all done on paper. It's likely the process will be moved online soon.

MIDI encourages you to prepare your CSQ application as you gather documents for your IRCC application and while you wait to hear from the IRCC. This way you can submit your CSQ application as soon as you are able to and can avoid unnecessary delays.

Who can sponsor you

Canadian citizens, First Nations people, and permanent residents over the age of 18 can sponsor a spouse, common-law partner, or dependent child under the age of 22. You can't sponsor a partner if you've been convicted of a violent crime.

Sponsors have to convince the IRCC and the MIFI that they can support themselves and their family, although there aren't any specific income requirements. They can do this by showing proof of income, proof of savings, a job offer, or explaining their plan. They may not be able to sponsor someone if they've recently declared bankruptcy. They may not be able to sponsor someone if they're still required to support a former spouse or de facto spouse they've previously sponsored.

What you have to do

To qualify as a spouse or de facto spouse, you need to be over the age of 16 and admissible to Canada.

Dependent children need to be under the age of 22 and unmarried. If your dependent child has a child, they can be included in your application, although you will face greater financial scrutiny. You can sponsor a child over the age of 22 if they rely on you due to a mental or physical health issue that predates their turning 22.

You need to fill out the Demande de sélection permanente – Catégorie du regroupement familial (Application for permanent selection – Family reunification class). This application is available only in French.

When your application is complete you need to give it to your sponsor, who will submit it to MIDI on your behalf.

What your sponsor has to do

Your sponsor has to complete an Undertaking Kit, legally agreeing to be financially responsible for you. Their legal responsibilities and the forms required differ based on their relationship to you. They also need to demonstrate that they are capable of providing for you financially and, of course, they need to pay an application fee.

The undertaking kit, your application, all required documents, and payment information are all submitted to MIDI together.

MIDI provides a guide for sponsors, which is only in French.

When you have your CSQ

MIDI's will directly contact the Canadian visa office for your country with their decision regarding your CSQ application. If your CSQ is issued, you will be issued a CoPR and a visa (if your nationality requires a visa to enter Canada). Congratulations, you can finally go to a port of entry to declare yourself a landed immigrant!

The Québec skilled worker program

The Québec skilled worker program (QSWP) has undergone many well publicized changes recently (like when they trashed the backlog of 18k applications and started fresh) and it now bears a striking resemblance to express entry. However, it's an entirely separate system.

Instead of applying through myCIC, you use the Arrima system. The Arrima system is only available in French. Instructions and requirements are kept up to date in French. When accessing English pages on the MIDI website you will likely find that they have a notice telling you to view the French version for accurate information, because the English instructions are out of date.

This system launched in September 2018, so any instructions from before that time are no longer accurate.

How does the QSWP work?

1. You create a free profile (your "expression of interest") and are entered into a pool of candidates.

2. Candidates with the highest scores are selected from the pool and invited to apply. You then have 60 days to gather documents and submit your application for a Certificat de sélection du Québec (CSQ). If things go according to plan, you get your CSQ within six months.

3. When you have been granted a CSQ, you submit a paper application for permanent residence to the federal government. You likely also need to submit biometrics and may have an interview.

4. When your federal application has been approved, you receive a Confirmation of Permanent Residence (CoPR) form and a visa (if your country of nationality requires a visa). You present this to a government official at a port of entry and become a permanent resident.

QSWP basic requirements

In order to qualify to submit an expression of interest for the QSWP, you need to be over the age of 18, have a secondary school (high school) general diploma, and show proof of settlement funds.

For a single person in 2022, the required proof of funds is just over C$3k. That may be the minimum amount required by the program, but it would be a struggle to relocate to a new country with so little money, especially without a job offer lined up and family to stay with.

While Québec manages its own immigration programs, you must still meet all of the federal requirements. Thus, if you're inadmissible to Canada, your application will be rejected.

Like express entry, you do not need a qualifying job offer to get PR through the QSWP. However, having a qualifying job offer increases your chances of being issued an invitation to apply (ITA) and having a successful application.

Speaking French is not a requirement, but is highly encouraged. The application and most instructions are only available in French..

Who gets priority?

There are three types of people whose Arrima profiles get priority processing in the new QSWP system:

- people with a qualifying job offer from an employer in Québec

- people whose CSQ application was thrown out when they switched to the new system and who were temporary residents of Quebec when they applied

- people whose CSQ application was thrown out when they switched to the new system and who were in Québec on a student visa or a temporary work permit when they applied

When Arrima was first launched in 2018, only 5k profiles were accepted. These three groups were not subject to the caps. Participants in the Québec experience program (Programme de l'expérience québécoise or PEQ) were also exempt from the cap.

Who can come?

Your spouse (or de facto spouse) and dependent children should be included in your expression of interest and final application. Everyone who is included on your application will receive permanent resident status once your application is approved and you all become landed immigrants.

If you are planning on immigrating without your spouse or common-law partner, you do not need to include them in your expression of interest profile. If you get an ITA, you would need to include them as a non-accompanying spouse on your application. If you would like them to join you later, you will need to go through the sponsorship process.

If you wish to immigrate with your child (or children) but without the other parent, you will need to demonstrate that you have legal permission from the other parent.

Do I need an immigration attorney?

Many people hire immigration representatives to help them. Going through the process on your own involves a lot of paperwork, a lot of annoying online forms, and a lot of checking to make sure you filled things out correctly. It's very tedious and navigating this process in French (or using a translation tool) can be challenging.

You know how much your time is worth and how comfortable you are outsourcing important tasks. Like express entry, Arrima is designed to be used without an immigration consultant or attorney.

Selection criteria

You're awarded points based on your:

- age
- language proficiency in French and English
- time spent in Québec and/or family in Québec
- financial self-sufficiency
- education
- area of training
- work experience
- qualifying job offer
- the characteristics of your spouse or common-law partner

- your accompanying children (as in, if you have them and how many)

They provide a tool to estimate the number of points you'd be given, based on your factors.

There is a potential total of 1,320 points: 580 are based on you and your family, 740 are for how well your abilities and experience align with Quebec's labour market needs A single person needs at least 50 points. The minimum for candidates with a spouse or common-law partner is 59 points.

If you're between 18 and 35 years old, you get the maximum number of points for age. The number of points awarded begins dropping at 36 until you receive zero points for being 43 or older. This is a program designed to bring young skilled workers into the country, so the older you are, the more impressive your other factors need to be. Once you receive an ITA, your ages (and the ages of accompanying family members) are 'locked in' and the number of points awarded for your age does not change.

Your French gets you points from the High Intermediate (B2) level and above. You are awarded a smaller number of points for speaking English at the Intermediate (CLB 5-8) or above. You will only be awarded points based on a recognized language exam, even if English or French is your native language or you have completed a diploma in the language.

You get a point for having spent more than two weeks in Québec. Having stayed for three months or more, gone to school, or worked in Québec will get you even more points.

You will get points if you have a spouse or common-law partner in Québec. You will also get points for having a child, parent, sibling, or grandparent in Québec.

Your financial self-sufficiency is a single point and it's the yes/no question of having the required proof of settlement funds.

You're required to have a secondary school diploma and will receive an increasing number of points for higher levels of education. Your area of specialization is not taken into account here, it is evaluated in the area of training section.

The government of Québec periodically releases a list of areas of training that outlines the number of points awarded for different types of degrees, certifications, and other diplomas. The official list is only available in French, although several websites provide translated versions.

If the list of areas of training is updated after you submit your EOA to the pool or after you submit your application, the number of points you are awarded may change.

You are awarded points for your paid work experience, with points allocated for amounts of time ranging from six months to 48 months or more. This is full-time work or the part-time equivalent.

If you have a qualifying job offer you will receive points for that. The number of points awarded depends on the geographic region the position is located in, with Montreal resulting in the fewest points.

If you have a spouse or common-law partner, you will get points based on their age, language, education, and area of training.

You get points for having dependent children, with more points awarded for children under 13.

You can calculate your score based on information from the Ministère de l'Immigration, de la Diversité et de l'Inclusion website or use a third-party score calculator.

Document checklist

Québec

You will be provided with a personalized document checklist by MIDI when you receive your ITA. However, some documents may take more than 60 days to procure, so it is helpful to be prepared. You are likely to need:

- Birth certificates for all applicants
- Passports for all applicants
- Marriage certificate or proof of common-law partnership
- Certified true copies of diplomas and transcripts
- Verification of work history (similar to that required for EE)
- Language exam(s)

Many of the documents required in order to apply for the QSWP must be certified true copies. Documents that are not in English or French must be translated by a recognized translator. Original documents and translated copies must both be provided. The document must be translated in its entirety.

Federal

- Biometrics
- Police certificate(s)
- Medical exam

Language tests

You have to take a language exam to demonstrate your proficiency in French and/or English if you want to get points for it.

For French, you can use scores for any of these exams:

- Test d`Evaluation du Français (TEF/TEF Canada)

- Test d`Evaluation du français adapté pour le Québec (TEFaQ)

- Test de connaissance du français (TCF)

- Test de connaissance du français pour le Québec (TCFQ)

- Diplôme d`études en langue française (DELF/DALF)

For English, they use the International English Language Testing System (IELTS).

All of these exam scores expire after two years. Your score needs to be valid when it's submitted, but it is still accepted if it expires while your application is being processed.

The application process

The process has several different steps as your application goes through the provincial and federal government offices. Here's how things unfold.

Submit an expression of interest

No documentation is required at this time. However, if you are selected from the applicant pool you will need to provide documentation to verify all information in your profile within 60 days.

You can update information in your EOI profile in Arrima at any time, even if you've already submitted it. Changes must be submitted within 30 days of the event (as in, if you earn a degree you need to update your profile within 30 days of it being awarded).

Your Arrima profile expires after 365 days. If you are not selected and issued an ITA by that time, you can create a new profile.

Because the QSWP and EE are separate systems, you can create profiles for both to increase your odds of being selected.

Receive your invitation to apply

If you are selected from the pool, you'll be invited to apply (ITA) for a Québec Selection Certificate (Certificat de sélection du Québec, or CSQ). You have 60 days to submit your application. You will be provided with a personalized documentation checklist.

While you won't have your personalized documentation checklist until you get your ITA, it's not terribly difficult to guess at what documents they will require.

If your ITA expires before you submit your complete application, you can simply submit a new expression of interest.

Request your CSQ

Once you've been invited to apply, you submit your application for a CSQ using the Mon projet Québec platform. This is where you upload documents to verify the information you provided in your expression of interest.

The final step in submitting your application for a CSQ is to pay the fees.

Now you wait. You can track your application and keep it up to date on Mon projet Québec.

Once you have your CSQ you can move on to the next step.

Submit your application for federal immigration

Now that you've been approved by Québec and have your CSQ, you need federal approval.

Québec has already assessed your likelihood to be economically and socially successful as an immigrant. The federal government is primarily concerned with confirming that you are admissible to Canada. They evaluate your medical exam and perform a security check.

The medical exam requirements are the same as for the EE system.

Your application needs to be mailed to the Case Processing Centre in Sydney, Nova Scotia:

Centralized Intake Office – Québec Skilled Workers (QSW)
P.O. BOX 8888
Sydney, NS B1P 0C9
Canada

You need to pay your application fees and biometrics fees when you submit the application or it will not be processed. This must be done online. You do not have to pay your right of permanent residence fees until your application is approved.

If your application is found to be incomplete it will be returned to you or they may request additional documents. You can add in any missing information and resubmit it without having to pay additional fees.

You will probably be required to submit biometrics: a photo and fingerprints. This must be done at a Visa Application Centre (VAC) or Application Support Centre (ASC). This was not required prior to 2018 and has been waived for some applicants during the pandemic.

The IRCC has a tool to help you determine if you need to provide biometrics.

During this time the IRCC may request additional documents or require you to have an interview.

Wait for the final approval

You can begin to prepare for your move while you wait for the IRCC to process your application.

Québec offers several tools, in French only, for holders of a CSQ. The Service d'intégration en ligne has forums, chat rooms, and loads of information about the integration into Québec life. There are also online French courses, information on getting your qualifications recognized, and a job placement tool.

You can check your application status online while it's being processed. The IRCC may contact you for more information.

It's important to keep your information current with the IRCC. Contact the IRCC and update your information if:

- your address, telephone number, email address, or any other contact information you've provided has changed

- you get married or divorced, or if you begin or end a common-law partnership

- you have a child, adopt a child, or a child dies

Any situation where you are ending a partnership or child custody is unclear will delay your application.

Receive your confirmation of PR and visa

When you get a letter in the mail saying your application for permanent residence in Canada has been approved, you'll also get a confirmation of permanent residence (CoPR) paper for yourself and any other family members that you applied to immigrate with. The CoPR paper is very important, though it's not obvious by looking at it. This is your permanent resident visa.

If you're coming from a country that requires a visa to enter Canada, you'll also receive a visa for that.

You aren't a permanent resident yet, even with your CoPR. The final step is when you sign the paper in front of a border agent during your final immigration interview.

The CoPR is a single legal-sized piece of paper with your personal details and a big stamp across it that says "NOT VALID FOR TRAVEL." It actually looks a bit like a temporary driver's license. Keep this in a safe place – Canadian customs officers will not allow you to cross the border and declare that you are moving to Canada without your CoPR.

Take careful note of the "valid to" date, which will be exactly one year from when your panel physician submitted the results of your medical exam. You need to declare landing in Canada before this date passes.

If you applied to immigrate with other members of your family, you can land before they do, but they can't land before the primary applicant. They can, however, enter Canada as a visitor and return to declare landing after you've become a permanent resident.

Every family member who is coming with you to Canada needs to declare landing before their CoPR expires. If your spouse or children do not declare landing before their CoPR expires, you will have to go through the family sponsorship process for them to join you in Canada.

Timeline & fees

The goal is for applications to be processed within 12 months. In July 2019 the anticipated processing time was 15 to 17 months. With the pandemic, processing times are erratic.

You can check application processing times for the federal portion of the application on the IRCC website.

- Québec application processing fee: $798 for the principal applicant / $171 for each accompanying family member
- Federal application processing fee: $550 per adult
- Right of permanent residence fee: $490 per adult
- Federal fees for dependent child: $150 per child
- Biometrics: $85 per person / $170 maximum per family

Programme de l'expérience Québécoise

Once you've studied or worked in Québec, you can participate in Québec Experience Program (Programme de l'expérience Québécoise or PEQ). The intention is to allow people who are currently living in Quebec to stay, so you need to demonstrate an intent to stay in Quebec permanently. You need to be living and working in Quebec when you apply.

Your family can be included in your PEQ application. All children need to be listed on your application, even if they're not going to be living in Quebec with you, unless they are already Canadian citizens. Children who are 22 and under will be able to get PR status.

While official information about PEQ is only available in French, documents can be submitted in English or French.

This program has undergone major changes in 2019 and 2021, so the experience of anyone who got PR through PEQ in the past is probably not helpful, aside from making you jealous of their 20 day processing times and lax requirements.

Language Requirements

You need to demonstrate that you can speak French. You can include a family on your application, but as of July 2021 your spouse will also have to show that they can speak French. The primary applicant needs at least a 7 and the spouse a 4 on the Quebec Scale of Proficiency in French for Adult Immigrants.

You can prove your language proficiency with:

- A transcript showing three years of full-time study at the secondary or post-secondary level (that's high school or college for us Americans),

- A professional license valid in Quebec or test results from the Office québécois de la langue française for professional orders,

- Test results or diplomas from TEF, TCF, or TEFAQ, or
- Proof that you completed a French course in Quebec if you were enrolled in or had completed that program prior to July 21, 2020.

Applications are submitted through the Arrima portal. There are no longer paper applications.

PEQ applications are generally processed within six months.

If you qualify for PEQ, you also qualify for the Québec Skilled Worker Program (QSWP). PEQ processing times are generally seen as being faster than QSWP, but it's hard to say if that will remain true with the most recent changes once pandemic delays have been resolved.

Work experience

For the purposes of PEQ, any job where you are working 30 or more hours per week is considered full-time. Your work experience doesn't have to be continuous and can be for multiple employers. Part-time work, freelance work, and self-employment don't count.

Québec graduates / Diplomé du Québec

To be eligible for PEQ as a Quebec graduate, you need to have completed your degree in the 36 months before you apply. Eligible programs are at least two years (1,800 hours) and run by an institution recognized by the Quebec Ministry of Education.

If your studies in Quebec ended with a university degree or diploma of college studies, you need 12 months of work experience in Quebec in jobs with a NOC level of 0, A, or B.

If your studies in Quebec ended with a diploma of professional studies (DEP) or diploma of vocational studies (DEV), you need 19 months of work experience in Quebec in jobs with a NOC level of 0,

A, B, or C. Work experience in NOC C jobs needs to be related to your program of study.

Up to three months of mandatory internships conducted as part of your studies can count towards your work requirements. Work done on a post-graduation work permit or through the IEC program does count.

Applicants who received their diplomas prior to January 1, 2021 don't need to meet the work requirements. Applicants who completed their degree before December 31, 2020 who are applying with a spouse don't need to prove that their spouse speaks French.

Temporary foreign workers / Travailleur étranger temporaire

To qualify for PEQ as a temporary foreign worker, you need to have worked in Quebec full-time for 24 months within the last 36 months.

Since the requirement for a spouse to speak French is new, it's waived If the primary applicant had a valid work permit prior to July 21, 2020.

Moving to Québec through express entry

People sometimes refer to the QSWP as "Quebec express entry," but the QSWP and EE are entirely separate systems managed by different organizations.

If you take the IRCC test to find out if you're eligible to apply for express entry and indicate that you intend to move to Québec, you'll get a message letting you know that you don't qualify for express entry. If you intend to move to Québec, you'll need to submit your intent directly to Québec through the QSWP.

Other options

Aside from the QSWP, Québec offers three ways for people to become permanent residents of Québec.

The documents required and their formats differ for each program. Any documents not in French or English have to be translated by an approved translator.

It's relatively likely that you'll be asked to have an interview with immigration officers. These take place around Canada at various times of the year and last about an hour and a half.

The Québec immigrant investor program, entrepreneur program, and self-employed workers program all provide pathways to citizenship. These programs only accept a limited number of applicants, but people with advanced intermediate French proficiency are exempt from the cap and receive priority processing.

Québec immigrant investor program

To participate in the Quebec immigrant investor program you (and your partner, if applicable), must:

- Have at least C$2 million of legally acquired net assets
- Have at least two years of professional management experience
- Make a five year investment of C$1.2 million with Investissement Québec - Immigrants Investisseurs Inc. and sign an investment agreement with a financial intermediary authorized to participate in the Investor Program
- Intend to settle in Québec

This program is on hold as of 2022. It's likely that the program requirements will be different if and when it opens to new applicants.

Québec entrepreneur program

If you plan on starting, relocating, or purchasing a business in Québec, you may qualify for the Québec entrepreneur program.

- Stream 1 requires support from a business incubator, business accelerator, or university entrepreneurship center.
- Stream 2 requires:
  - a deposit of C$300k for businesses in Montreal or C$200k outside of Montreal
  - a legally acquired net worth of at least C$900k

There are additional requirements, including regarding what type of businesses qualify and the percentage of ownership. You'll need to present a business plan to MIDI.

This program is on hold as of 2022. It's likely that the program requirements will be different if and when it opens to new applicants.

Québec self employed workers program

If you plan on creating your own job, you may qualify for the self-employed workers program. You'll need:

- to have at least two years of professional experience as a self-employed worker in the trade you wish to practice
- legally acquired net assets of at least C$100k
- to make a deposit of C25k or C$50k

When evaluating your application, MIDI will take your ties to Québec, financial self-sufficiency, language skills, work experience, and the factors of your partner into consideration.

This program receives far more applicants than there are available spots. All spots have been allocated through 2022. People who speak French are not subject to this cap and are still able to apply.

Landing in Montreal

When you're within 30 days of your arrival in Canada, you can set up an appointment to get help with settling in Québec.

Most immigrants declaring landing in Québec fly into Montreal. Immigration-Québec's reception service located on the first floor of the restricted area for international arrivals, in the room called Immigration 2 – Accueil Québec. The Immigration-Québec reception service is generally open from noon to midnight. They will provide you with information on getting settled in Québec.

If you arrive outside of their opening hours, arrive at a different port of entry, or have additional questions, you can contact them at 514-864-9191 or 1-877-864-9191 (toll-free).

At the airport, the first customs agent you talk to will ask you what your current status is in Canada. This is when you explain that you are declaring landing as a new permanent resident. You will need to show your completed customs declaration card, passport, and visa document at this initial stage.

They will direct you to a secondary screening area where you will show your CoPR, your biometrics will be verified, and your luggage may be searched. See the information in the main landing in Canada section for information on bringing your belongings into Canada.

A second customs agent will sign your CoPR form and return it to you. You are now a permanent resident of Canada. Congratulations!

Getting your PR card

Your official Permanent Resident card will arrive in the mail at the address you list on the CoPR form in six to eight weeks. Until then, the CoPR form will serve as both your temporary proof of permanent resident status and a record of your landing in Canada.

Your first year in Canada

You've finally become an official resident of Canada! There's a few things you'll need to take care of within the first few weeks, like applying for a SIN, signing up for provincial health insurance, and getting a driver's license or non-driver ID.

Canadian provinces and territories each have slightly different processes for these things, but the general idea is the same. I moved to Ontario, so that's what I'll be talking about.

Settlement services

The IRCC maintains a database of government funded settlement programs that are available to all newcomers to Canada. The database is not very useful. It provides general contact information, rather than connecting you with the specific resource it's trying to direct you to. For example, it will provide the main phone number for Ryerson University or the Toronto YMCA as a resource for job search support, rather than the office that handles these services.

Each program has its own eligibility requirements and usually the only way to learn if you qualify is to call, set up an appointment, and share a considerable amount of personal information.

Rather than attempting to locate appropriate services yourself using the directory, you can set up a needs assessment meeting. A social worker will then help match you with programs that will help you get settled and that you qualify for. Your local library can connect you with local organizations that do needs assessments.

The Toronto YMCA runs the Newcomer Information Centre. You can set up an appointment for a needs assessment, during which they'll go over what services might help you and connect you to service providers.

Services offered include professional guidance for finding housing, jobs, and legal assistance. They may also organize events (informational, networking, and social), language support, and educational programs.

Settlement services generally provide support for transportation, translation, and child care to ensure you can actually participate in the program. Naturally, if you have disabilities they are required to accommodate any support you need. Services are generally available both online and in-person, making it easier to get support if you're living outside of a major city.

The most obvious time to seek out settlement services is when you first arrive. However, settlement services remain available to permanent residents and refugees, even if you've been here for years. Some services are open to all immigrants to Canada, even after you've become a citizen. Most settlement services are cut off once you become a citizen.

Your SIN

The social insurance number (SIN) is the Canadian equivalent of a social security number or national insurance number. You will need this number in order to register for the provincial insurance plan, set up some types of bank accounts, access public benefits, and legally work in the country.

If you're lucky, you were able to get a SIN when you became a resident at the port of entry. However, if you drive across the border or weren't able to get it at the airport, then you can take care of it at any Service Canada location. You don't even need to fill out any forms, just bring your passport and visa (or CoPR or PR card) to prove you're a legal resident. There are Service Canada locations all over and they're even open on weekends, so this is simple and quick.

The Canadian government does not issue you any sort of physical card. Instead, they'll print out a piece of paper for your reference, so make sure to write it down somewhere where you won't lose it.

Your PR card

If you've moved to Canada as a permanent resident, the government will automatically mail your new permanent resident card to the address that you listed on your CoPR document. This usually takes six weeks. The IRCC has a tool that estimates the current processing time.

If you don't have an address in Canada on file with the IRCC when you become a PR, you have 180 days to provide an address to the IRCC. Once they have your address they'll mail you the card.

If there is a mistake on your PR card, you can apply for a new one. Your name is limited to 28 characters, so the IRCC may shorten it. This isn't a mistake and they will not change it.

If you don't receive your card, you lose it, or it's damaged, you can request a new one by submitting a solemn declaration. It generally takes up to 120 days for them to process your declaration and mail you a new card.

Entering Canada without a PR card

Occasionally the news will feature stories of Canadian permanent residents who get stranded after a vacation, because they missed the memo that they need a valid PR card in order to re-enter the country. Part of why this is so common is that, contrary to what the government says, they'll allow most people into the country without a valid PR card. It's only occasionally that they require people to have a permanent resident travel document (PRTD), as they'll typically accept alternate proof of residency or simply look you up in the system using your foreign passport.

Immediately after moving to Canada

If you need to leave the country before you receive your PR card, you probably don't need to worry. Bring your CoPR with you and be prepared to answer a few questions at the airport. Many people aren't able to wrap up their lives within six months, so the border agent you talk to won't find it unusual if you need to return to sell your home or take care of family matters.

However, this is at the discretion of the border agent. This unofficial policy of allowing new PRs to travel with a CoPR could change at any time and you may be required to obtain a permanent resident travel document (PRTD) to return to Canada.

After your first six months in Canada

It's important to have a valid PR card if you leave Canada. You may have trouble if you try to re-enter the country by commercial plane, train, bus, or boat without one. There's more information on entering Canada with an expired PR card or without a PR card in the section on renewing your PR card.

You can only renew your PR card from within Canada and you cannot have someone else pick up the card on your behalf. It's unpredictable whether they will mail your PR card or require you to pick it up in person.

Maintaining PR status

Letting your PR card expire does not mean you've lost your PR status. Maintaining your PR status requires that you spend every two out of five years, or 730 days out of 1825 days, physically in Canada. The time does not have to be continuous and is calculated on a rolling basis. You will need to submit a travel journal when you apply to renew your PR card.

Your phone

If you're moving to Canada, it makes sense to get a Canadian phone plan. Canada is known for having expensive phone plans. Plenty of people opt to keep their foreign service if it works in Canada and is less expensive than switching to a Canadian plan.

Getting a Canadian phone plan

Getting a phone plan as a new resident can be a little tricky. You'll probably need to choose a bring your own phone (BYOP) plan, because choosing a plan that includes a phone requires a Canadian credit history. You'll need to make sure whatever phone you have (or purchase separately from a phone contract) will work with your new provider.

When choosing a plan, be careful to check the coverage area and roaming fees. Some plans are Canada-wide, while others may consider calls outside of your area code long distance and charge you extra.

Make sure you understand how much it will cost for you to call or text your home country (or wherever your friends and family are).

The Wireless Code of Canada provides you with certain rights, including the right to suspend service at no cost if your phone is stolen and to have your phone unlocked.

If you'd like to keep your US number, you can transfer it to Google Voice and use it for free calling and SMS over data/wifi. This needs to be done while in the US (or using a VPN) and, of course, before you cancel your US phone plan.

Prepaid plans v. contracts

With a prepaid phone plan there is no contract. Each month you pay in advance for your services. This is helpful, because it won't require a credit check. Some prepaid plans offer a flat fee for monthly services, while others are pay-as-you-go based on your actual usage. You can buy a set amount of minutes, data, and SMS and simply pay for more when you're out.

A plan with a contract will likely require a Canadian credit history, a security deposit, or a co-signer. If you have friends in Canada already, consider joining their phone plan and splitting the cost.

If you have a contract, be careful if your plan is not unlimited. The cost of going over your allotted minutes, data, or SMS can be exorbitant. There are likely fees associated with ending your contract if you've had it for less than two years. With a prepaid plan, your service will be suspended when you run out of funds, so it's annoying but you won't run up a huge bill.

Most phone plans require you to have a credit card or at least a debit card that works like a credit card. Phone providers like Lucky Mobile allow you to buy a SIM card and top up your plan using cash at lots of different stores.

Life without a Canadian phone plan

The cheapest option is to not have any phone plan at all and use your phone on wifi only and make all of your calls over WhatsApp, Signal, Skype, etc. If you're in a city where wifi is ubiquitous (and you're very stubborn and dedicated to saving money) this could work for you.

Keeping your foreign plan

Most countries have cheaper, better cell phone plans than Canada. If your phone plan will work in Canada without roaming charges, keep it!

Check the details of your plan, because some providers reserve the right to terminate your plan without warning if you don't connect to a tower in your home district within a certain amount of time, typically 180 days. While it's possible your phone service will be cut off, quite a few people report keeping their international plan for years without any issues.

If you're coming from the US, you may opt to keep your T-mobile, Verizon, or Google Fi plan. All three provide excellent global coverage with no roaming and unlimited data. If you're in a city near the US border, like Toronto, it's not uncommon to occasionally connect to US towers, so you won't have any issue with them cutting off service for being outside of the country too long.

Getting a Canadian VOIP number

It's helpful to have a Canadian phone number so people can call you without worrying about international charges. If your building intercom is connected to your phone, you'll need a local number for that. You can get a VOIP number through Fongo or iPlum. Fongo isn't totally reliable and has a lackluster SMS interface that doesn't send or receive photos.

I kept my US plan for a few years, since it included global coverage. When Google Fi separated from Google Voice, I somehow ended up with my main number as a Google Voice number and a new number connected to my Google Fi plan. Since I now had everything connected to two VOIP numbers (Google Voice for the US and Fongo for Canada) I got a data-only plan from Lucky Mobile. I'd been paying around US$30/month with Google Fi and my Lucky Mobile plan was only C$15.

Your new home

Finding an apartment before you arrive in Canada can be difficult. Border agents gave me the impression that it's common for the primary applicant to declare landing, get started at work, find a home, set it up, and then have their family join them before the arrival deadline.

Most people plan on staying in a hostel, hotel, or vacation rental for the first days or weeks they're in Canada if they don't have friends or family to stay with. This gives them time to look at homes in person. Hostels in major Canadian cities frequently reach capacity for much of the summer, so you may need to book well in advance. The pandemic has made signing a lease without having seen an apartment, or even buying a home sight unseen, more common.

Another option for finding temporary housing before your arrival or immediately after is through a nonprofit serving newcomers.

Renting an apartment

Trying to secure an apartment when you're not there in person and looking in an unfamiliar market can make you vulnerable to scams. If you can't be there in person to find an apartment, working with a broker dramatically reduces the risk of getting scammed. A good real estate agent can help you pick out a great apartment, negotiate the price, and manage the paperwork. They can also save you the hassle of scheduling viewings.

Since the landlord pays the agent's commission, it costs you nothing. However, brokers typically don't bother with inexpensive properties, so if you're looking for a budget studio, you may be better off working with a settlement organization.

A real estate agent or settlement organization may be able to help you find a home without the standard tenant requirements. Most landlords will want to see:

- Proof of income
- Your Canadian credit history (some landlords will consider foreign credit scores)
- A reference letter from a Canadian landlord

As a newcomer, you may not be able to provide any of these. Individual landlords (like someone renting out the basement apartment in their home or a single condo they own) are more likely to accept tenants who don't have standard paperwork. If you're working with a settlement organization, they'll connect you with landlords who are open to newcomers who may lack standard rental application documentation.

You'll likely need to fill out a rental application with information on who'll be living with you, any pets you have, previous landlord contact information, and employment information.

It can help to have your deposit ready. Moving money around accounts takes time, so make sure you can get a bank draft or certified cheque for first and last month's rent. Most landlords also accept interac transfers, which are faster and easier.

249

While it may be illegal for a landlord to require you to provide post-dated rent cheques or to pre-pay rent, offering to do so is a way to get a landlord to accept you without proof of employment. If you do this, be sure to detail the agreement in writing.

In Toronto, apartment listings typically appear one or two months before they're actually available to move into. That's because landlords and tenants are required to give 60 days notice. Of course, if you need to move tomorrow, you'll be able to find places available immediately, but there will be fewer apartments to choose from.

Before you sign a lease, read it over carefully and check with the local laws. Ontario rentals use a standard lease. Most apartments don't include utilities, so you'll probably be responsible for hydro (electric), water, and internet/cable/phone. Be sure you understand what's included in your rent and what's not.

Most leases are for 12 months and automatically become month-to-month afterward. If you're on a month-to-month lease, tenants are required to give 60 days notice before moving out.

Laws governing housing vary from place to place, so check with your province and municipality for local regulations.

Shared apartments

If you're having difficulty finding a landlord who will accept you without the proper paperwork or if you're worried about being able to afford rent in an expensive city while you get settled, you can find an apartment sublet or a room in a shared home.

Plenty of people have roommates in Canada to save on expenses. One of the potential downfalls is that co-tenancy means you're jointly responsible for the lease — if they don't pay, you'll be stuck paying their portion of the rent. Technically, all tenants share the whole apartment.

Some landlords will allow each roommate to sign a separate lease. In this case, each tenant has a bedroom and access to the kitchen and bathroom are shared. This, however, may mean your apartment is technically a boarding house, falling under different laws.

In Ontario, if you share a kitchen or bathroom with your landlord, you are not covered by the Residential Tenancies Act that protects most tenants.

Buying a condo in Toronto

You hear it all the time: Toronto is way too expensive to buy anything! In fact, houses downtown are over a million dollars!

What's wrong with this statement? The idea that you need to live in a house right downtown. No one talks about buying *houses* in Manhattan or central London. Torontonians need to join their urban brethren and learn to live in condos, co-ops, and apartments like the rest of the world. Houses are for the rich and for the suburbs.

Luckily, Toronto has uncommonly nice real estate. Most condos are less than twenty years old and boast luxurious amenities: concierge, fitness centers, party rooms, indoor and outdoor pools, saunas, billiard rooms, show kitchens, pet spas, roof decks, grill areas, coworking spaces, and gardens. Toronto's real estate is less expensive than other comparable cities.

What's a condo?

A condominium most commonly refers to a residential unit in a high-rise building, but plenty of condos don't fit that description. Condos can be commercial units, townhouses, triplexes converted to sale, or any number of other styles. You own the condo unit and share ownership of common elements, such as the building and grounds.

While condos are pretty similar all around Canada (and the US), the laws and terminology differ from place to place. You should always check with your local real estate attorney and real estate agent before making any important decisions.

The condo board

Condos are run by a board of directors, typically made up of owners in that building. All condo owners have certain rights, including the right to attend general meetings and vote on decisions. You'll get annual reports and updates about any changes. If the condo is sued, that includes everyone, including you.

The buying process

Early on in the buying process, I started dropping by all the condo centres we passed. There are a lot of them in Toronto. This is a great way to see your options, since you're presented with all the floor plans for building units. If you like the floor plans and amenities in one building, you can also check out resale condos in other buildings by that developer. It helps to visit apartments in older buildings by the same developer even if you know you want to buy on spec, so you can see how their properties age.

In Ontario, you sign an agreement with a real estate agent when they start showing you properties, stating that they represent you as a buyer and will get a commission on any purchase you make for a certain timeframe. You don't pay the real estate agent, your seller does.

After buying and selling a co-op in Brooklyn, buying a condo seemed incredibly easy. I found a realtor, put in an offer, haggled a bit, and soon had a completed agreement of purchase and sale (APS). I then provided a bank cheque for the deposit. The hardest part of the sale was getting the money transferred internationally.

Prior to closing, I wired the balance of the funds to my attorney's trust and signed some paperwork. Once all of the papers were filed and the funds were released to the seller, I went back to my attorney's office to pick up the keys.

Real estate information

Your realtor can provide you with previous sales for your unit, building, or neighborhood. They can also provide you with information on how much a unit would rent for. Nothing is guaranteed, but this is important information to make such a big investment decision. Ontario's privacy laws restrict what information you can access without a realtor.

Have your real estate attorney review the condominium documents and status certificate. If you don't have access to these prior to putting in an offer, you can make your offer contingent on your lawyer's review.

Financing a condo purchase

If you're buying with a mortgage, you'll want to get prequalified or preapproved before you start looking. This shows agents and sellers you're serious, as well as demonstrating how much money you can have access to. You are under no obligation to get a mortgage from the bank that provided the prequalification or preapproval. Remember to account for closing costs and the cost of moving.

As a new resident to Canada with a minimal credit history, it can be a challenge to get a mortgage. You may be able to find a mortgage through an international bank that will recognize your foreign credit history or use a bank that offers programs for newcomers. The down-payment required can vary significantly, from 5% to 20%.

Pre-approval for a mortgage is no guarantee that you'll qualify for a mortgage, especially when you buy pre-sale and have a months or years long gap between pre-approval and actually getting the mortgage. Unless your pre-sale contract has a financing contingency, you will be responsible for payment, even if your mortgage is denied.

If you buy a pre-construction condo, your mortgage interest rate may rise between when you make your offer and when your building is actually registered. You may be able to get your bank to guarantee the rate for much longer than normal for pre-construction purchases.

If the value of your condo at completion is less than the pre-construction price, your mortgage may not cover the complete cost you've agreed to in the contract. You'll need to find cash to cover the difference.

Maintenance fees

New construction projects are notorious for having artificially low maintenance fees to lure in buyers, which skyrocket during the first few years of ownership.

Older buildings may have higher maintenance fees because they're carefully budgeting for future repairs and upgrades to keep the building in great condition. They're also likely to include some of your utilities — that "high" fee may include your hydro and water costs.

Buildings with nice amenities will inevitably have higher maintenance costs, although large buildings and building complexes can spread the costs of a pool over a larger number of units. The roof, elevators, and other utilities all require upkeep and upgrades over time. Buildings pay for snow removal, cleaning services, landscaping, security, and insurance costs.

A well-managed building will charge enough in maintenance to effectively pre-pay for large expenses over time, so costs can be taken out of the building's reserve funds. If the building doesn't have enough money to cover necessary repairs, the owners will have to split the costs by paying an assessment.

Property taxes

Property taxes are not included in maintenance fees unless you are buying a co-op or co-ownership unit.

In a resale unit, you can find out what owners paid last year and what the anticipated costs will be for this year.

In a new unit, you can find out the estimated property taxes.

Insurance

Your mortgage bank and your condo board will probably both require that you have insurance. Square One is one of the few insurance companies that will write policies for new residents without a credit history. They're also probably a lot more open to short term rentals than your condo board.

Setting up your home

Setting up a new home can be a lot of fun. It can also be a hassle. Here are the basics you'll need once you've found a place to move into.

Utilities

If you live in an apartment or condo, some or all of your utilities may be included in your rent or maintenance. This information should be in your lease or purchasing documents.

Each area has different utility companies. You can find all of your local utility providers in the Yellow Pages. You can also just ask the landlord, previous tenants, neighbors, realtor, or condo board for their recommendations.

You'll want to call the utility companies up to a month before you move in to create an account and schedule installation. Some utilities will charge you to set up an account and install service.

Some utility companies will want a previous address in Canada or a SIN. As a new resident, you may have to call around to find a service provider who will provide utilities to your home. If you don't have a Canadian credit history, they may require a security deposit. The security deposit should be returned to you, with interest, after a year of on-time payments or when you close the account.

Most utility companies bill you on a monthly basis. Some will bill you quarterly. Each bill is typically for the quantity you consumed in the previous month, although some utilities will have a flat fee paid in advance of service.

You can pay bills through the mail, on the company website, directly through your bank, automatic withdrawal, or over the phone. If bills aren't paid on time, you'll be charged a late fee. You'll usually have two weeks from when you get the bill to when the bill is due. You can have paper bills mailed to you or you can have electronic bills delivered.

If you can't afford to pay your utility bill, call the company and negotiate a payment plan, rather than simply not paying the bill. If you don't pay your bills, they can disconnect your service and charge you fees, in addition to the money you already owe, to reconnect service.

Internet & home phone services

Many telecom companies offer bundled deals, consisting of multiple services, including home phone, cell phones, internet, and cable TV. Both cable and DSL internet services are available. The phone, cable, and internet lines are typically owned by the main providers, but they also rent the lines out to smaller providers. Each province has different regulations for the telecommunications market.

You can compare plans at canadianisp.ca or comparemyrates.ca. Generally it'll take a few days or weeks to get service installed and there will be a fee to do it. Companies regularly run promotions to waive install fees, provide a free modem, or offer low introductory rates. Make sure you understand the contract terms, introductory/regular rates, and cancellation fees. Any equipment provided will usually have to be returned.

Internet in Canada is billed based on how much you actually use. You can get plans for certain usage levels or unlimited service. Unless you choose an unlimited package, most companies will send you alerts when you're getting close to your maximum usage so you can either avoid the internet until the billing cycle ends or upgrade your plan. You can also choose between different internet speeds.

Depending on where you live, you'll probably be able to get service from Bell, Rogers, or a third party that uses the lines of Bell or Rogers. Some third party providers, such as TekSavvy, are cheaper and provide better customer service for literally the same product.

Canadian phone numbers have 10 digits — a 3 digit area code, followed by a 7 digit local number. Canada and the US share the 001+ country code.

Domestic long distance is 1+ the number. International long distance from Canada is 011+ country code + the number.

Insurance

Even if you don't own your home, it's important to have insurance. Like health insurance, it can feel like wasted money—until you need it. Some leases, condos, mortgages, and provinces require insurance.

If a guest falls and is injured in your home, you let the tub overflow and it damages your apartment and the neighbor's apartment, or someone steals your laptop, you'll want to have insurance to cover the costs.

Each insurance policy is different, so check the terms carefully before buying insurance. Be sure to notify your insurance company if you buy an expensive item, renovate your home, get a dog, or make other changes to your home that would impact your insurance policy.

Insurance policies can be paid annually or monthly. Make sure you're not getting charged interest on that monthly payment option. It's a good idea to review your policy and update it each year.

As a new resident, quite a few insurance companies wouldn't offer me coverage. Square One Insurance offers policies to new residents. They also offer flexible options, like covering people doing short term rentals. They're also significantly more expensive than competitors, unfortunately. Once I'd been in Canada long enough to qualify for coverage from competitors, I switched to a more affordable insurance provider.

What's covered

Insurance will be for either the actual cash value (ACV) of an item (which considers depreciation) or replacement value. If you have an old TV, ACV insurance will pay for what it was worth, which may be much less than the cost of buying a new version of the same TV.

Look over the policy and make sure it covers what you own—and doesn't charge you for coverage on things you don't. If your kitchen is ready to be torn out, don't pay for more coverage than you need. You can save money by increasing your deductible or opting for a plan that pays the ACV.

There are different levels of coverage. Basic coverage is known as fire coverage, since that's basically what it covers. Mid-range and top-of-the-line policies cover much more. Sewer backups and theft can be expensive without insurance, but some people are comfortable with that level of risk.

Electrical appliances in Canada need to be Canadian Standards Association (CSA) approved. Home insurance will typically not cover damage caused by appliances without CSA approval.

Insurance will only cover what you can prove you owned. I periodically take photos of everything in my home—including under the sink and inside my cabinets—to have a record of what's where and what condition it's in. I also keep photographs of receipts for expensive items. If you imported things from abroad, your B4 or BSF186 is a record of everything you brought into Canada and its value. These photos and documents are a huge help if you have to file a claim.

Tenant insurance

If you rent your home, your landlord's insurance covers the apartment itself, but not your things. Tenant, or renter's, insurance will cover damage to your possessions, accidental damage you cause to the apartment, injury to visitors, and personal property that's stolen outside of your home.

Homeowners insurance

Home insurance typically covers damage to your personal possessions, injury to visitors, and accidental damage to others property. Don't insure more house than you own. Remember that when you bought your home, you paid for the land, too.

Condominium insurance

Condominium insurance covers damage to the interior structure of your unit, damage to your belongings, unit improvements, injury to visitors, and accidental damage to other units or the common areas. Anything that's not included in the standard unit will be covered by your personal insurance. The definition of the standard unit for your building will be in your purchase documents. The condo will have insurance for the building itself and common areas. If your building doesn't have a definition of a standard unit, adopting one can reduce your building's insurance rates and speed up the settling of claims.

Mail

Apartment buildings in the US commonly have a slot to collect outgoing mail near the resident's mailboxes. In Canada, a slot in the mailroom is probably a paper recycling bin for junk mail. Don't accidentally recycle your outgoing mail! Similarly, you probably can't leave outgoing packages with your concierge or in the lobby, like you would in the US.

Outgoing mail needs to be put in a pickup point or dropped off at Canada Post. Luckily, Canada Post has boxes along main streets and in front of shops like grocery stores and pharmacies. They also might have a location in your local pharmacy or gas station, as they're more likely to be inside another shop than to have their own storefront.

Furnishing your home

Canada isn't known for its excellent online shopping. I knew I wanted to buy a condo and furnish it so I could move in immediately, months before I shipped anything from my old apartment in Brooklyn. I didn't want to deal with the hassle of trying to find good deals on a million websites or coordinate pickups from Bunz and Kijiji. Which is how I ended up furnishing my entire apartment from IKEA.

There's a certain beauty to being able to buy furniture, mattresses, linens, kitchenware, and pretty much everything you need from a single store. I was able to look at items in the showroom in Brooklyn and place an order from one of the Toronto stores. If you're in a time crunch to get everything set up in a weekend, this is the way to go.

US stores like West Elm, CB2, Urban Outfitters, H&M and other stores sell furnishings and have stores in Canada. Their offerings are typically the same everywhere, so you can get an idea of what you want to buy without being in Canada.

Trying to order things online from international chains was kafka-esque. I tried to order a rug online from West Elm and eventually gave up after my support ticket was open for a month. They theoretically ship to Canada, but their online ordering system was down for weeks and they don't take international orders over the phone. Most stores are more open about not shipping to Canada, even if they have stores in Canada. Be prepared to pick up your purchases in person.

Canadian Tire is trying hard to fill the gap left by Target's departure from Canada. Their latest furniture lines are much more stylish. Home Sense is essentially the same as Home Goods. Walmart is self explanatory. Their online shopping experience is a bad knockoff of Amazon that's generally not worth bothering with.

Your driver's license

If you want to drive in Canada, you'll need to get a new driver's license. The rules depend on where you're living now and where you're moving from. In Ontario you can probably continue to use your current license for two months, but should apply for an Ontario license within 60 days of moving.

If you have a valid driver's license from Australia, Austria, Belgium, France, Germany, Ireland, Japan, Korea, Switzerland, Taiwan, the UK or the US, you are automatically granted some driving experience in Canada. You can simply exchange your driver's license. If you don't drive, the 60 day rule isn't super important, but you can't exchange your license after your current one expires.

If you can't exchange your license, don't worry, you probably don't have to start over. Check with your province to see what the process is for the country you're coming from.

US driving records

You only need to prove two years of driving history in order to be eligible for a full license. However, if you own a car you'll want to prove your entire history as a driver in order to keep your insurance rates low.

In order to get your full driving history you can request an official letter that outlines your history as a driver in that state. Most DMVs will have an option on their website where you can request your lifetime driving record for a small fee.

Your driving record must be in a sealed envelope mailed from the DMV. They will not accept printouts from a website or an envelope you have opened.

Exchanging your license

In Ontario, you go to your local DriveTest center to exchange your license. Bring your passport, visa document or PR card, and your current foreign license. If you happen to have any expired licenses you should bring those, too, as they may accept these as proof of the length of time that you've been driving.

If any of the names on your current or old licenses are different from your current legal name on your identity documents, make sure you also bring documentation to confirm the change of name (such as a marriage or divorce certificate).

You'll need to pass an eye test and pay a fee, and that's all there is to it. After dealing with DMVs in the US for so long, I expected this experience to be awful, but it was easy and quick.

Buying a vehicle

Much of Canada is rural and suburban, requiring a car to get around. Canada's bus service is surprisingly robust and reliable, but I wouldn't want to rely on it in most places. Many people have cars, even in Canada's most walkable cities.

If you buy a car from a dealership, it's likely to come with a warranty. If you buy a car from an individual, it's your responsibility once the title is in your name.

The seller will usually have a transfer of ownership form ready to go. These differ in each province and you can get them from the provincial road registry. You'll need to file this with the province, get a bill of sale, and pay the transfer tax. It's easiest if you do this with the seller.

You'll need to get the car inspected before you register it. Often the seller will have the car inspected before they list it for sale. You'll have to buy new license plates when you register the car.

Car insurance is mandatory throughout Canada. Specific requirements (and prices!) vary from province to province. Government agencies run car insurance companies in British Columbia, Saskatchewan, Manitoba and Quebec.

Your money

When you arrive in Canada, your credit score starts at zero. It can be difficult to get a credit card – or even rent an apartment – without a credit history. Some institutions will consider your foreign credit score, especially if you're from the US, UK, or Australia, but things are much easier once you establish your credit history in Canada. You'll build your credit by getting a credit card, paying rent, and other things you'll probably do automatically as you get settled.

You don't need a credit score to open a chequing or savings account. You don't even need a Canadian address. I opened a bank account while I was in Toronto as a tourist and had no problem. It seemed like most of the staff at my bank in Toronto were also born in another country, so they were familiar with all sorts of scenarios faced by newcomers and temporary residents. You might have a different experience in a small city or with a less international bank.

Many Canadian banks offer special accounts, credit cards, and mortgages for new permanent residents. Generally you can enroll in these programs for the first two years after you become a permanent resident. This is important, because otherwise it can be very difficult to access credit without a credit history.

If you don't qualify for a newcomer credit card, you can build your credit with a secured credit card. This is when you put down a deposit with a bank and can charge up to that amount, in order to demonstrate your ability to keep up with monthly payments.

Most Canadian bank accounts have a small monthly fee, but it's easy to get these waived for at least a few months. Some banks will give you a free account if you have multiple products or keep a certain account balance.

Interac e-transfer is how everyone pays everyone else north of the border. They allow you to send payments with someone's email or phone number, so they don't have to share their account information. If someone asks you to pay by email or text, this is what they're talking about. It's not uncommon for your bank to charge a fee of a dollar or two to send them.

When you open a bank account in Canada, your banker will probably be eager to get you to open a RRSP, RESP, and a TFSA. This is not good advice. You aren't eligible for a RRSP, RESP, or TFSA until after you've filed taxes. If you're a US citizen or greencard holder, your TFSA and RESP won't necessarily be tax free. Before you get talked into opening anything beyond a chequing account, do your own research or talk to an accountant.

Do you need a Canadian bank account?

You don't necessarily need a Canadian bank account. If your foreign bank has low foreign ATM withdrawal fees and you have a debit or credit card that doesn't charge for foreign transactions, you could comfortably continue using your current bank for quite some time.

I opened an account with RBC before I moved up and it's been very useful for things like condo maintenance fees and property taxes. However, since my income is primarily coming from the US and I have a no-fee US credit card, I continue to use my US bank account as my primary account.

If you're moving to Canada permanently or even working in Canada temporarily, it's easiest to bite the bullet and set up a Canadian bank account. Just remember that if you close your foreign bank account, it may be difficult or impossible to open a new one after you've moved.

Ways to bring money into Canada

Transferring money from one country and currency to another can be quite expensive. People devise all sorts of strategies to minimize fees. Different methods are best based on the amount and frequency of transfers.

If you'd like to move all of your money in one go or travel a lot, you can simply withdraw large amounts of cash from your foreign bank and deposit it into a bank in Canada. Or change it into Canadian dollars or whatever you want to do with it. It's weird, but quite simple.

You need to declare this money at customs if it's over C$10k. They won't charge you a fee, but they may ask for documents to show that this is money you earned legally and you aren't using it to fund terrorists. Paperwork showing that the amount corresponds with cash withdrawn from your savings account, proof of income, or a letter from your bank will make sure you don't spend all day getting grilled by customs agents.

Bank cheques, US cheques, and money orders

Many Canadian banks will accept American cheques for a fee, ranging from $5 to $20. You can simply write a cheque from your US account to yourself at your Canadian account. US banks will similarly accept Canadian cheques.

You can also request an international money order or bank cheque from your foreign bank, which you may have to do in person.

This isn't the fastest way to transfer money, as foreign cheques take an extra long time to clear, usually from 10-21 business days.

Wire transfers

Wiring money from your foreign account to your Canadian account typically happens instantly. Unfortunately, some banks will require you to be at the branch in person to initiate this process, which means you have to do it from outside of Canada. Typically there is a fee for both sending and receiving wire transfers.

In addition to checking the wire transfer fees, check the exchange rate. If you're not getting the sort of exchange rate you'd like, there are a number of businesses besides traditional banks designed to get your money across borders. Some of them charge a fee for the transfer, while others build this into the exchange rate. Wise, XE, and OFX are popular.

US/Canada cross-border banking

If you're coming from the US, handing your credit card over is the fastest way to out yourself as a foreigner. The need to sign is outdated enough that many automatic checkout systems aren't designed to allow it.

There are a few differences in banking between the US and Canada to note.

- Accounts without fees are much more common in the US than Canada. Credit card rewards and the like tend to be less enticing.

- You will be asked for your client card number instead of your bank account number. Your client card number is your debit card number.

- US bank accounts are insured by the FDIC for US$250k per account. The CDIC only covers C$100k.

If you spend a lot of time in both the US and Canada, it might be convenient for you to set up a cross-border account. While this is simple, it's probably not going to give you the best conversion rate.

Several Canadian banks have US branches. You may hear that HSBC has cross-border banking, but they are closing these in 2022. Even if a Canadian bank has branches in the US, it's not actually the same bank. Banks in different countries are separate legal entities, so there's limited services provided by the Canadian counterparts in America or vice versa.

Royal Bank of Canada

A few years ago RBC bought the Bank of Georgia so they can provide online US bank accounts for their Canadian customers. This is primarily a system set up for Canadians to bank in the US, but it also works in reverse.

When I need to add funds to my Canadian RBC account, I transfer money into my RBC US account. Once it clears, I can then instantly transfer it to my linked RBC CAN account. I can also deposit cheques directly into RBC US using their app.

RBC US is an online bank, but it could replace your US bank.

- You can get a US credit card and US mortgage using your Canadian credit score.

- You can also use ATMs with your RBC US debit card.

- They don't charge you ATM fees and will reimburse you for fees on some accounts. You can use PNC Bank ATMs without a fee.

- There are a bunch of ways you can move money into your RBC US account.

- You don't need to use a fake US address to open an RBC US account.

Theoretically, I could get an RBC CAN credit card and they'd take my US credit score into account.

RBC's regular Canadian accounts will also accept US cheques without charging fees. To confuse things further, they also have Canadian US dollar accounts.

Many of RBC's ATMs will dispense American dollars. Their ATMs are a little dated compared to what I'm used to. The first time an RBC

ATM failed to dispense cash because it was out of cash without displaying an error message, I panicked. Apparently that's normal here. Just like it's still normal to make ATM deposits using an envelope.

TD Bank

Once again, TD's cross border accounts are designed for Canadians banking in the US.

TD is the logical choice for cross border banking, since they have a ton of branches in both the US and Canada. However, they don't make it as easy as RBC does to transfer money between countries.

- You can move $2,500 a day between the US and CAN online or up to $100,000 a day over the phone using a wire transfer and they'll refund the fees.

- TD Bank will recognize your Canadian credit history in the US, so theoretically they may count it in the other direction.

- You can use ATMs in either country without any fees, but bank staff can only help with the account for whichever country you're in.

- They offer travel medical insurance while you're in the US.

- You don't need to use a fake US address to open or keep your TD US account.

- You do need a US address to have a TD bank US credit card.

Bank of Montreal

Like RBC, the Bank of Montreal has acquired a US bank in order to provide online banking for Canadian snowbirds. You can link your BMO and BMO Harris accounts online and easily transfer up to $25k in each transfer from Canada to the US. Each transfer takes up to two days to clear.

Transfers from the US to Canada have to be done via wire transfer and initiated in person. BMO Harris has over 600 branches in the US.

They make it easy to view accounts on both sides of the border in one place. They also offer a Canadian US dollar credit card.

Taxes & retirement planning for Americans

If you are a US citizen or greencard holder living in Canada, you need to file taxes in both countries every year. It's also to your benefit to understand the differences in the tax code so you can plan your future.

For detailed information on this, see my book *Cross Border Taxes: A complete guide to filing taxes as an American in Canada*. This book includes information on:

- Filing your taxes in Canada for the first time
    - dealing with currency conversions
    - filing when you're missing documents
    - ending your state tax obligations
- Understanding the tax treaty
    - Foreign earned income exclusion
    - Foreign housing exclusion
    - other tax credits and deductions for expats and immigrants
    - when your spouse is not a US tax resident
    - when you have income in both countries
- How the tax code differs between the two countries in regards to:
    - real estate (personal and investment)
    - self employment
    - inheritances
    - disability income

- Filing your US taxes as a resident living outside the US
  - FBAR
  - FATCA
  - filing back taxes in the US
- Getting audited by the CRA and IRS
- Planning for your future
  - power of attorneys and living wills
  - tax-favored retirement plans
  - tax-favored accounts
  - social security and old age pensions
  - estate planning
  - retiring abroad
- Ending your dual tax obligations
  - relinquishing US citizenship
  - relinquishing your US greencard
  - the Canadian exit tax

Mortgages

As a newcomer, you have access to special mortgage deals at some banks for your first two to four years as a permanent resident. They'll either waive the requirement for a Canadian credit check or evaluate your foreign credit history.

If you have a job in Canada, down-payments are often only 5%. If your income is foreign (such as rental income from properties abroad or working remotely for a company outside of Canada) you'll have to put somewhere from 20% to 35% down.

Oddly, your interest rate is higher if your down payment is between 20% and 30%. If your down payment is below 20% you're low risk because you're required to get mortgage insurance. If it's above 30% you're considered low risk because of your personal finances. If it's between 20% and 30% you're thus a higher risk than someone with a lower down payment!

Unlike in Australia, your full credit card limits aren't treated as debts, only your outstanding balance.

The mortgage application and approval process in Canada is much faster than in the US. It's unusual for it to take more than a week to get a final decision and you may get a decision in as little as a day.

Carefully check the terms of your mortgage before you agree to it, including fees, payment terms, overpayment and early payment options. You'll have the option to insure your mortgage in case of job loss or death.

In the US, a fixed rate mortgage locks in the rate for the entire duration of the mortgage, which is often 30 years. In Canada, fixed rate mortgages renew every five years (or less), so the rate will change.

Mortgages in both countries stipulate rules about payments in excess of the minimum. In the US, you can generally pay off your mortgage in full when you sell the property and not face any penalty. In Canada, this is usually not the case. Ending a mortgage early to sell a property is considered breaking a mortgage and there may be costs involved, typically based on the interest you would have paid had you kept the mortgage for the full term.

In Canada, mortgages are open or closed. With an open mortgage there are no prepayment penalties and you can switch to another lender to get better terms. They also have significantly higher interest rates.

With a closed mortgage, you get a lower interest rate. However, you face potentially steep prepayment penalties. You can switch lenders, but it only makes sense if the terms outweigh the penalties you'll have to pay.

Mortgage terms

Mortgages in Canada work differently than in the US. A 30-year mortgage in Canada needs to be renewed every 2-5 years, as if you are refinancing it at set intervals. This means that you could be denied a mortgage at renewal if your financial situation or the market changes. Your rate will change with each renewal, even if you have a fixed rate mortgage. This also gives you the opportunity to switch banks to get a better deal.

Breaking a mortgage

If you sell your home when your mortgage isn't up for renewal, this is referred to as 'breaking' your mortgage. Your bank will charge you a fee to do this and you may have to pay a portion of the interest you would have paid on the loan.

Your children

Public education is free in Canada for primary and secondary schools. The school year generally runs from September through June, with no school in the summer. School calendars are available far in advance, for ease of scheduling childcare. Education is overseen at the provincial and territorial level, but education is overall of a high caliber.

Classes take place from Monday to Friday. Most school days are shorter than the typical nine to five working hours, so you will need to arrange for childcare before and after the school day. If your child will miss school, you need to inform the school so they know the child is safe.

Teachers are required to be licensed or certified. Children's grades are sent home in report cards, typically quarterly. Parents are expected to meet with a child's teacher to discuss the child's progress at designated parent-teacher conferences. You may also contact the teacher to meet with them if you have concerns to discuss.

Schools typically have a nurse, counselor, and settlement worker on staff. If your child needs additional support, they can help you locate it and make referrals.

Schools are run by the locally elected school board. Most funding comes from the provincial and local level, which can lead to inequalities based on the wealth of a locality. Some provinces allocate funding per pupil, regardless of local funding levels.

Your children will likely attend a school based on the catchment area in which you live. In some circumstances, you may be able to request 'cross-boundary' enrollment to place your child in a school outside the catchment zone. This is most common for students with disabilities or in cases of shared custody. In areas undergoing rapid growth, like downtown Toronto, spaces may not be available in your neighborhood school.

Students with disabilities are entitled to receive support, either in a regular school or in a school specifically for children with specific needs.

Transportation is provided by most schools, depending on the distance to school and the walkability of the area. Textbooks are provided by the school. Other school supplies must be supplied by the students or their families.

School choice

You may be able to choose between school programs in English, French, or a mix of the two.

Some religious-based schools are publicly funded in Ontario, Quebec, Saskatchewan, Alberta, and Newfoundland and Labrador due to Section 93 of the Constitution Act, 1867. In Ontario this only includes Catholic schools. British Columbia has Sikh, Hindu, Christian, and Islamic schools. Students of any faith, or no faith, can attend these public schools. Canada's secular schools descended from Protestant schools.

Alberta has publicly funded charter schools.

In addition to publicly funded schools, which are free of cost, you can enroll your child in a private school or educate them at home. Home schooling is legal throughout Canada. Each province has its own regulations regarding home schooling.

Enrolling your child in school

Contact your local board of education for enrollment instructions and forms. Some popular schools have waiting lists, so it's worth enrolling earlier rather than later to ensure your child gets a spot in your top choice.

Documents for school enrollment

Each school has its own enrollment requirements, but documents generally include:

- Proof of age (passport or birth certificate)
- Proof of residence (utility bill, lease, or bank statement)
- Proof of immigration status (Confirmation of Permanent Residence (IMM 5292), Record of Landing (IMM 1000), PR card, Canadian birth certificate, or Canadian passport)
- Information about your child's medical history, including immunizations
- Proof of guardianship, if you are not the child's parent

Most schools require that students be immunized for polio, DTP (diphtheria, tetanus and whooping cough) and MMR (measles, mumps and rubella or German measles). A tuberculosis screening may also be required.

While schools may ask for proof of immigration status, all children aged 6-18 can attend school in Ontario, regardless of their immigration status or the immigration status of their parents.

Evaluating previous school records

Children enrolling in school in Canada are generally assigned to a grade based on their age if they are in primary school.

Secondary school students are placed in a grade based on an evaluation. This assessment is based on math and the language of instruction. Previous report cards, coursework, and other information will also be considered.

If your child needs support to learn English (or French), they will be placed in language classes. In Ontario they will be placed in at least one 'mainstream' class to help them interact with English or French speaking classmates.

Your child's grade placement isn't final. They'll continue to be monitored as they adjust to their new school.

Canadian schools recognize the importance of retaining a child's native language, in addition to learning English and/or French.

Childcare

Paying for private childcare is very common in Canada. Daycare costs vary widely by location. Provinces typically provide a child care subsidy in addition to the federal Canada child tax benefit and universal child care benefit.

Canada has licensed and unlicensed childcare. Unlicensed care is provided by babysitters, nannies, and unlicensed daycare.

Licensed childcare programs are overseen by the province, but not run by them. Staff are required to have a certain level of training and the childcare center is inspected. These include daycare, pre-schools, and out-of-school care.

Daycare

Daycare centers generally watch children from 18 months to the age at which children are required to enroll in school.

Family daycare is usually in someone's home and provides care for children of any age.

Unlicensed daycare programs are legal in some provinces, with restrictions on how many children can be watched simultaneously.

Pre-school

Pre-school is not provided for free like primary, intermediate, and secondary schooling.

Pre-school options include (in order of cost from least to most): non-profit co-operative schools, church-affiliated schools, local community schools, and private schools. Church schools do not require that children be of the same faith as the school and the amount of religious instruction varies widely.

Out-of-school care

Out-of-school care provides childcare before and after the school day. They also provide care during school holidays.

Summer camps

Many parents send their children to summer camps while school is not in session. Camps may run during the day, like school, or be sleep-away camps, where children stay at the camp for a week or even the entire summer. Camps may have academic, athletic, or religious themes. The cost of summer camp programs vary widely.

Primary and intermediate school

Kindergarten typically begins at the age of five for children born before December 31st of the year of enrollment. In Nova Scotia,

Ontario, Quebec, and the Northwest Territories kindergarten lasts two years (junior and senior kindergarten) and begins at the age of four.

The age at which education becomes compulsory varies between five and seven, depending on your location.

Students in primary school generally have one teacher for all subjects. In intermediate or secondary school students switch to having different teachers for each subject.

Childrens work is graded throughout the year. They may be held back to repeat a year or moved forward, skipping a year.

Secondary school

It is not uncommon for secondary schools, especially those in large cities, to have an academic or vocational specialization. Secondary school students have a core curriculum that is required and the remaining credit hours are electives. Students receive career counseling and guidance regarding universities and other training opportunities.

Public education is compulsory until the age of 16 (or 18 in Manitoba, Ontario, and New Brunswick). Some exceptions to this are possible as young as 14, including for students who complete secondary school early.

In order to complete secondary school, students may need to earn a certain number of class credits, pass several tests, and complete community service hours.

Ontario offers students the option of a 13th year (or 12+). This is jokingly referred to as a 'victory lap.' While this has not been required since 2003, many students still opt to complete this optional year.

In Quebec students attend high school until grade 11 and then attend a general or vocational college for two to three years, depending on the program.

Extracurricular activities

Extracurricular activities are seen as an important factor for being accepted into selective universities. They can also be a factor for earning scholarships.

Sports are a big part of life at most Canadian schools. Training and practice happens outside of school hours. Most schools require students to maintain a certain grade point average in order to participate in sports.

Other common extracurricular activities include: band, choir, drama, the newspaper, the yearbook, language clubs, nature clubs, and student government.

Your health coverage

Canada encourages you to sign up for private health insurance so that you're covered in the interim period before you're able to access the provincial insurance. You can also receive basic medical care at community health centers and pay out of pocket for services.

Each province and territory has its own health insurance plan. Most require you to wait three months after moving before you're eligible to access benefits. You can generally enroll before you're eligible and they'll mail you the card right before you can access services.

Stop by your local Service Canada location to sign up. Bring your passport, visa or PR card, and something that verifies your proof of residency.

Check which documents will count as proof of residency in your province or territory. A lot of the documents that validate your residency aren't readily available if you've just moved to the country. The easiest things to get your hands on are some sort of utility bill, bank statement, or driver's license. They may require that it be mailed to you and in an original envelope.

In Ontario you'll get your health card a few days before you can start using it, which will be exactly three months from the date that you moved to the province. Or, if you apply after that three month window, it will be valid as soon as you receive it. You'll want to keep this in your wallet in case of emergencies.

Finding a doctor

You'll have to find a family doctor or general practitioner (GP) in Canada to act as your gateway to prescriptions and specialists. This is similar to many kinds of insurance plans in America, where plans require referrals from your primary care physician to access specialists.

You may have to look around to find a GP that is accepting new patients. Some areas, like Vancouver Island, have critical shortages of GPs and you'll have to get on multiple waiting lists in hopes of eventually finding a doctor.

One trick is to look for new practices that don't already have a full patient roster. Ask your coworkers or neighbors if they have a GP they like who might be accepting new patients. Another option is to contact your local hospital and see if they have a family practice unit that's accepting new patients.

If you're in Ontario, you can register with Health Care Connect once you have your OHIP card and the Ministry of Health and Long-Term Care will match you with a GP who's accepting new patients. The College of Physicians and Surgeons of Ontario also maintains a directory where you can search for a doctor.

You can still access health care without a GP through walk-in clinics, urgent care, and the emergency room.

Healthcare in Canada vs. the US

When I first started talking about moving to Canada, I heard a lot of blanket statements from Americans about how disappointed I would be with socialized health insurance. In fact, I even heard that from Canadians. Americans seemed to think that healthcare in Canada would be more expensive and of a lower quality than I was used to receiving in America. Some Canadians would warn me that I would wait forever to see a doctor and would find that it provides less coverage than what I could get in America.

You might say I was skeptical from the start. My work puts me in the position of hearing healthcare horror stories from both countries, so I can confidently say that the worst case scenario is much better in Canada. How many people have experienced healthcare in both American and Canada? Canadians may spend less on healthcare, but they still have a longer life expectancy than Americans.

If you have health insurance in the US provided by your employer, you've probably watched as the amount you paid for insurance went up each year. The annual deductible probably went up every year too, along with co-pays for doctor's visits, medical procedures, and medications. At one point, my annual deductible was 25% of my annual salary. When I moved to Canada, my job in the US didn't provide any health insurance at all. In the US it's very common for people to go several years without health insurance between aging out of their parent's coverage and getting a job with benefits. Even then, you'll see $300 or more deducted from each paycheque.

In the US, you are pretty much guaranteed to have a totally different health plan any time you start a new job. Or even a new plan every few years when you stay with the same job. This means changing your doctor and pharmacy and losing coverage for things like pregnancy for the first year.

In Canada I'd have health insurance coverage, no matter where I was working. I've found it much easier to get an appointment with a doctor, even with a specialist, in Toronto than in New York. People I know who've experienced serious injuries or illness in Canada are generally very happy with their care. It's the quasi-medical costs and loss of income from time off caused by debilitating chronic conditions that are an issue, since they're not covered by insurance. This problem is hardly unique to Canada.

What's covered

Your provincial health plan will cover most things so long as they are considered "medically necessary." For example, you can't count on the government to pay for cosmetic surgery. You can count on your health care plan covering physician visits, medically necessary surgeries and procedures, diagnostics, and preventive care.

Since you're not bound by a single health insurance plan with a provider network, you can go to any doctor in the province. That means no looking around for an in-network provider. You're also covered for emergency medical needs if you're traveling within Canada, and can see doctors in other provinces if you first clear it with your provincial plan.

Many people have supplemental coverage for things like prescriptions, vision, and dental. If you can't afford your prescriptions, your pharmacist or doctor may be able to help you.

Supplemental health coverage

Many employers will offer supplemental health coverage plans, which Canadians refer to simply as "insurance." Unlike health insurance in the US, you can't opt out of supplemental plans if they're made available to you. Your spouse and/or dependents must sign up for any supplemental plan offered through your employer. The only exception to this is if your spouse is already signed up for a supplemental plan through their employer.

Supplemental plans aren't universal, so they'll be different depending on what your employer offers. Most cover all or part of costs related to vision, dental, physiotherapy, pharmaceuticals, and travel insurance. You can generally count on a supplemental plan to help with whatever isn't covered by your provincial plan.

Most insurance plans will only cover the majority of costs of generic medications (for example, some cover 90% of the price and you're left to pay for just 10%). Often times you're on your own for brand names...sort of. There are some programs that will help pick up the difference between brand name and generic if your insurance plan won't cover the (often super high) cost of brand names.

Even when insurance plans fall through, there are still other things in place to help pick up the slack. Pharmaceutical programs differ by province and even by pharmacy, so ask your local pharmacy about what sort of options they have that might help.

Your new career

The idea of moving to another country without a job waiting for you can be, well, terrifying. Canadian immigration programs require that you either have a job offer, money to support yourself, or a pledge of financial support from someone else. Plenty of people have come to Canada without jobs lined up and found their footing in their new country.

Getting a job in a different country can be incredibly challenging, especially if you require a LMIA, aren't fluent, or need to get international credentials recognized. Even if you don't get a valid job offer before you arrive, these steps will help set you up to find a job once you're in Canada.

Economy & industry

- Three in four Canadians work in the service industry.

- International trade is a large part of the economy. Canada has free trade agreements with much of the globe.

- Canada is one of the global leaders in the software industry.

- Logging, mining, and oil are major industries.

- Canada is a major exporter of wheat and other grains.

- Canada's fishing industry is the 8th largest in the world.

- Film, television, and entertainment industries are growing.

- Tourism is increasing, with most visitors coming from the US.

- Toronto is the financial center of Canada.

- Jobs in Québec will often require French proficiency, as will most jobs for the government or subcontractors.

- Many companies provide bilingual services, so speaking French is an asset at work anywhere in the country.

- There is a large manufacturing sector in central Canada, led by the automobile and aircraft industries.

Finding a job in Canada

Finding a job in Canada before you arrive can be difficult, especially if you require a work permit. However, it's not impossible. Your chances differ dramatically depending on your industry, experience, and personal connections. Arranging for a work permit adds a layer of expense and complexity for employers. Even if you don't require a work permit, employers may prefer local candidates who they can meet with multiple times before making a hiring decision. Many newcomers struggle with employers wanting to see candidates with "Canadian experience."

Finding a job before you come

One of the best ways to find a job in Canada before you actually move is to apply to jobs from abroad and schedule interviews during visits to Canada. Obviously, this may not be realistic for your situation. If you have friends in Canada, list their address on your resume, or simply list the city you'll be moving to. You can get a VOIP number so you can list a local phone number and have it ring to your cell phone anywhere in the world.

Finding a job requires a multi-pronged approach. Use your personal network, apply to job postings, and reach out to companies you're particularly interested in. While you shouldn't expect an employment agency to find you a job, it's still helpful to register with them and follow up to keep yourself at top of mind. Many cities have job fairs, where you can meet hiring managers, practice your interview skills, and see what sort of skills are in demand.

Don't overwhelm and discourage yourself by applying to 50 jobs in one day. Aim to spend a few hours each week sending out actual applications, but make sure to get out to meet your new neighbors and rebuild your professional network.

Finding a job through the express entry job bank

If you're applying to become a permanent resident through express entry, you have access to Job Match. You can't register with Job Match until you create your express entry profile.

Once you create your express entry profile, you'll get a message saying your profile is accepted and directing you to the Job Bank. The message will contain a PDF with your Job Bank Validation Code. You need this code to create your Job Match account.

Job Match will connect potential employees with companies that have job openings with LMIAs. After going through the regular interview process, employers will provide candidates with information to include in their express entry profile. This will award you an additional CRS points and you'll almost certainly get an invitation to apply.

Getting your credentials recognized

Unfortunately, qualifying for permanent resident status in Canada or an open work permit is not a guarantee that your credentials will be recognized by employers.

If you are in a field that requires licensing or certification, you will need to contact the licensing organization to find out what requirements there are to get your credentials recognized. You should start this process before you immigrate to Canada. In fact, it's a good idea to see what the requirements are before you decide to immigrate.

Bridging programs are designed to help people with international training get set up in their field in Canada. These programs are organized by your local immigrant-serving organization. You can also look into related jobs so you can get a job in your field while you wait to get your credentials assessed or get re-licensed in Canada. Settlement services will support you in the process of getting your credentials recognized, provide you with training to familiarize yourself with Canadian norms in your field, and help you rebuild your network.

Employment support through settlement services

There are numerous organizations funded by the federal and provincial government to assist newcomers in acclimating to life in Canada. These services are provided at no cost to you. Finding a job is a big part of the services they offer. Employers who hire someone through a settlement organization may be able to have part of your salary subsidized as an incentive to hire newcomers.

People I spoke with had mixed experiences with settlement services. It can be difficult to find a service that you qualify for. Because the funding comes from the government, the services you have access to are based on your immigration circumstances. It can be frustrating to figure out what services you qualify for and to distinguish between seemingly identical organizations. The directory of settlement resources on the IRCC website often links to general organizational homepages, without providing details of their settlement services and how to enroll, even when the organization in question is something like a university that offers many services.

You can only be enrolled in one employment program at a time, meaning it can slow things down if the one you try first isn't a good fit. Many programs are restricted to people who are unemployed, so if you take a survival job you can find yourself unable to access support to get your career back on track. I heard over and over how a career counselor would ask detailed questions about their background and aspirations, then suggest they take a low-paying job unrelated to their field. The process can be demoralizing.

Other people found employment programs to be very helpful. The variation depends on the specific staff member who's supporting you, as well as your specific circumstances. They match newcomers with mentors in their field, arrange informational interviews with potential colleagues, and organize career fairs. I know people who've established new careers in Canada and were happy with the experience. When I tried to get matched with a mentor I was turned down! So, it's a mixed bag.

While the career fairs are full of employers recruiting for 'survival jobs,' which tend to be low-skilled and low-pay, they also connect newcomers with large corporations looking to recruit from diverse and well-educated candidates. Big banks and other corporations are eager for "diverse candidates" to show that they're not racist. Channel those stock photos of diverse offices when you're choosing your outfit for a career fair.

I originally took a cursory glance at the available settlement services, then dismissed them as resume workshops and job boards. Coming from the US, I wasn't concerned about employers not recognizing my experience. I'd run a resume writing workshop for a settlement organization in Brooklyn, so I doubted there was much to learn from taking one myself once I arrived in Toronto.

Later, I came to question my decision, wondering if I'd missed out on opportunities to rebuild my professional network in Canada. A few months before I became a citizen I tried to connect with several settlement organizations. I was turned down at a speed mentorship matching event. I went to a virtual career fair that seemed to just be selling my data to grad schools. I never managed to talk to a career counselor, even though three of them said they'd get back to me to set up an appointment. The amount of hassle involved in trying to find help made it easier to become ineligible for these services when I became a citizen.

Networking

Many job vacancies are never advertised. This hidden job market consists of both jobs that haven't been posted yet and jobs that would be created if the right person comes along. In order to find out about these jobs, you need to know the right people.

Former coworkers, friends, family members, and acquaintances can be great sources for job leads. Hiring managers feel more comfortable interviewing candidates who come through a referral, since presumably you wouldn't have been referred if you weren't worth interviewing.

Even if you don't know anyone in Canada, your family, friends, and coworkers do. Let people know you're moving and will be looking for a job. Use your school alumni network. Use Facebook and LinkedIn to see who's in Canada who you can be introduced to. People you know who work for international companies may be able to get you in touch with Canadian hiring managers.

Once you're in Canada, or even if you're here to check things out before you move, get out and meet people. As you rebuild your social network, you'll inevitably meet people who will help you in your job search. Join professional organizations, social clubs, sports teams, religious organizations, or whatever's interesting and relevant to you. Register with Meetup.com and go to professional events related to your career field. Volunteering is a great way to make connections and get used to life in Canada.

It's not enough to simply join a professional organization. The more you get involved with organizing events and participating on committees, the more you can build relationships with other members and demonstrate your abilities.

If there is a certain organization you'd like to work for, get connected. See if you know anyone who could make an introduction. Go to events where people from that company will be presenting and talk to them after the presentation or in a follow-up email. Interact with them on social media. Nothing is guaranteed, but if you've got your heart set on working for a certain company, it's worth trying.

Advertising yourself

Put yourself out there to find employers. Make sure you have:

- A profile on LinkedIn,
- A personal portfolio website, and
- Are active on social media.

Finding job openings

Many people find applying to job openings incredibly frustrating. Job postings often list off impossible qualifications or require creating an account and filling out dozens of fields. Some job postings will even ask that you complete a task before you've even come in for an interview.

While job listings don't have the success rate that personal introductions do, they're a necessary evil. Lots of people find jobs through job postings.

- The Job Bank aggregates general job postings from several sites around Canada
- Canada.ca lists federal public service jobs
- Charity Village lists nonprofit jobs
- LinkedIn lists jobs in all industries.
- Twitter can be used to search for job postings in your field and set up a list of companies and people you'd like to work for.
- Glassdoor lists jobs as well as reviews from current and previous employees so you can get an idea of what it's like to work for specific companies

Settlement.org maintains a more extensive list of job search sites. There are also many specialty job search sites.

Employment agencies & executive search firms

Recruiters provide employers with a short list of pre-screened candidates. If you make the short list of the most qualified candidates you'll move on to an interview with the company. Remember that recruiters work for the employer, not you.

Many employment firms specialize in a certain industry, which increases your odds that they'll have multiple openings you'd be a good fit for.

Volunteering

Volunteering while you look for a job can be a great experience. Direct benefits for your job search include:

- Getting Canadian work experience.
- Re-building your professional network and make friends.
- Getting someone who can serve as a reference for you.

- Keeping your spirits up and keeping you busy during your search for work.

You can find volunteer opportunities at Volunteer Canada, Charity Village, or by reaching out to a nonprofit that seems interesting to you.

Your resume and cover letter

If you've never written a Canadian style resume and cover letter, or just want someone to help you proofread it, your local immigrant services organization can offer you help. Your local library may also have services to help you with your resume and job hunt.

Writing a cover letter in Canada

Cover letters should be short and conversational. Write a generic cover letter and then customize it for each position you apply for. If you're applying for several types of positions, write a generic cover letter for each one. Be sure to have someone else proofread your resume and cover letter for you.

Address it to a specific person whenever possible. Be sure to include:

- What makes you uniquely qualified for this position

- Why you want to work for this company

- A reference to anyone you know in common, if you went to the same school or are from the same city, or any other connection to the company or hiring manager

- Your contact information

Canadian resumes

Resumes in Canada and the US are virtually indistinguishable.

You do not need to include your work permit or residency status on your resume. Employers may ask if you're legally authorized to work in Canada, but you don't need to offer up that information unless they ask.

- Use keywords from the job posting in your position descriptions

- Include any relevant volunteer work, especially if it was in Canada

- Include a summary of qualifications

- Quantify outcomes and achievements whenever possible

- Keep it to one page unless you're applying for an executive level position

- Include only relevant work history, or simply list the dates, job title, and company for unrelated work

- Use formatting to make it easy to skim

- Don't include a mission statement or "references available upon request"

The interview process

The recruiting process varies considerably from one company – or even one department – to another. There's no one set process that everyone follows. Be prepared for common interview questions and ask around to see what to expect.

Topics that are taboo in job interviews include citizenship, race or ethnicity, physical appearance, affiliations, marital/family status, disability, age, religion, and arrest record. It's considered best practice to pivot the conversation away from these topics, like a politician turning a problematic question into one they are comfortable answering. Rather than answering the question directly, answer an adjacent unasked question that allows you to highlight your ability to do the job.

An insightful classmate told me that the interview process highlights how Canadians tend to be polite, without being kind.

Phone interviews

When you have a phone interview scheduled, make sure you can be somewhere private and quiet at the appointed time.

- Look at the company website and social media accounts beforehand. Read any recent news coverage.

- Make notes with key points you want to make during the call.

- Have a copy of the job posting and your resume available for you to look at during the call.

- People find it helpful to stand and smile when they're on the phone.

- Take notes and always send a thank you email to follow-up afterward.

In-person interviews

It's not unusual for companies to ask you to come in for multiple rounds of interviews before making an offer.

Some interviews can last all day. When scheduling an interview, be sure to ask how long you should expect it to last and if there's anything you should bring.

- Research the company before you go. If you have the names of the interviewers ahead of time, find out their background and look for common ground.

- Find out the dress code. Look for photos of employees on their website or social media accounts. Ask people you know at the company or in the field. You want to dress one level above what you'd wear on a typical day in that position. Startups tend to have very casual dress, so you don't want to show up in a suit.

- Make sure you're on time. Aim to be in the area ahead of time so you have time to collect yourself and to not have to worry about transit delays.

- Arrive about 10-15 minutes ahead of time. Give yourself time for security procedures.

- Ask questions. Show you're interested and look for red flags about the company, team, and role.

- Follow up. A thank you note is a great way to stand out and reiterate important points – or add in something you forgot to say.

Individual hiring managers have strong opinions on following up and they vary widely. The best way to know what to expect for the timeline is to ask during the interview. If they tell you they'll get back to you in five days and you don't hear back, it's good to wait an extra day or so before following up.

If you don't get the offer, it's still a learning experience. If you felt you connected with an interviewer, go ahead and follow up to see how you could improve for next time. You may never hear back, but you may also get incredibly valuable feedback – or gain a mentor.

References

You can still use your references back home for a job in Canada. Be sure to let them know to expect a call or email. Brief them on what job you're applying for and anything you'd specifically appreciate they could mention in terms of your strengths.

You can use old bosses, coworkers, clients, and professors as professional references. One way to get local references is to volunteer in Canada during your job search.

Be sure to follow up with your references. Thank them for their help and let them know if you got the job.

Salary negotiation

Many hiring managers won't discuss your potential salary until they're ready to make an offer. Many job postings will ask for your current salary or your expected salary. As a newcomer with a salary in a different currency and potentially a place with a very different cost of living, it's best to simply put your expected salary range.

When considering an offer, find out the details of the benefits package and consider things like what your supplemental health insurance will cover.

Employers who won't budge on base salary may be open to negotiating paid time off, paid training, business trips, bonuses, or other perks. Be sure these verbal agreements make it into your job contract.

Even if it seems like your dream job, don't sell yourself short. It's not going to be a dream job if you can't pay your bills or if you feel undervalued. Of course, sometimes it makes sense to accept a job knowing it's a choice you need to make to pay the bills while you look for something that's a better long-term fit.

Accepting an offer

When you get a verbal job offer, you don't have to give an answer right away. It's perfectly normal to spend a week or two negotiating details of the hiring contract, as well as getting some time to think about the offer. Thank them for the offer and find out when they need a final answer. You'll also need to agree upon a proposed start date.

If the offer doesn't meet your needs or expectations, you can make a counter offer and negotiate the details of the contract. If you decide to turn the offer down, be polite. The world is a small place, so it's best to avoid insulting someone.

Be sure to see if there are any restrictions on what you can do after you work for the company. Post-employment restrictions and non-compete agreements are increasingly common. It's also important to read and understand the termination clause.

After you've accepted the offer, either verbally or via email, you'll need to sign the contract. Look it over carefully to make sure it includes all of the terms you agreed upon. If you have questions about benefits or details of the contract, you can ask to speak to a human resources representative.

Once you're satisfied with the contract, you'll need to sign it and return it. It's usually at this point that you'll fill out any required paperwork to begin your new job.

When you can't find work

It's not unheard of for newcomers to struggle to find work in Canada, even when they'd never had a hard time finding work before. Finding a job is very different when you don't have a strong network to rely on, especially when you're dealing with cultural differences.

It's not uncommon for newcomers to take 'survival jobs' for a few months or even years as they get settled in Canada. This is especially common for professionals in licensed professions, who require months or years of retraining before your qualifications are recognized.

If you have PR status, you're free to work as a consultant or start your own business. You can also work remotely for a business outside of Canada.

Working in Canada

In Canada it's rare to work for a single company for your entire career. The three most common types of employment are permanent employment, part-time employment, and freelance employment.

The most common type of job is permanent employment. This typically includes a base salary, supplemental insurance, a retirement plan, and any other perks that come along with your job, like paid time off. Generally, employment insurance, Canada Pension Plan contributions, income tax, union dues (if applicable), and the cost of supplemental insurance (if applicable) will be taken directly out of your paycheck. If you lose your job through no fault of your own, you'll be eligible for employment insurance payments.

Part-time employment works the same as permanent employment, although it's common to be paid hourly and not receive additional benefits.

You can also be a contract or freelance worker. This means you're paid a fixed amount (generally per hour or per project) with no additional benefits. Because income tax deductions are not made automatically, these must be paid at the end of the year or periodically if your income is over a certain amount. In some instances, you may qualify for employment insurance. Contributions to employment insurance and the Canada Pension Plan are optional. As a freelancer, you need to get a GST number from Revenue Canada.

Work culture in Canada is very similar to work culture in the US. Because Canada is so diverse, even if you feel at home in your Canadian office, you'll likely still be working with people adapting to a new office culture.

- Watch how coworkers respond to how close you are when standing or talking, as the distance between two people talking that feels right varies considerably between cultures.

- Avoid interrupting, pointing, or waving.

- Being on time is important. If you're running late, call or email to let people know.

- The ability to shift from teamwork to independent work is valued.

- Participation in group discussions and asking questions is important.

- Workplaces are casual but respectful. You'll likely be on a first-name basis with your executives.

- It's okay to say no to your boss, but do it politely and explain why.

- Avoid discussions of age, pay, religion, and politics when in the office.

- Sometimes it's normal for coworkers to become close friends outside of work, sometimes it's not.

- It's generally considered unethical to date a coworker, client, or customer.

- Talk to your supervisor about your career goals.

- Misunderstandings can often be resolved or alleviated by having a private, non-confrontational conversation.

Salaries in Canada vs. the US

I've heard a lot of conflicting information on what to expect of life in Canada in terms of salary and general cost of living. People in Toronto seem to think they'd make five times as much money in New York or San Francisco. That's probably only true for a very small percentage of people. Rather than trust the anecdotes, I dove into the data.

Average salaries are about the same between Canada ($49,000 per year) and the US ($46,482 per year). Taxes are generally higher in

Canada, but they're used to fund social benefits like the single-payer healthcare system. That means that while your taxes will be higher, you pay very little for healthcare and won't see paycheck deductions for health insurance. I've paid $600 a month for lackluster health insurance in the US and that's when I was lucky enough to have health insurance provided through my employer. At the end of the day, you'll likely take home about the same amount of pay in Canada as you did in the US unless you earn quite a bit of money.

The cost of living in Canada is less than the cost of living in America. This will vary depending on location and certain things will cost a lot more than you're used to paying for in the US, but in general you'll pay less overall.

If you're moving from a large city like New York or San Francisco, you'll probably find that you'll pay less wherever you move to in Canada. On the other hand, if you were living in a small town or city and moved to Toronto or Vancouver, you'll definitely notice everything costs more because large cities tend to be more expensive.

Are you a member of the middle class? If so, living in Canada means that you are now a part of the richest middle class in the world, a title held by middle-class Americans until 2014. Canada has a higher rate of social mobility than the US.

Canadians have seen wages increase faster than in the US, growing 22% since 2007. In the US, incomes have not been keeping up with inflation and economic growth, so people pay more each year but often earn the same as they the year before. On top of all that, the Canadian government has been more actively involved in the redistribution of income, preventing the kind of larger than life discrepancies found in the US.

At 331-to-1, the ratio of CEO-to-worker pay is double in the US as compared to any other country, Canada included. So, if you're a top executive, you'll probably make less in Canada than in the US. If this

298

applies to you, you're probably not trying to immigrate to Canada anyway.

The federal minimum wage in the US is $7.25 per hour. For professions that receive tips, such as wait staff and bartenders, the minimum wage is just $2.13. The minimum wage goes all the way to $13.25 in DC and some individual cities have increased their minimum wage to $15 (San Francisco and New York).

Canada doesn't have a federal minimum wage. Instead each province/territory sets the minimum amounts, which range from $11.06 to $15 per hour. Some provinces have separate minimum wage amounts for people that receive tips, which range from $9.20 to $10.70 per hour. Some professions are further defined by special minimum rates per hour, day, week, or month. For example, a car salesperson in Alberta would make a minimum of $446 per week.

If you're coming from a city with a large job market, like New York, you may earn less when you move to Canada, but not a lot less. Different types of jobs might have higher or lower average salaries in Canada versus the US. You can use tools like payscale.com or glassdoor.ca to find out what sort of salaries you can expect to find in Canada for your profession.

Learning French

A surprising number of Americans think all of Canada speaks French. I'm curious to know if these are the same people who think Canada is a US territory. While not all of Canada speaks French, a significant portion of the population does. If you're in Quebec or New Brunswick it's helpful to at least know basic French. There are Francophone communities throughout Canada.

Government language classes

As with all settlement services, it can be difficult to determine whether or not you qualify for government language courses. Anyone who is a newcomer to Canada who speaks *neither* English nor French is eligible for classes. If you speak English *or* French, your eligibility is determined by your immigration pathway and native language. Some provinces provide language courses for temporary residents. While the program is federally funded, it differs by province or territory and is carried out by numerous private organizations.

Enrolling in courses through language instruction for newcomers to Canada (LINC) is not as simple as it seems. Officially, you need to contact a newcomer support organization and get a formal language assessment. Then you enroll in a language school. Courses are available online and in-person, at various times and full-time or part-time. Supposedly childcare and transportation support are available.

Other permanent residents who came from English speaking countries kept insisting I qualified for free French courses. Every time I asked an organization offering free French classes, I was told I didn't qualify. Then one day someone from the YMCA was advertising their settlement services at the library and this time I was told, yes, I qualified.

A few days later I heard from someone on their language assessment team, who confirmed my eligibility and told me that the wait list for beginner French classes was very long and I should call her back when I worked my way through DuoLingo, Mango Language, or another similar program. Once I was ready, she'd schedule my language assessment. I later learned that there were over 400 people on the YMCA's waiting list.

A week later, someone else from the YMCA called and asked if I was able to do the assessment later that day, due to a cancellation. I was able to fit it into my schedule, despite it being a four hour test. She emailed me several pages of forms to fill out and requested copies of my landing documents and other immigration paperwork.

Given that my French training consisted of seven days of DuoLingo and memorizing a few phrases before past trips to Quebec and Belgium, it consisted of four hours of shrugging, saying 'je ne comprends pas,' and guessing at multiple choice questions. Later the same day, I had to retake part of it, because there was an issue with the computer system.

A few days later, I was told I actually didn't qualify, since English was my native language. She referred me to the resources available for free through the Toronto Public Library.

A few days later, she contacted me again saying I did qualify for language classes, provided my assessment paperwork, and said I could enroll immediately. She asked about my availability, offered two class times to choose from, and said I'd hear from the school shortly.

Later that day I heard from someone at Collège Boréal, who confirmed all of my personal information and requested the forms I'd been provided with by the YMCA.

Two days later, I heard from my French instructor, who welcomed me to the course. Classes are capped at 15 students. Each course was designed to be a loop, so students could join the class at any time. At the end of the loop, each student would be evaluated. If you were ready, you could advance to the next level, if there was space available. In my program we were grouped into levels 0-1, 2-3, 4-5, 6-7. No courses were offered beyond level 7, which is considered upper intermediate on a scale from 0 to 10. Level 7 is the equivalent of B2 and at that point you are considered bilingual.

French programs funded by the IRCC are currently allowed to choose their own course materials. Soon, they will be moving to a curriculum on Avenue that is heavy on Canadian pride. Exercises include quizzes where you identify the flag of each province. You no longer have to feel bad about missing out on third grade civics classes!

The new curriculum does have practical information on how to navigate Canadian life, like getting a call from your kid's teacher, filling out common forms, and reading a prescription.

My French class was two hours long, twice a week. Previously, they were offered four times a week and have been reduced because of budget cuts. My instructor made it clear that two hour classes twice a week are not going to make me fluent in French. I still needed to spend a significant amount of time studying the course materials, which he put online for us. He encouraged me to use Mango Language as well as to watch movies in French.

There are many free language programs, including paid programs that are available for free from your library. Read reviews and test out a couple to decide which ones are the best fit for you. Using more than one program, in addition to my classes, means I'm learning information in different ways at different times. For me, this is helpful reinforcement that leads to a deeper understanding.

Rosetta Stone aims to be entirely intuitive. Mango Language provides clear grammatical and cultural information. I enjoy how DuoLingo allows me to learn grammar intuitively and its gamification means I look forward to it. I appreciate Memrise for the variety of voices it uses. Memrise has a supplementary module with French Canadian vocabulary.

Government language classes in Quebec

Naturally, Quebec offers different French language programs than the rest of Canada. For more information on what courses are available and how to qualify, visit: quebec.ca/en/education/learn-french/

Life in Canada

The paperwork does not end once Canada starts to feel like home. After you've been living in Canada for a while, staying requires ensuring you continue to have a valid work permit, becoming a permanent resident, renewing your PR card, or applying for citizenship.

Renewing or changing your work permit

You need to begin the process of renewing your work permit at least 30 days before it expires. The process is slightly different for employer-specific work permits and open work permits. Regardless of the type of work permit you have, you need to apply to renew it in order to continue working after it expires. You have maintained status while you wait for your new application to be processed, which means you can remain in Canada and maintain your authority to work under the terms of your expired work permit.

If you apply to renew or update your work permit online, the IRCC will provide immediate confirmation that you have the legal right to work in Canada under the terms of your current work permit for 120 days. If you apply on paper you will not have this proof of status.

While you're a legal resident according to the IRCC while on maintained status, it may be difficult to get other institutions to recognize this. If your drivers license expires while you're on maintained status, you may be unable to renew your license. If you're going to move to a new province or do anything that will require proof of status, you likely need to take care of things before your old work permit expires or after you get your new one.

Your work permit can't be valid beyond the expiration date of your current passport, so you may need to renew your passport before you get started.

If your work permit expires before you apply to extend it, you may be able to restore your status, as long as you apply within 90 days.

If you leave Canada after your old work permit expires and while your work permit renewal is processing, you may be required to enter Canada as a visitor, in which case you won't be able to work until the new application is approved.

Open work permit

You can apply for a new open work permit online. The IRCC has a quiz that will provide you with a custom document checklist. Once you've submitted copies of all of the required documents, you'll instantly be provided with a letter confirming your ability to work under the terms of your current work permit.

If you can't apply online, there is also a paper application process.

Employer-specific work permit

If you have an employer-specific work permit, you need to apply to change the work permit if any of the conditions of your job change. This includes:

- Changes in your pay.
- Changes in your responsibilities and/or work performed.
- Taking a different job with the same employer.
- Working for a different employer.

If you have an employer-specific work permit and are subject to unsafe conditions, you're eligible to apply for an open work permit.

You're allowed to stay in Canada while your work permit renewal is processed. You can continue working under the terms of your current work permit, even after it expires. None of the terms of the new work permit apply until the new work permit is approved.

In 2021, the IRCC began allowing some current work permit holders to begin following the terms of their new work permit before it's approved. You can apply online and the IRCC will notify you via email once you're approved to begin following the terms of the new work permit.

Your employer's responsibilities

If your employer had to perform a LMIA to obtain your initial work permit, they'll have to go through the LMIA process again.

They also need to submit an offer of employment and pay the employer compliance fee.

Your responsibilities

You can apply for a new employer specific work permit online. The IRCC has a quiz that will provide you with a custom document checklist. Once you've submitted copies of all of the required documents, you'll instantly be provided with a letter confirming your ability to work under the terms of your current work permit while they process the new work permit.

If you can't apply online, there is also a paper application process.

Getting a bridging open work permit

If you've applied for PR status and your work permit will expire before the IRCC is likely to make a decision, you can apply for a bridging open work permit (BOWP).

In order to be eligible you need to already be living and working in Canada, so you cannot apply from outside of Canada. You also need to be applying for PR through one of these programs:

- Express entry: federal skilled worker program (FSWP), Canadian experience class (CEC), or federal skilled trades program (FSTP)
- Some provincial nominee programs (PNP)
- Quebec skilled worker class (QSWC)
- Caregiver: caring for children class or caring for people with high medical needs class, with an application submitted before June 18, 2019
- Agri-food pilot (AFP)

It's not enough to submit an expression of interest for express entry. You need to have gotten an invitation to apply and have submitted your application.

If you're applying for PR through a provincial program, your BOWP will be restricted to that province.

Spouses aren't included in your BOWP. They'd need to apply for a spousal work permit once your BOWP is approved. Dependent children won't be eligible for a work permit based on your status.

Previously, you had to wait until four months before your work permit expired to apply for a BOWP and couldn't apply if your work permit had already expired. Now you can apply for a BOWP as soon as you apply for PR, even if your work permit is already expired.

You can apply online following the process for an open work permit. The paper application is also available.

Moving out of Canada temporarily

If you're a permanent resident, you're allowed to live outside of Canada temporarily. You don't stop being a resident when you leave Canada, so long as you have status in Canada and maintain ties to Canada. People who've lived in Canada for five years or more are sometimes surprised to hear from the CRA and discover they are still required to file taxes in Canada unless they tell the CRA that they have permanently left Canada. If the CRA doesn't believe you've cut ties permanently, they can still require you to file!

You can apply to renew your PR card and apply for citizenship while living outside of Canada temporarily. However, you need to be able to demonstrate that you have settled in Canada and intend to remain there permanently.

The list of ways to prove that you've left Canada permanently provides guidance as to how to demonstrate that you've established permanent ties in Canada:

- Maintain Canadian chequing, savings, and retirement accounts.

- Continue filing taxes with the CRA.

- Keep your Canadian drivers license.

- Establish and maintain a home. Rent your home on a short-term lease or leave your things in storage to demonstrate your intent to return.

- See if you can maintain provincial health insurance. Provinces have policies for people moving abroad temporarily, often intended primarily for students and applying in this situation.

- Have a job in Canada.

- Be active in community organizations and professional organizations in Canada. If you're working in a licensed profession or a member of a union, maintain your standing.

- Arrange to have a way to receive mail in Canada.

Plan ahead and get creative. If you're renting in Canada and don't want to deal with the hassle of subletting, consider moving into a friend's guestroom for a few months before you go abroad to establish that as a home address in Canada. Talk to someone at your bank to see if they'll waive account fees while you're abroad.

Consider the expiration date on your PR card. You need to be physically in Canada to receive a PR card, as it can only be mailed to an address in Canada and the IRCC may require you pick it up in person.

You need to be in Canada to take the oath of citizenship. You can return to Canada to take the oath and leave the country immediately afterward, assuming you will have the necessary travel documents to return.

Renewing your PR card

I had been warned that it's typical for it to take up to six months to get a new PR card, so I should submit my renewal application early. This was good advice. I submitted my PR card application over six months before it expired. My application was processed and my PR card was issued around when my PR card expired. Then I never got the card. I also didn't get instructions to pick it up in person. The IRCC didn't respond to my inquiries, beyond to say there were delays due to the pandemic. A year later, I still didn't have a valid PR card. A border agent suggested that it had likely gotten lost in the mail.

I finally got a letter from the IRCC saying I needed to appear in person to prove my ties to Canada so they could determine whether I qualified to receive a standard PR card, valid for five years, or one that is only valid for one year. I was unable to attend the meeting and never received a reply to my request to reschedule. A few weeks later I became a citizen, saving me from the hassle of sorting this out.

The vast majority of permanent residents simply mail in their documents and get a new card in the mail a few months later. Thanks to my convoluted experience, I have more information to share.

Potential issues

There are certain circumstances making it more likely that your PR card renewal application will be selected for investigation:

- You don't check "yes" on section F of the application, giving consent for the IRCC to review your tax information.

- If you were granted PR through a PNP and are not living in that province when you renew your PR card.

- If you're working remotely for a foreign company.

- If you don't have a stable address in Canada.

- There are issues with your tax filings.

There's also the possibility that your application will randomly be selected for close scrutiny as part of their quality assurance program.

If this is the case, you'll be required to attend an in-person meeting at your local IRCC office to present original copies of the documents included in your application, as well as provide other information at their request.

The application

In order to apply for a new PR card you have to:

- Have become a PR more than 180 days ago and never received your PR card in the mail.

- Have less than nine months remaining on your current card.

- Certify that your PR card was lost, stolen, damaged, or destroyed.

- Have changed your name and/or gender.

- Need to correct your birth date or another error on your original card.

You need to include:

- The application form (IMM 5444)

- A photocopy of an acceptable ID that includes the document type and number; issue and expiry date; your name; your photo; and your date of birth. An acceptable ID includes:

  o Your current passport

  o The passport you used to enter Canada, including the page showing your passport stamp

  o A certificate of identity or travel document issued by the Minister of Immigration, Refugees and Citizenship Canada or a foreign country

  o If you cannot provide any of these, you can submit a statutory declaration or any identity document issued outside Canada before you came to Canada.

- 2 passport photos taken within six months

- A copy of the receipt showing you paid the application fee

- The document checklist

- Proof of residency requirements (the physical presence calculator)

- Your birth certificate and proof of school records, if you're under 18

- Your biometrics, if you were under 14 when you got your current PR card and you're now over 14

- Legal documents to show you've changed your name, if applicable

- The Request for a Change of Sex or Gender Identifier form (CIT 0404), if applicable

You likely have all of these documents from your initial PR application. Any documents not in English or French must be translated by a certified translator or accompanied by an affidavit. You must include copies of both the original document and the translated version. You cannot translate your own documents and they cannot be translated by your parent, guardian, sibling, spouse, common-law partner, conjugal partner, grandparent, child, aunt, uncle, niece, nephew, or first cousin.

If you have your PR card, you need to include a photocopy. If your PR card is damaged, you need to include the physical card in your application packet. If your PR card has been lost, stolen, destroyed, or you never received it you need to include a solemn declaration (IMM 5451).

They are particular about the photos you submit. I submitted the same photos for my PR card renewal and citizenship application. They were rejected for my PR card and accepted for my citizenship application.

You will need to include information for everywhere you've lived, all jobs you've held, all schools you've attended, and every time you've left Canada in the past five years (or since you became a PR).

At present, the application needs to be printed and mailed to the IRCC.

If you send it by regular mail:

Case Processing Centre — PR Card
P.O. Box 10020
Sydney, NS B1P 7C1
Canada

If you send it by courier:

Case Processing Centre – PR Card
49 Dorchester Street
Sydney, NS
B1P 5Z2

Residency obligations

If you've had PR status for five years or more, you must have been in Canada for at least 730 days in the past five years (1,825 days) to maintain your status. If you have had PR status for less than five years, you need to have been in Canada long enough to show that you could be in Canada for 730 days by the time you've had PR status for five years. If you've had PR status for less than five years you typically only have to prove that you remain eligible to retain your PR status if you've caught the attention of a border agent when re-entering Canada.

In order to apply for a new PR card, you'l need to show that you met (or will meet) all residency requirements. If you can fit all of your trips outside of Canada onto the form, you can fill that in. If not, you can use the PDF form (CIT 0407), the physical presence calculator, or create your own spreadsheet.

If you were in Canada for less than the required time, you'll need to show that you were:

- Accompanying a spouse, common law partner, or parent who is a Canadian citizen, or

- Working full-time for a Canadian business or public service (with a head office in Canada), or accompanying your spouse, common law partner, or parent who was doing so.

The IRCC will also consider "compelling humanitarian and compassionate factors in your individual circumstances"

Urgent processing

You can request urgent processing when you submit your application or through the IRCC webform. If you're requesting urgent processing in your initial application, write "urgent" on the envelope itself.

In order to qualify, you need to show that you have to travel in more than three weeks and less than three months because of work, your own serious illness, or the serious illness or death of a family member.

You need to write a letter explaining why you need urgent processing, along with documents to support your claims, like a letter from your boss, a letter from your doctor, or a death certificate. You need to provide your itinerary and proof that you've booked and paid for the trip.

I work for a US organization and while I work remotely, I typically spend quite a bit of time in the office. My office was closing and I needed to be there in person to oversee this. I submitted documents to request urgent processing. I got a generic response:

"Thank you for contacting Immigration, Refugees and Citizenship Canada (IRCC).

This message is to inform you that we have received your request for the urgent processing of your Permanent Resident Card (PR card).

We regret to inform you that your request cannot be processed urgently at the moment, because the following information is either missing or incomplete:

- *Proof of travel (copy of your plane ticket or itinerary),*
    - *showing your destination and travel dates,*
    - *issued for a future date,*
- *A copy of your receipt showing:*
    - *the full payment on the ticket,*
    - *the amount paid and your payment method,*
- *A letter explaining the reason for the urgency, and*
- *Proof of urgency (e.g. a doctor's note, death certificate, or letter from your employer),*
    - *please include a translation in English or French if your proof of urgency is written in another language.*

We invite you to send us the missing information by filling out the IRCC Web form and choosing Request urgent processing of renewal or replacement card and have already applied located in the drop down menu under the heading Enquiry.

What will happen next?

Usually, it takes us 2 business days to respond. Due to the impacts of COVID-19 however, it may take us longer to respond to your enquiry. We thank you for your patience.

Rest assured that we will make all the necessary efforts to speed up the processing of your application.

Important - Departure date in less than 3 weeks?

If you are travelling in less than 3 weeks, your application does not qualify for urgent processing.

However, we are pleased to inform you that we have a way to accommodate you if you are (or you will be) outside Canada without a valid PR card, and need to return to Canada on a commercial vehicle (e.g., plane, train, boat or bus).

You simply need to obtain a Permanent Resident Travel Document (PRTD) to travel back to Canada following the steps below.

A few useful tips

- If you need to leave Canada before you obtain your PR card, and you:
  - return by private vehicle:
    - you can present documents proving your PR status,
  - return by commercial vehicle (airplane, bus, train, or boat):
    - please apply for a travel document before you return to Canada.
- You can verify the status of your PR card application using the Client Application Status online tool.

We hope the information provided is helpful in assisting you with your enquiry."

No matter what I submitted, they either said my application was incomplete or that it didn't qualify. I contacted my MP, who replied with a polite version of "sucks to be you."

I showed my board of directors the replies I'd gotten from the IRCC and my MP and they opted not to fire me, which I appreciated.

I thought I couldn't reasonably travel from New York to Toronto because I'd have to cross on foot at Niagara Falls and there were no trains, busses, or rental cars at that point in the pandemic. Now I know I could have flown there and back without any issues!

I used to judge Americans who thought they weren't required to follow Canadian immigration rules and who insisted you can still enter Canada showing only your driver's license. The IRCC website makes it very clear that you need to follow the rules and have proper travel documents. This isn't true, though. Those entitled Americans are right – the IRCC doesn't enforce the rules evenly and it's unlikely you will need proper travel documents to re-enter Canada.

Of course, it's still a risk to assume you'll be allowed to re-enter Canada without the required documents. Enforcement can become strict at any point and you may just catch a border agent on a bad day.

Tracking your application

The IRCC will email or mail an acknowledgement of receipt (AoR) when they get your application. There is typically a delay of weeks or months between when the IRCC gets your application (and the package is marked as delivered in your tracking information) and when someone at the IRCC types that information into their system so it generates the AoR.

The online portal

You can check the status of your application online. If you have not yet gotten an AoR, it's likely your application won't show in the system, even if your mail service marks it as delivered.

The information shown in the portal is very limited. It says in process, decision made, or complete.

The processing timeline does not include all communication from the IRCC.

My timeline looked like this:

- We received your application for a permanent resident card on September 22, 2020.

- We sent you correspondence acknowledging receipt of your application(s) on November 24, 2020.

- We started processing your application on November 24, 2020.

- We sent you a letter on November 12, 2021. Please consider delays in mail delivery before contacting us.

They sent me a letter requesting new photos in December 2020. I submitted new photos in January 2021. My application status switched to "decision made" in February 2021. After I reached out through the webform, they confirmed receipt of the photos in March 2021. None of this was shown on the timeline. The letter they sent was actually an email.

The limited status information isn't necessarily accurate in terms of how we would make sense of the information. The national office made a decision and created a new PR card for me in February, when my current card was set to expire. They then sent it to the local IRCC office to send it to me. The local IRCC office determined that they needed more information before deciding whether the new card should be issued to me or sent back to the national IRCC office. The notice in November 2021 was a request for me to attend an in-person interview. An interview is something I would have assumed happens during the "in processing" stage of the application, not months after the decision has been made.

Decision made

The online portal states that "decision made" means a decision has been made.

"Your application will be either approved or rejected. You will be informed of the decision.

If your application is approved, you will be notified by mail within four weeks and invited to pick up your card at the IRCC office closest to you.

If your application is rejected, you will be notified of the decision by mail."

Other people said they received their new PR card in the mail a few weeks after their status changed in the portal. No one reported they'd received instructions on how to pick their PR card up at an IRCC office; everyone said it had been mailed to them. There wasn't an obvious pattern to how long it took to arrive.

I contacted the IRCC through the webform again in the summer to let them know I had never received the card or a letter with instructions for pickup. I got a generic response. I'd met all of my residency requirements and submitted the required paperwork, so I figured there was a backlog and the card would show up soon.

Of course, the IRCC website has a limit for how long they'll hold a card at your local IRCC office, so it was a little troubling as it got closer to 180 days since my application status had changed to "decision made":

"Your permanent resident card will be canceled if you do not pick it up within 180 days of receiving your first notice. You will need to submit a new application."

Then I was invited to take the citizenship exam. I thought maybe my PR card had been put on hold because I'd soon be a citizen. A border guard said they were separate and suggested that my PR card had likely been lost in the mail. I contacted the IRCC asking if my PR card had been mailed out and got no response.

Then I got an email from my local IRCC office saying I was required to appear in-person in ten days. In my case, "decision made" meant no decision had been made. While the portal said I had a certain number of days to pick up my PR card or I would have to start over, my file was sitting untouched for ten months.

I was traveling within Canada at the time, so I replied to them saying I could not attend the meeting and providing them with the date I would return to Toronto. I did not get a response. At this point I wasn't particularly concerned, since I was used to not getting a response and I had a date scheduled to take my oath of citizenship.

At my citizenship ceremony I was told I needed to submit a solemn declaration saying I had never received my PR card, since their records indicated it had been issued to me in February 2021. This was despite the letter I had from November 2021 clearly stating the card was at another IRCC office. The form was simple to complete and did not hold up the ceremony.

Review appointment

You may be required to attend an in-person meeting at the IRCC office processing your application. If this is the case, you'll get an email from the IRCC assigning you an appointment time. If you are unable to attend the meeting, you can request they reschedule it. The email will include a list of requested documents to bring with you.

The one-year card

You may be given a PR card that is only valid for one year, rather than five. These are known as limited mobility PR cards and mean your status is under review. This is given in instances where they are not convinced that you have met the requirements to retain your PR status.

Traveling without a valid PR card

If your PR card is expired or you don't have a PR card and you are a US citizen or permanent resident, you are unlikely to have any issues reentering Canada. You can provide alternative documents to prove your residency status and they will look you up in the system.

If you aren't a US citizen or greencard holder, you can fly into the US and enter Canada through a land border. While ostensibly you need to enter Canada on foot or a private vehicle, this depends on your tolerance for risk. People report having no issue entering Canada with expired PR cards when taking the train, bus, and ferry.

You can also fly to Canada and hope no one looks at the expiration date on your PR card before you board the plane. If you don't have a PR card you will need to have a US passport. They won't allow you to board the flight without an eTA or a US passport.

While the border agent will see that your PR card itself is expired, that's separate from whether or not you still have PR status. They are much more concerned with your status than the expiration date of your card. You may get a lecture on the importance of having a valid PR card. I had my AoR letters on hand when I crossed the border and a printout showing my oath of citizenship ceremony had been scheduled. I never took the papers out of my bag since the agent didn't even mention that my card was expired. Because of the pandemic far more people than usual have expired documents and the border agents are aware that there's a huge backlog.

If you cannot enter Canada through the US, don't leave Canada with an expired PR card. Be very careful that it's never lost or stolen when you're out of the country. If this is the case, you'll have to follow the rules and apply for permanent resident travel documents (PRTD) to re-enter Canada once you leave.

Permanent resident travel documents

The IRCC website advises people with expired PR cards who are outside of Canada that they need to obtain permanent resident travel documents (PRTD) in order to enter Canada.

I assumed this would be a simple process. I've known people who've lost their passport and still caught their scheduled flight home. That is not how PRTDs work. While the IRCC website says PRTDs are for anyone with Canadian PR who is outside of the country with a valid PR card, it's clearly for people who have moved elsewhere and are looking to reclaim their PR status.

The application

I compiled five years of utility bills, bank statements, and other documents showing that I really do live in Canada. I got more photos taken, carefully following their specifications. I accounted for where I was every day I was in Canada. I was hoping I could recycle the physical presence documents from my citizenship application, but that is an accounting of every day I was *outside of* Canada. I paid my fee and submitted it.

Theoretically, I would have gotten an email approving my application and providing instructions for me to mail them my passport or bring it in person to a Canadian Visa Application Center (VAC). They would add the PRTD, which is a counterfoil on the passport, and return it to me.

Instead, I got a confirmation email saying they were only responding to inquiries from people in war zones. This email included a set of instructions that was different from the instructions on the IRCC website. It also said repeat submissions would be ignored.

Notably, while the instructions on the IRCC required you to show proof of booked travel arrangements, these instructions said not to book any travel until they provided you with PRTD.

The alternate instructions

Here are the instructions that were emailed to me:

DUE TO HIGH VOLUMES, REPEAT ENQUIRIES WILL NOT BE ANSWERED.

1.   If you are not in possession of a valid Permanent Resident Card, you must apply for Permanent Resident Travel Document (PRTD) to return to Canada. Normally, you apply for a PRTD at a visa application centre (VAC). Due to COVID-19, many VACs are closed or offering limited services.

a.   Check if your VAC is open and accepting PRTD applications before you apply. If your VAC is open and accepting applications, find out how to apply for a PRTD through the VAC.

b.   You can submit your application for a PRTD by email ONLY if your VAC is closed and/or unable to accept PRTD applications.

2.   If your VAC is closed and/or unable to accept PRTD applications, you can apply for a PRTD by email:

a.   Read the instruction guide to make sure you prepare a complete application.

b.   You must submit ALL required documents in the Document Checklist.

i.   Electronic copies (scans) must be in one of the following formats: PDF, JPG, TIFF, PNG, DOC or DOCX.

ii.   Ensure that each document does not exceed the 5MB size limit.

c.   Complete, sign and scan the Application for a Permanent Resident Travel Document (IMM 5524) form.

d.   To avoid processing delays please ensure that:

i.   Your passport is valid for at least 6 months.

ii.   You submit an electronic copy of all pages of your passport(s) used in the last 5 years (including blank pages).

iii.   You submit proof of residency in Canada (see Document Checklist)

e.   If you are using a Representative, you must submit a signed Use of a Representative form (IMM 5476).

f.   If your PR card was lost or stolen you must submit a Solemn Declaration (IMM5451) form with your submission.

g.   To pay your $50 PRTD fee click on this link and provide a copy of the receipt.

i.   Select your country of residence

ii.   Select: Permanent Residence

iii.   Select: Permanent resident Travel Document'

h.   Send the scanned copy of your application package by email:

o   In the subject line, put: "PRTD application: (your name)"

o   Send   to: IRCC.COVIDPRTD-TVRPCOVID.IRCC@cic.gc.ca   (this inbox)

o   Find out what to do if your documents are too large

3.   Due to the impacts of coronavirus disease (COVID-19), we can't

- *Process applications normally*
- *Provide accurate processing times*

Once a decision has been made on your application, you will be notified by e-mail how/where to submit your passport.

Please do not book your travel to Canada until after you have received your passport with your PRTD sticker.

If you have already submitted an incomplete request, or have made a mistake in your submission, but meet the above criteria, please resend all required documents and information in a single email.

If you still need assistance, you may submit your question(s) through our webform at https://secure.cic.gc.ca/enquiries-renseignements/canada-case-cas-eng.aspx. Note: If you are submitting your question via the webform and do not know your UCI, you may enter 00000000 in the webform UCI field."

I concluded that I was not going to get PRTDs any time soon, if ever, and made arrangements to cross the border on foot at Niagara Falls.

A few days later I got an email from the IRCC saying my application was incomplete because I didn't provide my address outside of Canada. I replied asking for guidance, noting that I had not moved out of Canada and thus didn't have an address outside of Canada, aside from the itinerary for the trip I was currently on.

They replied six weeks later, saying if I did not have an address I should simply list the country in section 12B. By then I was already back in Canada.

Thankfully, there was a reason no other Canadian permanent residents had any idea what a PRTD is. That reason is that you almost certainly don't need one to return to Canada with an expired PR card or without a PR card.

Private travel

If you are crossing from the US into Canada on foot or in a private vehicle, you will have no problem entering Canada with an expired PR card. What matters is whether you have maintained your PR status, which is different from the validity of your PR card.

I had been warned to expect a lecture from the border agent for allowing my documents to expire. When I walked across the border at Niagara Falls the border agent didn't even mention it.

Flights, trains, busses, and other commercial travel

Officially, if you are a Canadian resident or citizen, you must use documents showing that status to enter the country. Canadian residents and citizens aren't supposed to get an electronic travel authorization (eTA) to enter Canada. Commercial transit companies will not let you board without showing an eTA and/or a valid travel document to enter Canada.

If you are a US citizen, you don't need an eTA. This makes it possible to board your flight/train/bus/ship using your US documents. When you are at the border you can present your expired Canadian PR card or other documents to confirm your identity. The border agents will then be able to pull up your information in their database and confirm your status.

If you have an expired PR card, it's likely you'll be able to board your flight/train/bus/ship without anyone noticing that your PR card is expired.

Using NEXUS

Officially, if you are entering Canada using your NEXUS card, you are supposed to have a valid PR card ready to present. When entering Canada on the bus or train I have always been asked to show my PR card. Having an expired PR card was not an issue.

Becoming a citizen

By the time your first PR card is close to expiring, it's likely you qualify to apply for citizenship. Some people choose to apply for citizenship as soon as they qualify, while others maintain their PR status for decades.

What it means to change your status

The most obvious reason to become a Canadian citizen is so you can vote. Even if you're not particularly interested in politics, there are other reasons to become a citizen.

Some jobs require you to be a citizen. If this is the case, you qualify for expedited processing of your citizenship application.

As a Canadian citizen, you have the right to come and go from the country at will. Canada was quite reasonable during the pandemic in regards to allowing permanent residents and temporary workers to travel, but that was at the discretion of politicians and border agents.

If you're from a country that has a less powerful passport and you like to travel, you're probably eager to get that Canadian passport.

The children of Canadian citizens are automatically Canadian, even if they're born abroad.

It's possible to lose your PR status. It's very difficult to lose your citizenship. If you are living outside of Canada for more than three years you'll most likely lose your PR status. Citizens always have the right to return to Canada.

Dual citizenship

If you become a citizen of Canada, will you lose your current citizenship? Maybe.

Canada allows you to keep your existing citizenship, but not all countries allow you to retain multiple passports. The US makes it very difficult to give up your citizenship.

Countries that allow dual or multiple citizenship include: Argentina, Australia, Bangladesh, Belgium, Belize, Brazil, Chile, Colombia, Cyprus, Denmark, Dominica, Ecuador, El Salvador, Fiji, Finland, France, Greece, Grenada, Hungary, Iceland, Iran, Iraq, Ireland, Israel, Italy, Jordan, Kenya, Latvia, Lebanon, Macedonia, Malta, Mexico, Montenegro, New Zealand, Peru, Philippines, Poland, Portugal, Romania, Russia, Serbia, Sri Lanka, St. Kitts & Nevis, Sweden, Switzerland, Syria, Thailand, Turkey, the UK, the USA, Vietnam, and Western Samoa.

Countries that do not allow dual or multiple citizenship include: Austria, Azerbaijan, Brunei, China, Germany, India, Indonesia, Japan, Nepal, the Netherlands, Norway, Saudi Arabia, Singapore, and Venezuela.

Each country has specific requirements and requirements can be quite complex. You should check the specifics for your country before applying for Canadian citizenship. Some countries only allow dual citizenship if acquired at birth or under special circumstances.

If you aren't sure if your current nationality allows you to be a dual citizen, contact your consulate or embassy.

Eligibility for citizenship

In order to apply to become a citizen of Canada, you must be:

- 18 years old or older (or your parent must file for you)
- Speak English and/or French
- A current permanent resident of Canada
- Have been physically present in Canada for 1,460 days during the last six years (unless you're under 18) and for at least 183 days during four of those six years
- Have filed and paid all applicable taxes as a Canadian resident
- Plan to continue living in Canada
- Understand the rights, responsibilities, and privileges of citizenship
- Understand Canada's history, values, institutions, and symbols
- Are not currently facing charges, on trial, in prison, on parole, or on probation, nor have been for the past four years

There are some reasons why you might be ineligible, but they're pretty unlikely to apply if you haven't committed immigration fraud or war crimes.

If you are a permanent resident with children who are also permanent residents, you can submit their applications for citizenship at the same time as yours or after you have become a citizen.

Calculating your physical presence

In order for a day to count, you must have been a Canadian permanent resident at the time.

Remember, there are two parts to the requirement:

- 1,460 days in the 6 years before your application

- At least 183 days in each of 4 of those 6 years

If you landed in Canada as a permanent resident before July, the soonest you could apply would be in four years. If you landed in July or later, you would not have spent six months of each of the four calendar years in Canada and would have to wait slightly longer.

The days you leave and return from a trip abroad both count, since you're physically in Canada for at least part of each day. You are still required to report any time you leave the country, even if you leave and come back the same day. If you cross the border frequently this will be an onerous task, but it's a required part of the application.

You don't need to get your history of entries from the Canada Border Services Agency (CBSA). You're advised to give permission to the IRCC to do so. The IRCC will look at your CBSA records to verify your information. Government departments can't share your personal information without your permission. However, this information is required for your application. If you do not give permission on your application, you'll likely be asked to provide additional information and your application may take longer than usual.

If you or your spouse (or common-law partner) were stationed abroad with the Canadian Armed Forces, federal public administration, or public service of a province or territory, that time counts as being present in Canada.

Time spent in prison or on parole does not count toward the 1,460 days. If you were convicted of a crime, time on probation does not count either.

The IRCC provides a physical presence calculator to help you figure out when you'll be eligible. You can register for an account to keep track of your days as you go. You can then provide this information with your citizenship application, instead of filling out the calculate physical presence form (CIT 0407). The date on your readout from the physical presence calculator must match the date on your application. The IRCC prefers the readout from the calculator to the paper form.

Language requirements

Canada requires that you have an adequate knowledge of English or French in order to become a citizen if you're between the ages of 14 and 64. You'll need to prove that you meet a level 4 or higher on the CLB/NCLC and potentially to talk to an immigration officer during an interview.

You don't need to be fluent in English or French to meet the language requirements. You merely need to be conversational. You can prove this by supplying results from an approved language test, a diploma from a college or university program in English or French, or proof that you completed a government-funded language program. Private language classes do not count as proof.

The CIC is very specific about the documents they'll accept. If you took a language test for your permanent residence application (such as for express entry), that counts as proof of your language proficiency and does not expire.

How long does it take to become a citizen?

You can check the current processing times for citizenship online. Prior to the pandemic, it took about 12 months for new citizenship applications to be processed. The IRCC had announced that it was working on eliminating their application backlog and reducing application processing times. I was surprised at how quickly my citizenship application was processed during the pandemic, since I'd assumed I'd essentially mailed my application to a black hole. I had a citizenship certificate in my hands 17 months after I mailed in my application.

If you do not give the CIC permission to request your CBSA records, do not pass the citizenship test, or are required to provide additional information, your application will take longer to process.

If you've served in the Canadian Armed Forces, you can apply through a fast-track process. You'll be eligible to apply for citizenship after serving in the CAF, and filing your taxes, for three years.

The application

There are three types of citizenship applications:

- Adults
- Minors
- Canadian Armed Forces

Along with your application, you'll need:

- PR card or Record of landing (IMM 1000) or Confirmation of PR (IMM 529 or 5688)
- Proof you speak English or French (unless you are under 14 or over 64)
  - Results of an accepted third-party test
  - Proof of a secondary or post-secondary program in French or English
  - Proof of CLB/NCLC level 4 or higher
- Passport pages with your name, photo, passport number, issue date, and expiration date
- 2 pieces of personal identification:
  - Canadian drivers license
  - Canadian health insurance card
  - Copy of your passport or travel document

- 2 identical photos taken within 6 months (original required)

- Your physical presence calculator record or CIT 0407 form: a record of the days you were or were not in Canada for the past 6 years or since you became a permanent resident (whichever is shorter) (original required)

- Police certificates for any country, other than Canada, where you spent six months or more during the 4 years immediately before your application (original required)

- To pay the fees online

Review the official document checklist before submitting your application. Do not submit original documents with your application unless specifically requested. Clear photocopies of both sides are sufficient for most documents. You'll need to bring the original documents with you when you take the citizenship test and attend the citizenship ceremony.

Bring along the specifications for the photos and provide them to your photographer. If they reject your photos they'll notify you by mail, giving you 30 days to resubmit. This will delay your application.

If you've had multiple passports in the past six years (or since you became a PR), include photocopies of all of them. If you have a gap of time between passports or lost a passport, you'll need to attach an explanation.

Any documents that aren't in English or French need to be translated by an approved translator.

You may also need to provide documents to prove your name has been changed, your sex designation has changed, or if the date of your birth has been corrected.

You must write in "N/A" for any question that is not applicable. Every answer field must have a response.

Don't forget to sign and date the application. The date on your physical presence document must match the date on your application.

You can submit your application online or on paper. If you mail paper applications in one envelope, they'll be processed together. If you send multiple applications together and one is incomplete, they will all be returned to you.

Cost

- Adult: $630 ($530 grant of citizenship + $100 right of citizenship)
- Child: $100

If you need to submit police certificates, request a university transcript, take a language test, or have documents translated, you will be responsible for those costs as well.

Digitization & COVID-19

The citizenship application process is currently being moved online. As of August 2021, single adults living in Canada and filing on their own behalf can apply online. By the end of 2022 the online application will be available to families, minors, people living outside of Canada as a crown servant or family member, and people working with an immigration consultant or attorney.

Based on the transition from paper to online applications with other programs, it's advisable to wait until you can apply online. When express entry and spousal sponsorship went online, online applications were processed so quickly that they were approved within three to nine months, while the backlog of paper applications still took two to three years to resolve.

I became eligible to apply for citizenship during the summer of 2020, when the IRCC was operating with a skeleton crew and citizenship ceremonies were on hold indefinitely. Prior to the pandemic, citizenship applications took a year to process. I mailed my application in September, assuming it would take at least twice that long.

It was the end of February 2021 when I got a letter acknowledging that they'd received my application. I was invited to take the citizenship test online in June 2021. I was assigned a date to take the oath of citizenship in August 2021. I became a citizen in January 2022. This isn't necessarily representative, as the amount of time applications take to process and the order in which sections of the application were processed appeared to be random during the time I was paying close attention in 2020 and 2021.

Waiting for your application to be processed

You can check your application status online.

Technically, you should contact the IRCC if you change your address, are going to leave Canada for more than two weeks in a row, if you are charged with a crime, or if you don't get confirmation that your application was received.

Traveling outside of Canada

You can leave Canada while your citizenship application is being processed. However, you still need to meet your residency obligations as a permanent resident. Make sure someone will be checking your mail, since the IRCC won't mail things abroad. Most communication is coming through email or the portal, but they still occasionally send physical letters.

You will need to be in Canada for any appointments with the IRCC, including your citizenship test, interview, and ceremony. If you can't make an appointment, you'll need to contact the IRCC immediately and let them know why.

Application updates

You'll hear from the CIC when:

- They've received your application
- They require additional information
- Your interview is scheduled
- Your citizenship test is scheduled
- If you need to attend a hearing with a citizenship officer
- Your application is approved or denied
- Your citizenship ceremony is scheduled

First, the Case Processing Centre will check to make sure you met the minimum requirements, included all required documents, and paid the fees. If it's complete, you'll get an acknowledgement of receipt (AoR) and the citizenship study guide. If not, it will be returned to you.

If the CIC requests additional information and you don't respond, your application will be closed.

Citizenship application tracker

The IRCC has two ways to track your citizenship application: the main portal that also shows your application for all IRCC processes and the citizenship application tracker (CAT). Neither provides email updates, so it's best to check them occasionally. The IRCC will occasionally physically mail documents and this will not be reflected in either tracker, nor are copies of those documents available online.

It was a complete surprise when I got an email in June of 2021 from the IRCC inviting me to take my citizenship test online within the next 21 days. None of the sections in my application had been marked as complete when I'd last looked. After getting the email I saw that none of them were complete, although now the citizenship test indicated it was waiting on me. Don't assume the steps will be done in order or that the citizenship exam will be the final step before your oath is scheduled.

Oath scheduled

When the CAT shows you've been scheduled to take the oath, it gives inaccurate information. It says:

"Follow the instructions we sent to you for information on:

- *how to attend the ceremony*
- *what documents you have to present*

The notice you'll receive is the official confirmation of the appointment. If you haven't received the notice by the date of the scheduled appointment, contact us."

They have not sent you any information yet. They'll send this information a few days before the ceremony, even if they assign you a date months in advance. I got my invitation seven days ahead of time. Many other people reported getting it 48 hours ahead of the ceremony.

Given that the webform typically results in a delayed response or no response at all, you're a brave soul if you follow their instructions and wait until the date of the scheduled appointment before reaching out to the IRCC.

The citizenship test

Anyone applying for citizenship between the ages of 14 and 64 must take the citizenship test. All of the information you need to know is in the Discover Canada study guide [PDF // MP3]. Theoretically they'll mail you a paper copy after you submit your application, although I never received one. You can also view sample questions. Their study guide is the only official study guide. The IRCC advises you against using third party materials to prepare for the citizenship test.

You have 30 minutes to answer 20 multiple choice questions. A passing score is 15 correct answers.

I hadn't bothered to start studying for the citizenship test when I was invited to take it, since I assumed I'd have another year before I heard anything. I took a couple of practice tests online, which varied considerably in the level of detail. Some asked general questions about civics and history. Having vaguely followed the news, read several books on Canadian history, and gone to plenty of museums in Canada, I passed these with no problem.

Other practice tests reminded me of why I didn't enjoy history classes until college. They asked about arcane details. They were written to be intentionally confusing. They'd ask me to choose the correct name or year. More concerningly, some were outdated (specifically with the number of ridings and names of current politicians) or outright wrong. These practice tests had me worried. They weren't random sites from the internet, they were sites recommended by the Toronto Public Library that said they were funded by the IRCC.

So, I crammed. I read through the Discover Canada booklet the IRCC provides as a study guide, taking careful notes. I rewrote my notes, organizing them into a timeline, a list of notable people, and grouping them geographically. I went through the study guide at Citizenship Counts.

Absolutely none of that was necessary. I would have gotten a perfect score even if I hadn't studied, because I'm a bit of a history nerd. Names were given in context. They asked about broad historical periods, rather than specific dates. This isn't designed to trick you.

Taking the test in person

If you're taking the test in person, the test may be written or oral. You'll need to bring the original copies of any documents you submitted with your application and your passport with you when you take the test.

You'll be told right away if you've passed the test or not.

Assuming you've passed, they'll either tell you when and where your citizenship ceremony will be right then after you've taken the test or they'll send you a letter. The citizenship test will generally take place within six months.

If you don't pass, they'll schedule you for a second test, usually in four to eight weeks. If you don't pass the second test, they'll bring you in for an interview with an immigration officer. This interview will give you 30 to 90 minutes to demonstrate that you meet the citizenship requirements.

Taking the test online

The process of taking the test online was simple. The IRCC's email included a PDF with instructions, which said a lot about the process of taking the test. They bury the lede about how to actually access the test online so you can take it. They do include a link to the IRCC page that has information on taking the test, which invites you to sign in at the bottom. You sign in using your application number and UCI, which is on the PDF they provided, as well as on the AoR letter.

There's no need to schedule a time to take the test. Once you login and request the test, you need to take it then. You do want to check the technical requirements ahead of time to make sure your browser is compatible. You'll need a private, well-lit place to take the test. You'll also need a stable internet connection.

You can sign in at any time during the 21-day window they assign you. When you sign in, you'll check a dozen boxes agreeing to various terms. Then you use your webcam to take a picture of your ID. I photographed my expired PR card, which they indicated was acceptable. I then took a picture of myself with my webcam. Then I requested a link to take the test.

An email with the link appeared in my inbox right away. It's automatically sent to the email address they have on file for you, so if you're applying through a representative it'll go to them. The link expires after 15 minutes.

The link took me to a page where I signed in again, using my application number and UCI. Then I was in the test. The timer started immediately. There is a little video feed from your webcam in the lower right corner.

The questions were not full of trivial details only a historian would care about. They stuck with key historic moments, like confederation. The questions and answers were worded clearly. Dates and names were presented in context. The civics questions seemed like things you'd want to know before voting, if you have any faith in democracy.

To be frank, the hardest part of the test was getting a picture of my ID using the webcam.

Once you submit your test, they show your score. You can print or screenshot this page for your records. This isn't an official score, since a person will review the photos of your ID, you, and the video feed of you taking the test to make sure nothing fishy was going on.

Some people who take the test online will get a follow-up email from the IRCC requiring you to attend a virtual meeting for a "citizenship knowledge test and/or verification of identity documents." People appear to be selected at random for this step.

The IRCC likely will not give you a more specific reason for the meeting or information on how to prepare. They may want to verify your documents, your language skills, or confirm that you passed and give you the date of your oath of citizenship ceremony.

It's advisable to have the documents you've included in your application and anything else you believe will support your eligibility for citizenship with you when you login to the meeting.

If you aren't invited to take the oath

If your application is denied, you can reapply. You can re-apply right away if it was denied because of missing paperwork, a missed appointment, etc, so long as you still meet the requirements.

If your application was denied, your application was closed, or you withdrew it after they began processing it, your fees will not be refunded.

The citizenship ceremony

The final step to becoming a Canadian citizen is the citizenship ceremony. If you don't attend the ceremony, you don't become a citizen and your application will be closed.

In-person ceremonies

In-person ceremonies are often hosted by community groups and they take place at various times throughout the year all around the country. The ceremony is presided over by a citizenship judge. You'll take the oath of Citizenship and get your citizenship certificate at that time.

The oath of citizenship entails affirming your allegiance to the Queen, observing the laws of Canada, and fulfilling your duties as a citizen.

Anyone over the age of 14 must attend the ceremony. Children don't have to go, although it's encouraged. You must bring all of your original immigration documents with you, including your PR card and your landing papers. If you'd like to take the oath over a holy book, you're asked to bring your book with you.

If you'd like to attend a citizenship ceremony, some are open to the public. When you attend your citizenship ceremony you can bring your family and friends to celebrate.

Virtual ceremonies

When the CAT is updated to show that you've been approved for citizenship, it will indicate the date of your oath ceremony. If you don't get your promised invitation, it's likely that you've been assigned to participate in a virtual ceremony. The CAT doesn't indicate if the ceremony is virtual or in-person. It also doesn't provide the time of the ceremony.

The invitation will be emailed to you no more than a week before the ceremony, sometimes only the day before. This means you will not know the time of the ceremony until a day or a few days before. My ceremony started at 8:30 am and lasted an hour. Supposedly it can take up to three hours.

You need to be physically in Canada to attend the ceremony. I've heard that people have been able to get permission to attend the ceremony from outside of Canada. You can also reschedule the ceremony for a time when you'll be within Canada, which can delay your becoming a citizen by several months.

You're supposed to login from a quiet place with a plain background. A few people, including both the IRCC agent and the judge, had Canadian flags in the background. You can sit throughout the ceremony, including during the oath, if that's more comfortable for you or easier for your camera setup.

You're asked to dress "respectfully" for the ceremony. Most people wore red shirts so I felt very conspicuous in my green sweater. Face coverings of any kind will need to be removed briefly in a private breakout room for identification purposes and can be worn the rest of the time. Your head and shoulders need to be visible.

They ask you to minimize any movement of the camera, so if you're using a phone or tablet use a stand or prop it up securely. Given the length of the video call, you may want to make sure you can plug in your device so your battery doesn't die.

You'll need to present your PR card (which can be expired) or your CoPR. You're required to cut up your PR card, if you have it, so you'll need a pair of good scissors. If you don't have a PR card, let them know ahead of time and they'll have you sign an affidavit. Adults will also need two pieces of ID, typically your drivers license and your passport. If you'd like to swear the oath on a holy book, have it ready to go.

The invitation

Since the invitation is sent out immediately before the ceremony, it's hard to know what to expect. Here are the instructions for the online citizenship ceremony as of January 2022:

NOTICE TO APPEAR: To Take the Oath of Citizenship by Video

Immigration, Refugees and Citizenship Canada (IRCC) is pleased to invite you to take the Oath of Citizenship.

To complete all requirements for Canadian citizenship, you are required to recite the Oath of Citizenship before an authorized official.

The Oath will be administered by video using Zoom on:

[Date, time, ceremony language, and zoom link go here]

1. *If you cannot take the oath at this date and time, send a message to this e-mail address as soon as you receive this invitation in order that we reschedule your ceremony. You (and any family member associated to your application) will be asked to cut up your Permanent Resident card(s) during the ceremony with an employee. If you need to travel urgently and will require your Permanent Resident card to return to Canada, contact us as soon as possible with details. Please be aware that we may not be able to process your request urgently; you may wish to postpone your citizenship ceremony*

temporarily. Also read the "Information about Passports" below.

2. By participating in this video oath ceremony, you are consenting to the use of your image on a third- party application (Zoom) for the purpose of administering the Oath of Citizenship by video. You also give permission to allow IRCC to take photographs, video and/or sound recording during the video oath ceremony of yourself, your minor* child(ren), if applicable, and any minor* child(ren) for whom you have also made an application, to release or use them in its future electronic or printed communications products (at any time, without compensation or notice). The images will be the exclusive property of the Government of Canada. Photographs, video and/or sound recording of the video oath ceremony may be taken by media or may be shared with media by the Government of Canada. By participating, you give permission to the Government of Canada to share your images taken during the video oath ceremony with media and to have your name(s) printed by any media. If you do not consent to these uses, contact us as soon as possible. *A minor child is a child who is under the age of 18 years.

3. By participating in this video oath ceremony, you confirm that you, and any family members associated to your application, will be taking the Oath of citizenship in Canada. If you are not currently in Canada, contact us as soon as possible in order for us to reschedule your ceremony.

4. If you cannot take the oath, i.e. you are not available at this date and time due to work, health, travel, or other reasons; you do not have the video/internet capability; you are physically unable or require accommodation; prefer an in-person ceremony; etc., contact us as soon as you receive this invitation with an explanation in order to be

rescheduled or to postpone - NOTE: a request for an in-person ceremony will result in delays in processing of your application. In your reply, change the e-mail subject line accordingly, i.e. Ceremony - New date/time needed, Ceremony - No equipment/Internet, etc. Pursuant to paragraph 13.2(1)(b) of the Citizenship Act, if you cannot appear and take the Oath at the date, and time indicated at the top of page 1, you must contact IRCC within thirty (30) days of the date of your appointment and provide a reasonable explanation for not attending. If you do *not* contact IRCC or if your explanation is not acceptable, your application could be delayed and you will receive a final notice to appear.

5. Canadian citizenship shall not be granted or the Oath of Citizenship shall not be taken in certain circumstances. These circumstances are based on when your citizenship application was signed. Visit our website at www.cic.gc.ca/english/citizenship/situations.asp to review details about the circumstances which could prevent you from becoming a Canadian citizen. It is your responsibility to review the circumstances described on our website and if you think any of these circumstances apply to you, you must inform IRCC on or before the day of your video appearance. Citizenship may be revoked if it has been obtained by false representation, fraud or by knowingly concealing material circumstances.

6. If you have special needs, e.g. hearing or vision impaired (and require an American Sign Language [ASL] or Quebec Sign Language [LSQ] Interpreter), please let us know by contacting us as soon as possible.

7. The video oath ceremony will take place in the official language of service indicated by you on the application form. If you have not been invited to a bilingual ceremony, and you (or your guests attending in the background)

would prefer to participate in a bilingual ceremony, contact us as soon as possible.

8. If your Permanent resident card was lost, stolen, destroyed or never received, contact us as soon as possible, complete a Solemn Declaration form and return it to us at this e-mail address immediately (and not at the Sydney, Nova Scotia address listed on the website).

Information about the video oath ceremony

A citizenship ceremony is a dignified and meaningful event. Most video oath ceremonies include multiple candidates. Conversation should remain respectful. Family and friends may be present in the room with you, however, they should not be disruptive.

A Presiding official and Clerk of the Ceremony from IRCC will oversee the video ceremony and administer the oath. The ceremony will last up to 2 hours and 30 min - there are 3 steps involved: the registration (in private), the video oath ceremony itself (speeches, oath taking, etc.) and the post-ceremony instructions.

A person aged fourteen (14) or older who is granted Canadian citizenship must take the Oath of Citizenship to become a Canadian citizen. Children under 14 years of age are welcome but not required to take the oath. A minor child must be accompanied by the parent/guardian who submitted/signed the application on their behalf.

Situations may arise where, due to circumstances outside of the control of IRCC, we are not able to proceed with this video oath ceremony as scheduled. Should this happen, we will communicate with you regarding an alternate video oath ceremony date/time.

Information about passports

Before applying for a passport or other government services, you will require your citizenship certificate.

It may take up to approximately 2 to 4 weeks to receive your certificate, and additional time will be required for you to apply for and receive your Canadian passport. You shouldn't finalize any travel plans until you get your citizenship certificate and then your passport. For up-to-date passport information, please consult the Coronavirus disease (COVID-19): Passports and travel documents webpage, as there may be delays.

[Contact email]

We look forward to your attendance on this very special occasion!

Regards,

Immigration, Refugees and Citizenship Canada

Steps to take BEFORE the video oath ceremony

Preparing a few days before the video oath ceremony

1. *Review the information available at www.cic.gc.ca/english/citizenship/cit-ceremony.asp to learn more about the sequence of events during a citizenship ceremony and how to prepare, i.e. practice wording of the National anthem. NOTE: Not all ceremonies are the same; the format or some steps may be different due to the pandemic.*

2. *Determine how you will sign the Oath or Affirmation of Citizenship form (at the end of this message) - you can choose to:*

a) *Print the form in advance, then sign it on paper after the ceremony - DO NOT SIGN THE OATH PORTION OF THIS FORM BEFORE TAKING THE OATH. OR;*

b) *Sign the form electronically after the ceremony (using the instructions below).*

NOTE: This form must be signed by you on the same day you recite the Oath, AFTER the Oath has been taken; it confirms the Oath has been recited and the effective date of Canadian citizenship. Each family members associated to your application must have their own form.

3. *Read the document below called "Checklist - Things you will need DURING the video oath ceremony" and ensure you have all of the documents/objects needed for your video oath ceremony.*

4. *Ensure you have the proper equipment to participate in a video oath ceremony. Try Zoom with family or friends in advance, if possible. If you know how, change your Zoom screen name to show your seat number.*

- *Internet, audio and video capability: Ensure that you have reliable access to the Internet with either a*
- *computer, tablet or cellular phone with both audio and video capability.*
- *Computer: Only the following web browsers are supported by Zoom: Internet Explorer, Microsoft Edge, Google Chrome and Mozilla Firefox.*
- *Tablet/Cellular Phone: Download the Zoom application from your corresponding application store. For iOS devices (i.e. iPhones and iPads), this will be available through the Apple App Store. For Android devices (Samsung, Huawei, HTC, etc.), this will be available through the Google Play Store.*

5. *Practice saying the Oath of Citizenship in advance by using these videos. During your video oath ceremony, you will be repeating the Oath of Citizenship after the presiding official in the official language of your choice, and encouraged to do so in both official languages.*

English:
https://www.canada.ca/en/immigration-refugees-citizenship/news/video/oath-citizenship.html

French:
https://www.canada.ca/fr/immigration-refugies-citoyennete/nouvelles/video/serment-citoyennete.html

Preparing on the day of the video oath ceremony

1. *Ensure your device is fully charged.*

2. *Appear on the same device as your family members, if applicable and possible.*

3. *Please dress respectfully for the video oath ceremony. You can wear traditional or religious dress and head coverings, however, avoid wearing a casual hat. You can wear headphones if you wish.*

4. *Sit in an area/room free of noises and disruptions (turn off volume of your telephone/cellular). You can sit for the duration of the ceremony, even during the Oath taking.*

5. *Choose an area with a plain background. Do not use Zoom "virtual backgrounds". You can display Canadian items or red and white colours, if you want to.*

6. *Adjust your camera or device (computer, tablet or mobile phone) in order to be in the line of sight (your head and shoulders should be seen on screen). Stabilize your handheld devices so they don't fall.*

7. *Take out the documents/objects listed in the "Checklist - Things you will need for the video oath ceremony".*

8. *Be prepared to show personal identification on screen for identification purposes. If you wear a face covering, you will be asked to remove it during registration, in a private room, for identity verification.*

9. *You will be permitted to take a picture of yourself and the Presiding Official on the screen at the end of the ceremony (as a "selfie"), if desired, with your own device. The Clerk of the Ceremony or IRCC staff will let you know when. Be aware that you are NOT permitted to take pictures or recordings at any other time during the registration and the ceremony. If at any point during the session you choose to ignore this instruction or any reminders given by staff, your ceremony may be paused, delayed or rescheduled.*

10. ****At the date and time of your Video oath ceremony:*

    a) *click on the Zoom link in your invitation (at the top of this email) to join the session;*

    b) *if your computer has a door covering its camera, open it for video use;*

    c) *enter the Meeting Password when asked;*

    d) *have your seat number on hand and, if you know how, change your Zoom screen name to your seat number;*

    e) *turn on your audio and video camera in order to enable audio and video for the meeting;*

    f) *you will be placed into a Zoom Waiting Room, and may wait up to 30 minutes to be admitted into the session;*

    g) *the IRCC Official will accept you into the meeting when ready.*

11. *If you get disconnected during your Video Oath ceremony, try reconnecting again using the same link and password we gave you. If you are not able to connect,*

   a) *check your phone, we may call you, or your email inbox for further instructions; or*

   b) *send a message to this e-mail address. You will be rescheduled on a different date and time.*

12. *At the beginning of the ceremony, during registration, validate your home address with the IRCC official, when asked, so that we can send you your citizenship certificate to the correct address.*

Checklist - Things you will need DURING the video oath ceremony

Have the following documents/objects with you:

For ALL STEPS

A device with reliable access to the Internet and both audio and video capability.

FOR REGISTRATION – once you join the Zoom session

Your seat number (at the top of this email);

All of the original documents in your possession: your permanent resident card if you have one (even if it's expired) or your confirmation of permanent residence (IMM5292 or IMM5688), as well as your record of landing (IMM 1000), if you became a permanent resident before June 28, 2002 and have one;

(If applicable) The permanent resident card for each of the minor children associated to your application, whether they participate in the ceremony or not);

2 pieces of personal identification (ID):

- one must have your photograph and signature on it, e.g. driver's license, health card
- one of them can be your Permanent resident card, if your second piece of identification is Canadian federal, provincial or territorial issued ID foreign ID documents must be government-issued, Canadian ones don't need to be government-issued if they're not in English or French, you must provide a translation with an affidavit from the translator minors are not required to show identification with a signature;

Examples of pieces of identification can be found here: Show identity, Minors - Gather documents;

(If applicable) Your Personal identification (ID), if you are the parent/guardian who submitted/signed the application on behalf of a minor child;

A good pair of scissors as you will be asked to cut up your Permanent Resident card during the session with an employee.

If you do not have all items in the checklist above, you may not be able to complete the video oath ceremony.

DURING THE VIDEO OATH CEREMONY ITSELF

[Optional] A holy book, of your choice, if you want to use one to swear the Oath of Citizenship.

AT THE END OF THE CEREMONY

[Optional] A cell phone or camera if you want to take a picture (i.e. 'selfie') with the Presiding official on screen – the IRCC official will let you know when the moment is right.

Steps to take AFTER the video oath ceremony

Immediately AFTER the Zoom session

You will be sent your paper citizenship certificate by regular mail within 2 to 4 weeks ONLY once we have received your signed Oath or Affirmation of Citizenship form (and the Solemn Declaration form, if applicable).

1. Sign the Oath or Affirmation of Citizenship form on paper (using a black pen) or electronically at both places indicated "Signature of applicant" (see yellow in example below); the completed form should include 2 signatures. If not already included, add your full name at the top beside "Applicant" and the date beside your two signatures. The date must be the date of your ceremony.

   a) If you printed and signed the form on paper, scan or take a picture of it;

   b) If you chose to sign the form electronically, see instructions below (under "Add Electronic signatures to a PDF", "Extract a page from a PDF") and extract only the last page corresponding to the oath form in a PDF file;

   NOTE: All candidates aged fourteen (14) or older must sign the Oath or Affirmation of Citizenship form as indicated above. Each member of the family associated with your application must have their own form.

   Minors under the age of 14 do NOT need to sign or send in the Oath or Affirmation of citizenship form. Parents or guardians also do not need to sign nor send the form on the minor's behalf.

2. Email us the PDF or JPG (PDF files are preferred) of the signed Oath or Affirmation of Citizenship form immediately; it should NOT be more than 2 days after the ceremony.

   NOTE: In the subject line of your email, include: "Oath form for [your file number], [your family name]". Family members should save the forms in separate PDFs, however, they can all be sent in one email.

There are free scanning Apps that can be downloaded if necessary. (Example : CamScanner, Adobe Scan, etc.) Ensure that each attachment is not larger than 1 MB (1000K).

If you recently moved but did not provide your new address during registration, please include it in your reply email so that we can send your certificate to the correct address. In the future, you don't need to tell us if you change your address.

Keep your "Record of Landing" or "Confirmation of Permanent Residence" as you may need it later, for example to obtain old age security benefit.

Take out your record of landing (IMM 1000), if you became a permanent resident before June 28, 2002, and have one, then write on it in a black pen the words "Holder is No longer a Permanent Resident" in the middle of the form.

Visit the IRCC website

1. Visit canada.ca/after-citizenship-ceremony for important information about applying for passports, registering to vote and learning about and exploring Canada. For example, the Institute for Canadian Citizenship, a national charity, invites you to celebrate your citizenship with Canoo! The Canoo mobile app offers new citizens like you a year of free admission to museums, science centres, art galleries, and parks across Canada! Learn more here.

Once you have received your citizenship certificate

1. Check that the personal information on the front and back of your certificate is accurate; if it contains errors, contact us immediately. Keep your certificate in a safe place.

2. If there are no errors, destroy your signed Oath or Affirmation of citizenship form. The Oath or Affirmation of

citizenship form is NOT proof of citizenship; the citizenship certificate is evidence that a person is a Canadian citizen.

3. Visit our website to find out how to apply for a passport or call the Service Canada Passport Call Centre directly at 1-800-567-6868.

NOTE: If you do not receive your certificate within 6 weeks of the date you submitted your Oath or Affirmation of Citizenship form, contact us.

Following this are the instructions for adding an electronic signature to a PDF and the personalized oath or affirmation of citizenship form.

The ceremony

As soon as I joined the video call I was pulled into a breakout room. After over a year of mystery, it was nice to talk to an immigration program assistant who had a face and was helpful. She quickly verified my IDs, sorted out my PR card debacle, and gave me instructions for submitting my signed oath after the ceremony. She also confirmed that I was currently in Canada and verified my home address.

She then had me cut up my PR card on camera with her. I felt nervous cutting it up *before* taking the oath!

I was then moved into a waiting room, where we were encouraged to have ourselves muted and could turn our cameras off. I spent a few minutes catching up on emails while I waited.

Then the ceremony began. Another IRCC agent welcomed us. The judge made a short speech on what it meant to be a citizen and spoke about how she felt as a naturalized citizen herself.

We were warned that if we didn't recite the oath we wouldn't be granted citizenship. The invitation suggests you practice the oath. I'd assumed we'd be able to read the oath off the screen, especially since we have to say it in both English and French. Nope. We were to recite after the judge. I could hardly hear it now that 73 people had their microphones turned on, with the inevitable babies and dogs in the background. I was worried that if I searched online to find the words to read it would look like I wasn't paying attention, so I nervously mumbled things that somewhat resembled the oath. If you, like me, lose the ability to repeat after someone under pressure, be sure to have a copy of the oath at hand.

Then we sang the national anthem. This time they did a screen share so we could read the lyrics off a karaoke video. Given the lag between the video and the audio and the fact that now all of us were muted, this was a very awkward sing-along.

We were then asked to all turn off our cameras so only the judge was visible on screen. This was our photo op to take a selfie with the judge. This was simultaneously sweet and dystopian.

Our final instructions included instructions on how to register to vote. Then we were congratulated and the zoom call ended.

After the ceremony

My citizenship certificate arrived a little more than a week after the ceremony. The back of the certificate has the oath in both languages, my basic details, and two bar codes. It left me confused as to why I need to mail the original for my passport application when there's a certificate number. I eagerly tried to register to vote and had my application rejected.

It didn't occur to me ahead of time that I would need to update my drivers license and health card because of the change in my status. Both of these records record your status, so it's good to make sure to update them once you have your citizenship certificate.

Traveling after the ceremony

American citizens, including those who also hold Canadian citizenship, can enter Canada using a US passport. If you're not a US citizen or don't have a current passport, things are a little more complicated.

Even if you didn't cut up your PR card, it would no longer be valid for travel. Border agents scan your PR card and would know it's invalid, since you no longer have PR status. This means that any travel between when you become a citizen by taking your oath of citizenship and when you get a Canadian passport will be a little complicated.

The IRCC says you'll get your citizenship certificate four to six weeks after the ceremony. Supposedly at the ceremony you can request they expedite this, if they find your reason compelling. At my ceremony I was told that the only option would have been to delay my ceremony, since they don't offer expedited certificates. It might depend on which IRCC office performs your ceremony.

Once you have a citizenship certificate you can cross the border on foot or a private vehicle. Just like traveling without a valid PR card, you can plan on entering Canada with commercial transportation. Just be prepared for the possibility that you won't be allowed to board or that you'll be turned away at the border.

If you'd like to fly and need an eTA, you can apply for special authorization to board your flight to Canada within 10 days of your flight. You can select a date of travel on the form. It only remains valid for four days, so let's hope there are no major weather delays.

If you can't get special authorization and they won't let you board your flight, you can contact the local embassy or consulate to figure out your options.

Applying for a passport

If you're able to attend an in-person ceremony and get a citizenship certificate the day you become a citizen, you must wait at least two business days between becoming a Canadian citizen and applying for a passport.

The steps for getting a passport are:

1. Fill out the passport application form
2. Gather your documents:
    1. Proof of Canadian citizenship
    2. Proof of identity
    3. 2 passport photos
    4. Any valid Canadian travel document issued in your name
    5. Documents to prove a name change or sex designation
    6. Form if you'd like to omit your place of birth
    7. Official translations of any documents not in English or French
3. You need a guarantor and 2 references:
    1. A guarantor certifies that you are who you say you are. They must be an adult Canadian citizen who has known you for 2 or more years. They must hold a valid 5- or 10-year Canadian passport. They can be a family member.
    2. References must have known you for at least two years and be 18 or older. References and guarantors must be different people. References cannot be family members. The passport office may contact your reference.

4. Mail your application and documents, along with your application fees.

If you mail your application, your new passport and original documents will be mailed back. Usually your new passport will be mailed to you separately from your original documents.

If you are traveling within a month, you'll need to apply in person at a passport office. If you applied in person, your receipt will list your pickup date. During the pandemic you're only allowed to apply in person under special circumstances.

A 5-year passport is $120, a 10-year passport is $160. You can have your passport processed faster for an additional cost.

Changing your immigration documents

You can update your immigration documents to change your name or gender. Canadian documents have three gender identifiers: m, f, and x.

You can update your name and gender designation on your work permit, protected person document, refugee protection claimant document, verification of status (VOS), PR card, or citizenship certificate. You cannot update your gender designation on your CoPR, which is considered a historical document.

Your foreign passport and foreign documents do not have to show the gender listed on your Canadian documents. Your gender designation on your eTA must match your foreign passport.

The process to change the name on your documents depends on whether it was a clerical error or if your name has legally changed.

Voluntary change

To update your immigration documents, you need to apply for a new PR card or citizenship certificate. If there are more than nine months remaining on your current PR card, you will need to explain that you are changing your name and/or gender or they will not process it.

If your name changed because of a marriage, divorce, or adoption, you can submit a marriage certificate, divorce decree, registration, declaration of union, revocation of declaration, annulment of union, or adoption order.

If you changed your name through the court, you need a copy of the legal change of name document or court order.

If you changed your name outside of Canada, you can show your foreign passport or other national authoritative document that shows your new name and an official document linking the old and new names.

Reclaiming your Indigenous name

If you're applying for a new PR card to show your reclaimed Indigenous name, you are not required to pay the usual fees. You can submit a legal change of name document that links your previous name to your reclaimed name or a statutory declaration along with proof that your request for a legal name change was rejected.

Correcting an IRCC mistake

If your immigration documents need to be corrected because of a mistake on the part of the IRCC, you need to submit the Request to Amend the Immigration Record of Landing, Confirmation of Permanent Residence or Valid Temporary Resident Documents (IMM 5218) to the Operations Support Center:

Operations Support Centre
P.O. Box 8784 STN T CSC
Ottawa, Ontario K1G 5J3

or, if sent by courier or registered mail:

Verification of Status or Replacement of an Immigration Document

Operations Support Centre
365 Laurier Avenue West,
Ottawa, Ontario K1A 1L1

Leaving Canada

What happens to your residency when you leave Canada? In a word: nothing.

Going on a trip, however long it lasts, doesn't mean you're not a resident of Canada. I travel often and for long periods of time, leading me to occasionally have to prove that I'm still a resident of Toronto, Ontario, or Canada.

I can be gone for as long as I want and I'll still be a resident. I haven't gotten rid of my apartment in Toronto or set up a new place somewhere else. I'm still covered under OHIP. I haven't gotten a new driver's license, registered to vote, or done anything that might suggest I've moved anywhere else. While I might be away for months, I'm rarely in one place for more than two months, so I certainly haven't established residency elsewhere.

Until I establish a permanent home somewhere else, I am a resident of Toronto who is currently traveling and is planning on returning to Toronto as far as the federal government is concerned. Because I'm still a resident as far as Canadian law is concerned, I'd be in trouble if I don't file my taxes with the CRA.

Permanent residents need to be physically present in Canada in order to maintain their status. As a permanent resident, I could still be a resident even if I don't set foot in Canada for three years.

Remember that different provincial, territorial, and private organizations have different residency requirements.

Ending your residency

Once you're a resident of Canada for 60 months (five years), you remain a factual resident until you can prove to the CRA that you have left Canada for good and have no plans to ever move back.

You can't just move away and be done with it. As far as the CRA is concerned, you can't accidentally stop being a resident of Canada. And you can't just move and stop filing your Canadian taxes.

You have to file a form with the CRA and convince them that you're gone for good. They can reject your claim and continue to consider you a resident.

Demonstrating that you've left

- Sell your home or rent it out on a long-term lease
- Move all of your things out of the country
- Establish a new home outside of Canada
- Be required to pay taxes in another country
- Get a job with a non-Canadian company or get transferred to a foreign office
- Get a new driver's license in another country
- Give up your Canadian work permit, study permit, or permanent resident status
- Get new health insurance coverage
- Have a reason for any Canadian bank accounts you're keeping open
- Quit your Canadian professional organizations or unions

- Join new community groups abroad

If you leave your spouse and kids behind or don't have to pay taxes to another country, they're going to require you to continue paying taxes on your worldwide income. They'll require that you provide a list of all of your assets so they can make sure you don't commit tax evasion in the future.

The CRA may even ask you to provide them with a copy of your foreign tax return to verify that you've really moved.

The CRA isn't kidding around with this. If you don't file they'll contact you, using the information they have on file. If you ignore them, they'll freeze your Canadian bank accounts and can put a lien on your Canadian assets.

Renouncing PR status

In order to stop being a permanent resident, you need to renounce your status. Neglecting to maintain your physical presence requirements doesn't cause you to automatically lose your PR status, it puts you in a legal limbo. If your PR card is expired, you don't qualify for a new PR card, and you want to visit Canada, you are advised to renounce your PR status. When you apply for an eTA, the IRCC will send you instructions allowing you to submit your renunciation packet electronically. The documents you need to renounce your PR status are:

- The document checklist (IMM 5783)

- The application (IMM 5782)

- 2 passport photos

- Your physical PR card, if it's still valid. If your PR card isn't expired but you don't have it, submit a solemn declaration (IMM 5451)

- A copy of your international passport or some other proof of citizenship or permanent resident status in a country other than Canada

There is no cost to renounce your PR status.

The application should be submitted electronically when requesting a eTA to visit Canada. If you're living outside of Canada and don't need an eTA, mail your packet to the Canadian visa office responsible for your country of citizenship or legal residence.

If you're living in Canada when you renounce your PR status, submit your packet to:

Renunciation of Permanent Resident Status
Citizenship and Immigration Canada Operational Support Centre
365 Laurier Avenue West, Ground Floor Mailroom, South Tower
Ottawa, Ontario, K1A 1L1

You'll become a visitor once they receive your packet. You then have six months to leave the country. Once the IRCC receives your application you lose the right to work or study in Canada.

If you qualify to receive Canada Pension Plan and Old Age Security benefits, you may still be able to collect these after you renounce PR status.

The exit tax

If you've been a resident for more than 60 months in the last ten years (five years in ten years, counted on a rolling basis) you're subject to the exit tax if you stop being a resident of Canada.

That sounds scary (and punitive!) but it's really not. It's designed to make sure you don't run off without paying capital gains taxes.

For tax purposes, the day you leave Canada forever (or die) you are considered to have sold everything you own and then re-purchased it at market rate. This changes the cost basis of everything you own and you theoretically owe capital gains taxes on the theoretical proceeds.

It's typical for people leaving Canada to not have to pay anything for the exit tax. You don't have to pay capital gains taxes on your primary residence, RRSP, or TFSA and that's where most people have all of their net worth. You're basically just reporting all of your assets and their current value to the CRA and promising to pay any taxes you're required to pay when you eventually sell them.

Canada doesn't tax you on capital gains on your primary residence, but once you move it's not your primary residence anymore. If you keep your former home you'll need to have it assessed to determine the new cost basis for the eventual capital gains tax determination.

You're not paying any extra money with the exit tax. If you do pay an exit tax, you're just pre-paying a portion of the capital gains taxes you'll eventually owe when you sell. It's very rare for the CRA to not grant requests to defer tax payment until the actual sale. If you sell everything before you leave, you're just paying normal capital gains taxes.

Want more information on Canadian tax law?

Okay, you probably don't. But if you're a US citizen or greencard holder living in Canada, you probably need it! I have a book on the topic: *Cross Border Taxes: A complete guide to filing taxes as an American in Canada.*

Appendix

Sample work verification letters

To whom it may concern:

This letter serves to verify the employment of [your full legal name]. She is the [current job title] for [employer name]. She has been an employee since [hire date]. From [start date] until [end date] she served as [original job title]. On [start date] she was promoted to [current job title] and is presently employed in that role. Her current salary is [salary].

In her role as [original job title], she was responsible for: [original job description].

In her role as [current job title], she is responsible for: [current job description].

Please don't hesitate to contact me for further information.

Sincerely,

[signature]

[full name]
[job title]

To whom it may concern:

[Your full legal name] was employed by [employer legal name] from [hire date] to [last day of employment], in the capacity of [job title]. Her schedule entailed a 40 hour work week. Her annual gross compensation was [salary]. While an employee of [employer name] the firm provided life/AD&D, short- and long-term disability benefits. The firm also covered the cost of her medical, vision, prescription, and dental benefits.

As a [job title], [your name] was responsible for: [job description].

Truly yours,

[signature]

[full name]
[job title]

To whom it may concern:

This letter is to confirm that [your full legal name] was a permanent, full-time employee with [employer name] as a [job title]. [Your name] worked at [employer name] from [hire date] until [termination date]. The terms of employment were:

Hours per week:
Starting salary:
Final salary:
Benefits:
Duties:

My business card is attached. Please contact me for any further information you may need.

Sincerely,

[signature]

[full name]
[title]

Immigration resources

While Canada has one of the most user-friendly visa and immigration programs, it's common for us to come across instructions or requirements that just don't make sense given our particular circumstances.

Thankfully, there are plenty of places where you can find answers to your immigration questions.

Essential Websites

The IRCC website to verify advice. This is the authority for all visa and immigration information.

Numbeo provides cost of living information.

The Conference Board of Canada's Immigration Centre provides economic analysis and forecasting.

Peer support

Moving to Canada requires a ton of research. There are many groups online where people share what they've learned. Once you make it through successfully all of that knowledge becomes useless unless you help other people with the process.

Remember that any advice you get should be verified by the IRCC. Requirements change periodically and people can misunderstand things. Why is potentially unreliable information still so helpful? It's a lot easier to fact check something than it is to figure it out on your own!

Facebook groups

Most of these groups are for a specific visa/immigration pathway. You'll have the best luck getting helpful answers if you join the appropriate group and ask clear questions.

Remember to check the pinned posts and files for helpful information. You can also search within a group, since usually someone has already asked the same question.

Canada Work Permit Visa, Student Visa, Citizenship

Canada Immigration & Work Permits for People from Asia

Canadian Citizenship - Support Group

Express entry

Express Entry (EE) Help Desk

Canada Express Entry Forum

Express Entry Canada

Canada Express Entry

Express Entry Canada Guidance

Express Entry Law

PNP

Saskatchewan Immigrant Nominee Program

Manitoba Provincial Nominee Program

Ontario Immigrant Nominee Program

Provincial Nominee Program – Canada

Provincial Nomination Programs - PNP

Canada PR & PNP Queries

International Experience Canada

International Experience Canada (IEC) – Ask Us Anything!

IEC Working Holiday Forum – Moving2Canada

Working Holiday Canada & now what?! From IEC to PR

Student Visas

Yes, all of these groups really do have the same name.

International Students in Canada

International Students in Canada

International Students in Canada

Canada Student Visa

Family Sponsorship

Canada Spousal Sponsorship Petitioners

Applying for PR Common-Law/Spousal Canada

Canada Spouse Open Work Permit

Canada Family Sponsorship Filipino Tagalog Group

Quora

Immigration to Canada

Canada Express Entry

Permanent Residency in Canada

Career Advice in Canada

Working in Canada

Living in Canada

International English Language Testing System (IELTS)

IELTS Preparation

Reddit

r/IWantOut

r/ImmigrationCanada

r/CanadaImmigration

Canada Visa

Part of a site run by an immigration law firm, the Canada Visa forum provides advice mostly from other immigrants. This is by far the most active forum for Canadian immigration, covering all temporary residency, permanent residency, and citizenship programs.

Personal Websites

I'm not the only one who's moved to Canada and then shared what I learned with other would-be immigrants. Here are a few other websites written by people who've moved to Canada.

Black Migrant Girl

Black Migrant Girl is Akata Salowo's blog about moving from Lagos to Toronto. She shares her experience finding a job and finding an apartment, among other things.

Moving2Canada

Moving2Canada is a website with a lot of immigration and visa information, run by Outpost Recruitment. They're a recruitment agency focusing on construction and engineering. Most of the articles have been written by people from abroad who are now living in Canada who are sharing their own personal experiences or writing guides based on first hand knowledge of the topic. If you're looking for an immigration consultant, here's who they recommend.

eKanada

This site has great information on the immigration process as well as what to expect about life in Canada in both Polish and English.

Expat Yourself

Learn how you can move to Canada from someone who's lived in 30 countries. His move to Canada pre-dates the changes to the immigration programs in 2015, 2016, and 2017, but he has great posts on dealing with taxes and other trials and tribulations of living abroad temporarily.

Gray Ninja's Guide to Canada

This blog provides a personal account of the journey from deciding to move to Canada through getting settled in Fredericton, New Brunswick. The author is a CPA who was able to find a job very quickly after landing, so if you're in a licensed profession you'll find his experience helpful. If you're coming from the Philippines or moving to New Brunswick, you'll appreciate his insights.

Lost in the Leafy City

The personal blog of someone moving from the Philippines to Calgary.

Off-Track Travel

While mainly a travel blog, this British-Canadian couple has done working holidays in Canada, New Zealand, and the UK. They provide step-by-step guides for the IEC process and lots of information on what to see and do.

Toronto Newbie

This is the story of a British journalist who moved to Toronto in 2012. She covers immigration stories as a journalist. While the information is still helpful in terms of knowing what to expect and discovering the best of the GTA, all of the immigration programs have changed significantly since her arrival.

The Expatriate Mind

This blog is written by an American who moved to Canada as a skilled worker in 2011, through the paper application. He's currently working on applying for Canadian citizenship.

An Aussie in Canada

This is an online course created by Sara Doole. As you've probably guessed, she's an Australian who moved to Canada through Express Entry.

Other blogs about expats in Canada

Sometimes you don't need detailed immigration information, you're just wondering what day to day life in Canada is really like.

Skippy or Bullwinkle: Australians trying to work out Canada

Correr es mi Destino

The Loud Americans

From Switzerland to Canada

A Singapore Story

Live from Waterloo

Moved to Vancouver

How's it Going, eh?

Expat in Toronto

Professional Support

- Arrive Prepared provides online courses to help immigrants prepare for the Canadian workforce environment. These courses are available only between when you've been approved to immigrate and before you've landed.

- Next Stop Canada is a program run by the YMCA that provides free pre-arrival services to young adults (12-19) and adults (16+).

- Canadian Immigrant is a magazine about the newcomer experience.

- If you prefer video over print, New Canadians is a web tv show.

- Prepare for Canada is an online magazine for skilled professionals preparing to immigrate to Canada.

Province Specific Resources

Ontario

- Settlement.org for Ontario housing and employment information.
- New Youth helps young people in Ontario get settled, from daily life to legal questions.
- CultureLink provides language help, school assistance, job placement, mentorship, and free outdoor activities in Toronto.
- Ontario's Ministry of Citizenship and Immigration connects newcomers to bridge training, language classes, and settlement services.
- WIL is a nonprofit employment center for newcomers to London, ON.
- The Cross Cultural Learner Centre provides settlement services in London, ON.
- Skills for Change provides career training to newcomers in Toronto.
- StartUp Here Toronto helps startups move to the GTA.
- Polycultural provides immigrant services in Toronto, including career services, language programs, wellness programs, and senior services.

- Newcomer Women's Services Toronto was founded by a group of Latin American refugees. They now help immigrant women with employment services, skills development, and language training.
- Ottawa Community Immigrant Services Organization provides settlement, employment, and language help for adults and children.
- Immigrant Women Services Ottawa provides culturally appropriate services supporting immigrant women and their children.
- The Ottawa Chinese Community Service Centre provides help with settlement, language, employment, and family services.

British Columbia

- New to BC is a clearinghouse of all the services available to newcomers in BC.
- ISS of BC connects newcomers with ESL classes, settlement and career help.
- Mosaic supports newcomers with translation services, intercultural training, language training, and income tax clinics.
- The Skilled Immigrant Infocentre is a program run by the Vancouver Public Library that helps newcomers learn how to find a job, choose a new career, or start a business.

Alberta

- Centre for Newcomers supports immigrants in Calgary.
- Immigrant Services Calgary provides language classes, translation, career support, and other settlement services.
- Calgary Immigrant Women's Association provides settlement services specifically for women and children.

- The Calgary Bridge Foundation for Youth provides in-school support, afterschool programs, and mentorship for children and young adults.

Immigration Attorneys & Consultants

You can access expert advice without having to pay an immigration attorney or consultant. How? Their websites!

- Matthew Jeffery
- Ackah Business Immigration Law
- Vancouver Immigration Blog
- Sas & Ing
- Warren Creates
- Meurrens on Immigration
- FW Canada

You'll find that many professional immigration blogs give you the impression that it's virtually impossible to get a visa or PR status in Canada without professional help. That's not the case.

Every year many applicants successfully apply on their own. The electronic application is a lot like applying for a job online. If you're capable of following instructions, using a computer, and getting the required documents, you'll be fine.

However, some circumstances will require the help of a professional. This is especially true if you have a criminal record or if one of your immediate family members may be inadmissible to Canada.

Remember that if you choose to hire an immigration consultant or attorney to help you with the process, you should always make sure they're authorized.

All consultants are authorized by the College of Immigration and Citizenship Consultants. Until 2021, they were authorized by the ICCRC.

It is illegal for someone to work as an immigration consultant who isn't authorized by the CICC, a Canadian law society, or the Law Society of Upper Canada.

Canada Visa

Canada Visa and CIC News are run by Campbell Cohen, a Canadian Immigration law firm. If you aren't sure if you qualify for an immigration stream, you may find their free assessment helpful.

Their website has easy-to-understand overviews of each immigration program. While they'll help you find the best way to bring yourself and your family to Canada, they're not giving away step-by-step instructions. This website is a great place to start. They also have a newsletter and social media accounts that will keep you up to date with the latest immigration news, PNP, and EE draws.

French language resources

The best way to learn French is to immerse yourself in the language. Of course, that's easier said than done, especially when you're starting out without knowing a word! These programs will help you get to the point where you can switch your TV shows, movies, podcasts, and news to French.

Online classes

Your local library likely offers pre-recorded beginner and intermediate French courses from Collins, DK, Gale Courses, Living Language, Pimsleur, and others. There are online courses available for free to all, including:

- Annenberg Learner: learner.org/series/french-in-action/
- Learn a Language: http://www.learnalanguage.com/
- Coffee Break French's podcast lessons are available at no cost: coffeebreaklanguages.com/coffeebreakfrench/
- MIT's Open CourseWare has online versions of their French language courses, as well as courses on French culture: ocw.mit.edu/courses/global-languages/

Apps and interactive programs

Your local library probably provides free access to Mango Language, Rosetta Stone, and the Pronunciator. Mango Language teaches you phrases so you can speak right away. They provide the literal translation as well as usage and cultural notes. Rosetta Stone presents things in a way that's intuitive, so you learn the grammar without memorizing rules and pick up vocabulary looking anything up or studying lists of words. Pronunciator is a mix of the two styles, while also providing flash cards and drills.

Mauril teaches French and English through CBC Radio programs. This program is only available in Canada, so you won't be able to download it ahead of time unless you update your app store location. TV5Mode is a similar app that's available worldwide.

There are numerous free and freemium apps providing French lessons, including:

- Babble
- Busuu
- DuoLingo
- Français Authentique
- HelloTalk
- Mango Language
- Memrise

- Pronunciator
- Rosetta Stone

One fun thing about many of these apps, including DuoLingo and Memrise, is that you don't need to learn French from English. You can dust off your high school Spanish and use that to learn French. Once you have a head start on French, you can start learning another language and use that as a handy review of the French you've already mastered.

Conversation practice

It's likely that your local library and Meetup.com have local opportunities for conversation practice. DuoLingo has conversation practice and live lessons on their website: events.duolingo.com.

Tandem, EasyLanguageExchange, Polyglot Club, and HelloTalk match you with a conversation partner who's fluent in French and wants to learn English (or another language you speak).

Canadian French

Most French programs teach European French. Here are a few resources for learning French for life in Quebec:

- Pronunciator offers Canadian French:
  https://www.pronunciator.com/

- Mango Language offers Canadian French:
  mangolanguages.com/available-languages/learn-french-canadian/

- The Memrise app has a module for Canadian French phrases:
  app.memrise.com/course/369487/quebec-french-quebecois/

Dictionaries & glossaries

- The place to go to verify your words is the Dictionnaire Québécois: dictionnaire-quebecois.com/
- There's also the Wikébec dictionary: wikebec.org
- Let's not leave out Acadian French: http://139.103.17.56/cea/livres/glossaire_index/glossaire.cfm

Official resources

- The Province of Québec offers a basic online French course that I found less than helpful: midiena.gouv.qc.ca/bnqex/
- They also have vocabulary lists organized by topic: oqlf.gouv.qc.ca/ressources/bibliotheque/dictionnaires/index_lexvoc.html
- The Université du Québec à Trois-Rivières has similar resources for learning Québécois and learning the history of Quebec: oraprdnt.uqtr.uquebec.ca/pls/public/gscw031?owa_no_site=1131&owa_no_fiche=39&owa_bottin= (or search for "Textes et narrations: français langue étrangère")
- The University of Laval offers their Labratoire de phonetique: phonetique.ulaval.ca
- The Université du Québec à Chicoutimi also has a phonetics library: phono.uqac.ca

Foreign Service Institute

The Foreign Service Institute offers numerous online language resources, including several for French:

- French fast:
  fsi-languages.yojik.eu/languages/oldfsi/languages/french-fast-course.html

- French basics:
  fsi-languages.yojik.eu/languages/oldfsi/languages/french-basic.html &
  open.spotify.com/album/1RwIpFUyyVKqY6Zuimky0E

- Pronunciation to reduce your accent:
  fsi-languages.yojik.eu/languages/oldfsi/languages/french-phonology.html

Self assessment

The CBL-OSA online self assessment isn't the same test used by professional language assessment organizations. It's a free and accessible tool for you to gauge your language level prior to scheduling an official assessment: nclc-ael.ca

Escape Guide

Not everyone is going to be eligible to move to Canada. Perhaps you've decided that life in Canada isn't for you. Maybe you never intended to stay in Canada forever. There are plenty of other options to live abroad — as an immigrant, expat, or nomad.

Ways to immigrate

If you want to settle in another country for the long-term, you probably want to have permanent resident status or citizenship. This ensures that your ability to stay in your new home is not dependent on renewing your visa paperwork every year or making periodic visa runs. These options all provide a pathway to permanent resident status or citizenship.

Family sponsorship

Most countries will allow family members to sponsor you for resident status. Often this is limited to sponsoring a spouse and children, although some countries have more expansive policies. They'll typically have to show that they can support you for a certain amount of time and may need to meet other requirements. Your sponsor may need to be living in your destination country.

Citizenship through descent

If either of your parents was a citizen of another country when you were born, some countries consider you a citizen even if you were born abroad. You're already a citizen, so you simply have to apply for proof of citizenship.

Other countries allow your parents to sponsor you for citizenship or apply using proof of your parents' citizenship.

Citizenship by descent can go back quite far, so even if you don't qualify through your parents, there may be other options.

Your Grandparents

Some countries allow you to apply for citizenship based on the nationality of a grandparent. These include Argentina, Armenia, Belize, Cape Verde, Chile, the Czech Republic, Finland, Germany, Hungary, Ireland, Italy, Latvia, Lithuania, Luxembourg, Poland, Portugal, Romania, Slovenia, Spain, and the UK.

A few countries go back beyond grandparents, as long as you can provide documents backing up your ancestry claims.

Jewish diaspora

You've probably heard of Jews living abroad moving to Israel. Immigration to Israel through the Law of Return is referred to as making Aliyah. People immigrating to Israel using this program have access to support to help them settle.

If you can demonstrate your Sephardic ancestry, you qualify to become a citizen in Portugal. You'll need to convince the relevant Jewish community organization in Portugal of your ancestral ties, who will issue a certificate of ancestry. Then you can apply with the Portuguese government.

Sephardic ancestry also makes you eligible for citizenship in Spain, although they have more stringent requirements and require you demonstrate the ability to speak ladino or haketia.

If your ancestors were stripped of German citizenship during the Nazi era, you can apply for citizenship in Germany.

African diaspora

If you're a member of the African diaspora you can apply for citizenship in Ghana and Sierra Leone.

Some African countries previously didn't allow for dual citizenship, meaning that those who became citizens abroad lost their status in their home country. Several countries have recently changed these laws, allowing people who lost their citizenship to regain it. It's unclear if a parent or grandparent regaining their citizenship would make you eligible for citizenship through them.

Skilled worker immigration programs

Canada isn't the only country with a program designed to bring skilled workers into the country. Here are some programs similar to Canada's express entry immigration system.

The Europe Economic Area

If you've worked temporarily within the European Economic Area (EEA), you may qualify for the Blue Card. This program allows temporary workers in any EEA country to work in any other EEA country, as well as eventually become permanent residents. There's also the Czech Green Card.

Australia

You can apply for a Skilled Migration Visa and become a permanent resident of Australia using Skill Select. You can apply for a Skilled Independent Visa, Skilled Nominated Visa, or Skilled Regional Visa.

If you meet the requirements for a Skilled Independent Visa, you can become a permanent resident without a job offer or family sponsorship. They use a points system, which makes the program easy to understand and helps you reliably predict your odds of being approved.

New Zealand

If you're under 55, you may qualify for New Zealand's Skilled Migrant Category. You can take a quiz to see if you're eligible or calculate your points yourself.

Retiring or working remotely

Quite a few countries are happy to welcome you if you're bringing money into the country, rather than looking for a job. Moving to a country with a low cost of living has long been a way for retirees to enjoy a higher standard of living. Some countries require people to be 'retirement age' in order to qualify, but most don't.

In countries with a lower cost of living than the US and Canada, the monthly income requirement can seem quite reasonable. Some require your income source be guaranteed. Guaranteed income includes government pension plans, private pension plans, disability income, certificates of deposit, and annuities. Some programs specify that the income must be guaranteed for your lifetime.

Usually passive income like rental income, income from businesses you own, stock market returns, and royalties are considered. You may need to demonstrate a certain overall net worth or amount of cash savings. You may need to put a required amount of cash savings into a local bank account or investment.

Some countries will allow people who are self-employed or work remotely to qualify for their retiree visa programs. This may be explicitly written into the program or it may be how the program is applied by the people processing applications. Others have created programs specifically for location independent workers.

The US, Canada, and Australia do not have visas for retirees or people of independent means. They do offer visas for participants in investment and entrepreneur programs.

Entrepreneur and investor immigration programs

You may not think of yourself as someone who has enough money to qualify as a business investor, but some countries offer investment and entrepreneur visas that are within the grasp of many Americans with retirement savings or proceeds from a primary residence. These programs may offer you permanent resident status right away. A few go directly to citizenship. These include Antigua and Barbuda, Dominica, Malta, St Kitts and Nevis, and Turkey.

Investing $250k in real estate can get you a Turkish passport in a matter of months. You also have the option of purchasing $500k in government bonds, VC funds, real estate funds, or leaving it in a Turkish bank account for three years.

A passport for the Caribbean nations will run around $100k.

Most investment and entrepreneur programs provide you with a resident permit that can eventually be used to gain permanent resident status. The most popular of these are mentioned later in this guide.

Some investor visas don't require you to personally be involved in running a company, they only ask that you invest in their country. Buying a nice house may be enough to get you a resident permit.

Expat life

Not everyone wants to move abroad permanently. If you're interested in spending a year or more in another country without worrying about eventually becoming a permanent resident, there are many options.

Most of these options will require you to have private health insurance. Some require police checks. Even if your record is squeaky clean, this can add a chunk of time to the process – getting a police check from the US can easily take six months. Translating and certifying documents can also be an expensive and time consuming hassle.

Work permits

The dream is to get your company to transfer you to another office in a country with worker mobility provisions in a free trade agreement. If you can talk your company into doing this, it's the easiest way to move abroad. Your employer's attorneys will take care of the paperwork for you and hopefully even provide a relocation consultant.

Nearly any country will give you a work permit if you have a qualifying job offer. Most countries require your potential employer to jump through hoops, like demonstrating that they tried to hire a local, showing you have unique skills, and paying fees.

Teach English

You probably know someone who's taught English abroad. You may know someone who went to teach English for a year and never came back.

South Korea, China, Japan, Taiwan, and the UAE are known for providing lucrative teaching opportunities. Many include flights, health insurance, and housing. Plenty of other countries have schools that hire native speakers to teach English, including those of Eastern Europe and South America. Countries in Africa are more likely to rely on volunteers.

You don't need a teaching degree or even a TEFL certificate to teach English abroad, although it certainly helps. Some schools will help you get any necessary certifications and provide training. Dave's ESL Cafe is the place to find out about how it works and find job postings.

Work as an Au Pair

An au pair is typically a young person (most often female) who takes care of children, cooks meals, and does some housework. Positions generally include room and board and a little bit of spending money. There's certainly no legal requirement that an au pair be female and typically there's no age requirement. The service placing you with a family will typically walk you through the process of getting a work permit.

Freelancing

Berlin and Prague are known as havens for expats on freelance visas. People are there using national immigration programs, so there's no need to only settle in these two cities.

Your options include Columbia, Croatia, Czechia, Dubai, Estonia, Germany, Georgia, Greece, Iceland, Italy, Japan, Spain, Malta, Norway, Portugal, and Romania.

You'll need to show that you have a stable income, so this is best for people with an established client base. Some of these countries require you to demonstrate you have current or potential clients in the country in order to qualify. They may require you to have a stable address in the country, making it less attractive for digital nomads who don't want to commit to spending a whole year in one spot. You may qualify for PR status after a few years.

Working remotely or living off investments

Many countries will welcome you to stay for a year or more if you're bringing money into the country. If there's a specific country you'd like to stay in, chances are good that they'll have a program for people working remotely for foreign companies or living off of passive income. It may be called a "person of independent means," "passive income," "retirement," or "non-lucrative" visa. Depending on the country, you may even be able to get residency qualifying for a formal program if you're able to meet with the authorities and make a case.

You will most likely be required to show proof of private insurance coverage. Check to see the tax implications of your stay, as some countries have special tax programs for participants, many have international agreements to avoid double taxation, and each country has different rules about who is considered a tax resident.

New programs are being introduced as countries update their laws and as countries scramble to replace tourism income lost due to the pandemic. Countries that are currently working on programs to attract remote workers and digital nomads include Belize, Cyprus, North Macedonia, Montenegro, Romania, Serbia, and Thailand.

Non-working resident visas

Many countries are happy to give you a resident permit if you can prove that you have a reliable source of income (such as investment income or a pension) or savings. Income requirements are higher if you have a family. Generally, the likelihood of your application being approved gets higher as your income increases.

While most of these programs are intended for retirees, not all of them have age limits. Even those that have age limits may be open to people in their 40s. As far as I know, all of these programs allow you to bring your family. They may require applications for each of you, to be processed together. Some define family to include parents and adult children. A few allow you to bring a foreign domestic helper.

- **Argentina**: You can apply for permanent resident status or citizenship after living in the country for two years with either of these two visas.

  o Rentista visa: Those with proof of income can get a visa for a year, renewable for up to three years. The official required amount is very low, but it appears that applications aren't approved with less than US$2,000k/month. You can establish a business or do freelance work with this visa.

  o Pensionado visa: This has a lower income requirement, around US$500/month, which must be guaranteed income.

- **Aruba**: You can get a residence permit in Aruba with an income of US$29k/year if you're over 55 or US$58k/year if you're under 55.

- **Belize**: If you have an income of US$24k/year, you can move to Belize as a Qualified Retired Person.

- **Costa Rica**: Proof of US$2,500/month will get you a rentista visa for two years. If you have guaranteed income, you only need to show US$1,000/month for a pensionado visa.

- **Cyprus**: An income of at least €10k/year qualifies you for a Category F visa. Your visa will automatically be canceled if you are gone for two years or acquire PR status abroad.

- **Ecuador**: You can move to Ecuador with a guaranteed income of US$800/month. It has to be guaranteed for your lifetime, such as social security, a government pension, or annuities. This visa allows you to work remotely, start a business, and freelance in Ecuador.

- **Guatemala**: The pensionado and rentista visas both have a USD$1,000/month income requirement. It takes three months for applications to be approved. They're valid for a year, and can be renewed.

- **Ireland**: If you have an income of €50k/year and savings to cover unexpected expenses, you can retire to Ireland as a person of independent means. There is no age requirement listed. Approval takes four months.

- **Italy**: You can retire to Italy with the Italian Elective Residency Visa. Income requirements vary, starting at €2,600/month. You'll need to show that you've signed a lease or bought a home. The initial visa is for one year and can be renewed for two years at a time.

- **Malaysia**: The My 2nd Home program provides a 10-year residence permit that's renewable. You can bring your family, including your parents. It welcomes those under 50 with an income of US$2,000/month who make a deposit of US$72k with the government. After a year, half of the deposit can be used to buy a home. The deposit requirement is lower for those over 50.

- **Mauritius**: The Premium Visa is valid for up to a year and can be renewed. The application is online, can be done from within Mauritius if you're there on a tourist visa, and takes 48 hours for processing (during business days).

- **Mexico**: Mexico's temporary residence permit allows visitors to stay for up to a year and it can be renewed for three years. This program welcomes remote workers, as long as they have an income of US$1,62/month for the past six months or US$27k in savings.

- **Nicaragua**: If you're over 45 and have an income of US$600/month, you can get a retirement visa. If you're under 45, you'll need to show an income of US$750/month.

- **Panama**: If you have a guaranteed income of US$1,000/month you can get residency in Panama. This is reduced to US$750/month if you spend US$100k in real estate. If you don't have *guaranteed* income, you can put US$170k in a National Bank of Panama CD, which will provide the necessary guaranteed income.

- **Philippines**: You can qualify for the special resident retiree visa if you're 50 and have a pension of US$800/month (only US$1000/month for couples). You'll need to deposit at least US$10,000 in a local savings account to apply. If your income isn't a pension, you can deposit a larger amount in savings to demonstrate your financial stability.

- **Portugal**: The D7 visa allows you to live in Portugal without working, as long as you can prove that you have an income greater than the minimum wage (currently €600/month). The higher your income, the better your chance of being approved. You have to apply from outside of Portugal in a country where you're a legal resident. It's valid for two years, can be renewed for another three, and then you're eligible to apply for PR status.

- **South Africa**: If you have a net worth of US$750k, you can become a permanent resident for a one-time fee of US$7,500. You can also get a resident permit for up to four years by showing a guaranteed income and/or a high net worth. You can renew this indefinitely as long as you visit South Africa once every three years.

- **Spain**: You'll need to show an income of €26k/year or enough savings to support yourself. Remote workers and freelancers qualify. You have to be a resident of your country of citizenship to apply. If you're from a Spanish speaking country, you're eligible to apply for citizenship in two years instead of the usual ten. It's possible that Puerto Rico may qualify for expedited citizenship. There's a list of villages eager to attract remote workers.

Remote work visas

Programs designed for remote workers are becoming more common. Freelancers will need to prove that they have a reliable income stream, such as long-term client contracts, or adequate savings.

- **Anguilla**: They're really trying to sell this program by naming it "Lose The Crowd Find Yourself. Work. Life. Bliss." You'll need proof of employment or a business license and a police check. You'll also need to import anything you bring with you. The visa is good for a year.

- **Antigua and Barbuda**: The Nomad Digital Residence visa is valid for two years. You'll need an income of US$50k/year and a police check.

- **Aruba**: I feel obligated to list this here because of the misleading media coverage it's gotten, even though it's a special tourist package and not an actual resident permit. The One Happy Workation visa for Aruba is only valid for 90 days and is only open to US citizens. You cannot arrange your own accommodations, this is a hotel package that comes with permission to work remotely. You'll need to buy into their state-run travel insurance program for your stay.

- **Bahamas**: The Bahamas Extended Access Travel Stay visa is good for a year and extendable for up to three years.

- **Barbados**: The Barbados Welcome Stamp program allows you to stay for a year as long as you can show that you have an income of US$50k/year.

- **Bermuda**: The Work from Bermuda visa allows you to stay for a year.

- **Cape Verde**: The Remote Working Cabo Verde program gets you a six month visa, extendable for up to a year, if you can prove an income of €1,500/month.

- **Cayman Islands**: If you have a salary of US$100k (or $150k for a couple) you can spend two years working remotely from the Cayman Islands with a Global Citizen Certificate.

- **Croatia**: If you have proof of an income of US$2,600/month, you can spend a year in Croatia. They require a police check, which can delay your ability to submit an application. Applications are typically approved in two or three months. Once it's approved, you can only leave Croatia for 30 days at a time and for a maximum of 90 days during the year. You have to register your residence, making moving around within the country difficult.

- **Curaçao**: If you can prove that you're a remote worker with a salaried job or stable client base, you and your family can get a six month visa for Curaçao. The application takes about two weeks for approval and you can renew it to stay up to a year. The application is done online and can be done in Curaçao as long as you have time left on your tourist visa.

- **Dominica**: If you earn US$70k/year you can spend 18 months in Dominica through their working in nature program.

- **Dubai, UAE**: Yes, Dubai is a city and this program is only valid for residence within the city. You need an income of US$5k/month to apply for this year-long visa.

- **Ecuador**: Ecuador will accept 9-V visa applications with a proof of income as low as US$400/month and a university degree. Applications are approved in about two weeks. It's valid for two years. You can then renew it for another two years or apply for permanent resident status.

- **Estonia**: If you have proof of an income of €3,500/month, you can apply from within the country or at an embassy and is typically approved within 30 days. It's valid for a year.

- **Georgia**: If you have an income of US$2,000/month, you and your family can spend a year on the Remote from Georgia visa.

- **Greece**: If you earn at least €3,500 as a freelancer or remote worker, you and your family can live in Greece for a year. The income requirement increases if you bring a spouse and children. You have to apply from your home country initially and can then renew it twice. Applications are approved in ten days.

- **Iceland**: If you earn US$88k/year as a permanent salaried employee you can spend six months working remotely in Iceland.

- **Malta**: If you have proof of an income of €2,700/month, you can get a year-long visa for Malta. This is renewable, just be sure to submit your renewal application at least 30 days before your visa expires. Processing takes 30 days and requires a police check.

- **Mauritius**: The premium visa is good for a year and doesn't have specific income requirements.

- **Montserrat**: If you earn US$70k/year you can spend a year in Montserrat. They boast a processing time of 7 business days.

- **Panama**: The Short Stay Visa for Remote Workers is valid for nine months and can be renewed for another nine. You need US$36k/year in income to qualify. This program is designed with remote workers in mind, but is also open to freelancers and business owners.

- **Seychelles**: The Seychelles Workcation program gets you a 12-month visa and doesn't have a specific income requirement.

Long-stay tourist visas

If you're living off of savings or passive income, you can live in a country on a tourist visa. Many countries will also allow you to work remotely on a tourist visa.

Most tourist visas are valid for 30, 60, or 90 days. Some countries offer much more generous tourist visas. You'll still want to be prepared to show proof of health insurance and funds at the border, even though you don't need to apply for a visa.

- **Albania**: US citizens can spend a year in Albania on a tourist visa.

- **Georgia**: Citizens of Australia, the US, New Zealand, South Africa, and other countries can spend a year in Georgia.

US citizens get automatic six month tourist visas for Antigua and Barbuda, Armenia, Barbados, Canada, the Cayman Islands, Curaçao, Dominica, Mexico, Panama, Peru, and the UK. Some of these reset if you do a visa run.

US citizens can easily apply to get extended tourist visas in Australia, Belize, Bermuda, Brazil, Chile, Columbia, Ecuador, India, Jamaica, Nepal, New Zealand, Peru, Sri Lanka, Thailand, and Uruguay.

While the Schengen Zone doesn't allow for your tourist visa to reset if you leave the country, it has quite a few exceptions, allowing longer stays in specific countries for people with certain nationalities.

- **Belgium** offers an additional two or three months for citizens of some countries.

- **Denmark**: Citizens of the US, Australia, Canada, Chile, Israel, Japan, Malaysia, New Zealand, Singapore, and South Korea can stay in Denmark 90 days past their 90 day Schengen visa, so long as they leave the Schengen Zone from Denmark.

- **France**:

- France will allow you to stay as a tourist for up to a year. You need to apply no more than 90 days before your arrival in France and the process takes 30 days.
- US citizens can spend an additional 90 days in France past their 90 day Schengen visa. You need to leave directly from France. This isn't well known and you may need to figure out a way to prove that you were in France, since there is no border control within the Schengen zone.

- **Poland**: US citizens can stay in Poland for 90 days after their Schengen visa. You need to leave the Schengen zone before you enter Poland in order to get entry and exit stamps in your passport showing you were in Poland.

- **Sweden**: Sweden will allow you to stay as a tourist for up to a year. You can apply from within Sweden and it takes two weeks for approval. You'll need to provide a compelling reason for your extended visit.

Start a business, move your business, or invest

The financial resources required to qualify for a business or investor visa vary widely. Some countries will consider a long-term lease or home purchase an investment, while others want to see a business plan and jobs for locals. These programs typically allow you to bring your family and often offer a pathway to citizenship.

- **Brazil**: In 2020 Brazil introduced a program offering a five year residency permit for an investment of US$130k. You can then apply for citizenship.

- **Curaçao**: This island nation has a tiered investment program, with US$281k getting you a renewable three year visa, US$420k getting you a renewable five year visa, and US$838k getting you an indefinite visa.

- **Greece**: An investment of €250k will get you residency in a few months, although there are also substantial fees. Your residency is valid for five years and can be renewed. After seven years you're eligible for citizenship.

- **Holland**: The Dutch American Friendship Treaty is a unique program to allow Americans to start a business in Holland with very minimal requirements. Here's how one freelancer got her DAFT visa and some FAQs. If you decide to become a Dutch citizen, you'll have to renounce your US citizenship.

- **Ireland**: Ireland's investor program is open to people with a net worth of €2 million or more. You can invest €1 million or donate €500k to an approved project.

- **Italy**: You can invest as little as €250k into a start-up, €1 million in an Italian business or philanthropic project, or €2 million in government bonds.

- **Mauritius**: There are several investment options for Mauritius, including the Integrated Resort Scheme (IRS), Real Estate Scheme (RES), Property Development Scheme (PDS), and Smart City Scheme (SCS).

- **Montenegro**: Purchasing a home or investing in a business in Montenegro makes you eligible for residency. In five years you qualify for permanent resident status and another five years makes you eligible for citizenship.

- **Panama**: If you're a citizen of one of 50 "friendly nations," purchasing US$200k in real estate or depositing US$300k in a fixed deposit account for three years will get you residency. You're eligible for permanent resident status in two years and citizenship in five years.

- **Portugal**:

- If you'd like to start a business or move it to Portugal, you can apply for a D2 visa. This option can also work for freelancers.

- There's also the well-known Golden Visa, which can be obtained with an investment as small as €280k or a donation of €250k. In 2022 the amounts required for some types of investments increased and restrictions were placed on the locations of eligible investment properties.

- **Spain**: Spain's residency by investment program starts at €500k. You can apply for PR status after five years and citizenship in ten. If you're from a Spanish speaking country you're eligible for citizenship in only two years.

- **The UK**: If you can get access to investment funds, you can get an Entrepreneur Visa in the UK.

Go back to school

It's generally relatively simple to get a student visa to attend university abroad — and there are no age limits. The tricky part is going to be the financing.

Luckily, if you're American and looking to use FAFSA, they do fund some international universities. There are scholarships available, too. And, of course, some universities are free or very affordable. You can compare European schools for bachelors, masters and PhD programs. Many universities offer programs in English.

The best course of action is to contact the specific universities you're interested in, as they'll provide advice for obtaining a visa and financial assistance.

Many countries make it possible to get a work permit after graduation.

Do a working holiday

If you're over 18 and under 35, you can work abroad for six or more months. You'll generally need to show that you can support yourself while looking for a job and have your own health insurance. The visa fees are generally quite low and it's a lot cheaper than doing a study abroad program.

If you're looking for help arranging a work exchange and managing the paperwork, Bunac or Swap can set things up for you. While you have the legal ability to work for local companies, there's no requirement that you do so. You can work remotely or live off of savings if you want.

If you're interested in staying after your visa is up, you have the chance to build your professional network in hopes of getting an employer to sponsor you for a new visa. You may be able to stay as a skilled worker, even without a job offer. You may also find a new love interest who would like to keep you in the country.

These are the working holiday programs for US citizens. There may be other options, as some countries allow people to participate even without an official reciprocal agreement, such as how Canada allows Americans to apply through a designated organization.

Australia

Australia recently expanded its work and holiday visa to include people up to the age of 35. You can stay for a year, but you can only work for 6 months for any one employer. Your significant other will have to get their own visa and you cannot bring any dependent children. US citizens can apply online.

Ireland

Ireland's Intern Work and Travel Pilot Programme allows US citizens to spend up to 12 months working in Ireland. You must either be a current full-time student or have graduated within the last year.

New Zealand

The New Zealand Working Holiday Visa is open to Americans 18-30 years old. It lasts for 12 months typically, or 18 months if you're working in agriculture or horticulture.

Singapore

The Singapore Work Holiday Programme is good for up to 6 months. You can apply for a new pass 12 months after your old pass expired. You need to be a student or recent graduate.

South Korea

You'll need to be a student or recent graduate in order to participate in the Working Holiday Program in Korea. You'll have to plan your trip, too, and provide a plan for where you'll be living and traveling. If you're 18-30, you can stay for up to 18 months.

Don't like any of these options? Check Just Landed and *Getting Out.*

Glossary

Acknowledgement of Receipt (AOR)

You get an AOR when the IRCC has decided your immigration application is complete.

Bridging Open Work Permit (BOWP)

If your work permit is going to expire while your PR application is under review, you can apply for a BOWP.

Canada Border Services Agency (CBSA)

The government agency responsible for immigration enforcement.

Canadian Language Benchmark (CLB)

This is the system for describing your language proficiency, on a scale from 1 (basic) to 12 (fluent). Your speaking, reading, writing, and listening are each evaluated and given a CLB.

Citizenship and Immigration Canada (CIC)

This is the former name of the IRCC.

College of Immigration and Citizenship Consultants (CICC)

The regulating body of immigration consultants in Canada as of November 2021.

Common Law Partner

Common law partners have a relationship that's similar to marriage in terms of commitment. To be considered common law partners, you need to maintain a common household for at least a year and, if you don't have a child together, have been together for at least two years.

Comprehensive Ranking System (CRS)

This is the points system for express entry. It's calculated based on your work experience, language ability, level of education, age, and adaptability.

Confirmation of Permanent Residence (CoPR)

Once you have your PR visa, you aren't actually a permanent resident yet. During your final immigration interview you sign a CoPR and become a permanent resident. Used to be called your record of landing.

Conjugal Partner

Conjugal partners are unable to marry legally or become common law partners due to factors outside of their control, like living in a country where divorce or homosexuality is illegal.

Dependent Child

A dependent child can be either biological or adopted. They have to be under 22 years old and can't be married nor in a common law relationship. Children who are 22 years and older but who are unable to support themselves because they suffer from a mental or physical condition are also considered dependents. These rules changed in 2017.

Draw

Selecting candidates from a pool of applicants. This is also known as an invitation round.

Dual Intent

If you show up at the border to get one type of visa while planning on applying for or being in the process of applying for another type of visa (or permanent residency), you have dual intent.

Educational Credential

An educational credential is any degree, diploma, apprenticeship, or trade credential.

Educational Credential Assessment (ECA)

An ECA determines if your foreign education credential is valid in Canada and, if so, what level of credential it's recognized as.

Electronic Travel Authorization (eTA)

People entering Canada who: are not Canadian permanent residents, citizens of the US or Canada, or come from a country that is not visa-exempt need to apply for an eTA before flying to Canada.

Excessive Demand

Your application can be denied based on excessive demand on the medical system. This is based on an illness or condition that would cost more than three times the average cost per person in Canada. This was updated in April 2018 to exclude certain common support services for people with intellectual disabilities as well as hearing and vision impairments.

Express Entry (EE)

Express Entry is the digital system of managing the Federal Skilled Worker Class, the Federal Skilled Trades Class, the Canadian Experience Class, and a portion of the Provincial Nominee Programs.

Express Entry Pool

Once you create an EE profile, you're placed in the candidate pool until you receive an ITA.

Express Entry Profile

The first step in EE is to create a profile, or expression of interest in becoming a permanent resident. This information is based on self-report and if you get an ITA you'll have to provide documents to verify your information.

Family Class

Citizens or permanent residents of Canada who are at least 18 years old can sponsor a spouse, conjugal or common law partner, dependent child, or other eligible relative to come to Canada through Family Class.

Immigration Consultants of Canada Regulatory Council (ICCRC)

The organization that regulated immigration consultants in Canada until November 2021.

Immigration and Refugee Protection Act (IRPA)

The main statute pertaining to immigration law

Immigration Representative

An immigration representative has your permission to interact with IRCC on your behalf. These are typically immigration consultants or attorneys, but it may also be a family member or volunteer.

Immigration Medical Exam (IME)

Exactly what it sounds like, but maybe you didn't know the acronym. These are done by a panel physician.

Implied Status

In some cases your current visa is considered to remain valid while your application to extend your visa is considered. This is now known as maintained status.

Inadmissibility

If you're deemed inadmissible to Canada, you aren't allowed to enter the country. If a family member is inadmissible, it can complicate your application.

International Experience Canada (IEC)

Commonly known as the working holiday program.

Invitation to Apply (ITA)

Candidates who are chosen in a draw from the EE pool are issued an ITA. You then have 60 days to submit your complete application or your invitation will expire.

Job Bank

This is a job posting database inside of EE.

Labour Market Impact Assessment (LMIA)

A LMIA verifies that hiring a foreign worker won't have a negative impact on the Canadian labor market. This used to be called a Labour Market Opinion (LMO).

Lock-In Age

Once your application and fees have been received by the IRCC, you and your dependents ages are locked in and you're still eligible based on the age at the time the application is received.

Maintained Status

If you submit your application to remain in Canada before your current visa expires, you can stay until a decision is made. You maintain your status while it is processed. This used to be known as implied status.

National Occupational Classification (NOC)

Your NOC is a four digit number that describes the type of work you do. This is used to determine your eligibility for EE.

Non-Accompanying Family Members

Even if your family members don't come with you to Canada, they still need to be included on your application, since you're still expected to provide for them and could sponsor them in the future.

Open Work Permit

If you have an Open Work Permit you can take any job you'd like without needing a LMIA.

Panel Physician

Panel Physicians, formerly known as Designated Medical Practitioners, perform immigration medical examinations.

Permanent Resident

A permanent resident has the right to live, work, and study in Canada, receive most social benefits like health care, be protected under Canadian law and the Canadian Charter of Rights and Freedoms, and apply for Canadian citizenship. A permanent resident cannot vote, run for political office, or hold a job that requires a high-level security clearance. Permanent residency status can be taken away if a permanent resident does not live in Canada for two out of five years or is convicted of a serious crime.

Police certificate

A police certificate is a background check, detailing any criminal record, such as an arrest, warrant, and conviction for the person being investigated.

Some countries require a consent form before issuing a police certificate. If you need a police certificate from one of these countries, you submit the consent form to the IRCC in place of the police certificate and the IRCC will then request a police certificate from that country on your behalf.

Port of Entry (POE)

The CBSA facilities at land crossings, airports, and other border crossings. You need to go to a POE in order to land as an immigrant.

Provincial Nomination Program (PNP)

PNPs allow provinces and territories to choose immigrants they believe will help their economy. These programs may be part of EE, in which chase you'll be awarded 600 CRS points if you're nominated. If you're chosen, you're a provincial nominee.

Quebec Selection Certificate (CSQ)

If you plan on immigrating to Quebec, getting a CSQ is the first step in the process. This means Quebec has approved you.

Relationships of Convenience

A sham marriage.

Registered Canadian Immigration Consultant (RCIC)

This is the professional designation given to immigration consultants.

Removal Order

This means you're being kicked out of Canada. There are three types. Listed in order of how much trouble you're in: departure order, exclusion order, and deportation order. You'll get one of these if you overstayed your visa, lied on your application, were convicted of a crime, or various other ill-advised things.

Settlement Funds

Money to support yourself and your family while you get settled in Canada. If you have a job lined up, you don't need to show proof of funds, but you probably should still have money saved for this.

This term sometimes refers to government funding providing newcomers with services.

Sponsor

A sponsor is a Canadian citizen or permanent resident who is willing to sponsor you to become a Canadian permanent resident.

Temporary Resident Permit (TRP)

Canada is a very reasonable country and if you're inadmissible, but have a really good reason to need to come, you can still get a TRP. If this applies to you, you want to talk to an attorney.

Temporary Resident Visa (TRV)

A TRV is a document giving you the right to visit, study, or work in Canada. It might allow you to enter the country multiple times or only once.

Still have questions?

If you have questions that aren't addressed in the book or have noticed an error, grammatical or otherwise, please let me know.

You can contact me here: bit.ly/3796070

If appropriate, I'll provide you with updated or additional information and correct future editions of the book.

I'm not an immigration consultant or attorney, so I can only provide general information. If you need guidance on a specific situation or would like someone to help you with applications, you can hire an authorized professional.

About the author

Cori Carl immigrated to Canada through express entry's federal skilled worker program in 2016. She writes about her immigration experience on WelcomeHomeOntario.ca.

Before moving to Toronto, she spent ten years in Brooklyn and grew up on the Jersey Shore. She is an avid traveler and history nerd who writes about her adventures in the sharing economy on RemoteSwap.club.

She works as a communications consultant for mission driven organizations and serves family and professional caregivers around the world as director of The Caregiver Space.

Cori has a BA in media and cultural studies from the New School University and an MA in communications from Baruch College, both in New York City.

Made in the USA
Middletown, DE
06 November 2024

64042146R00245